Beyond Reason

Beyond Reason

MARGARET TRUDEAU

**PADDINGTON
PRESS LTD**

NEW YORK & LONDON

Library of Congress Cataloging in Publication Data

Trudeau, Margaret, 1948–
    Margaret Trudeau: beyond reason.

    1. Trudeau, Margaret, 1948–   2. Trudeau, Pierre Elliott.
3. Canada—Biography.   4. Prime ministers' wives—
Canada—Biography.
CT310.T76A35   971.06'44'0924 [B]   78-26865

ISBN 0 448 23037 2 (U.S. and Canada only)
ISBN 0 7092 0776 X

In The United States
PADDINGTON PRESS
Distributed by
GROSSET & DUNLAP

In The United Kingdom
PADDINGTON PRESS

In Canada
Distributed by RANDOM HOUSE OF CANADA LTD.

In Southern Africa
Distributed by
ERNEST STANTON (PUBLISHERS) (PTY.) LTD.

For my three little boys

CONTENTS

ACKNOWLEDGMENT

THERE IS ONE person who must be acknowledged: Caroline Moorehead. Caroline was my disciplinarian, my lie detector, my writer. She took all my stories and with her tremendous talent, not to mention tact, deftly chose the words to put to page.

Picture Credits
Photographs on the pages listed below are supplied by kind permission of the following individuals and agencies:

MARGARET TRUDEAU 82 (above), 89 (above), 90 (below right), 92 (above), 179, 182 (below), 187 (both), 188 (below – photo: Margaret Trudeau), 189 (above – photo: Margaret Trudeau), 189 (below), 191 (above). CAMERA 5, INC. 191 (below). CANADA WIDE FEATURE SERVICE LTD. 81 (above right, below), 83 (above), 88 (above), 182 (above). THE CANADIAN PRESS 90 (above, below left), 96. ALFRED EISENSTAEDT 185, 186. JOHN EVANS 84. GAMMA/LIAISON 93 (above – photo: Gilbert Uzan), 94 (photo: Jean Gaumy), 188 (above). SHERMAN HINES 88 (below), 89 (below). ROSS KENWARD 86–87 (above). GEORGES PIERRE 192. UNITED PRESS INTERNATIONAL 87 (above), 91 (below), 177 (above), 178. *Vancouver Sun* 81 (above left). WIDE WORLD PHOTOS 82 (below), 83 (below), 85 (both), 86–87 (below), 91 (above), 92 (below), 93 (below), 95 (all), 177 (below), 180 (all), 181, 183 (both), 184, 190 (both).
Picture research by Karen Moline.

PROLOGUE

ONE SUNNY WEDNESDAY in August 1969, I caught the ferry from Vancouver to the Sechelt Peninsular. It was a brilliant blue morning, with a slight haze over the mountains, promising perfect beach weather. I was off to see my maternal grandmother, Rose Bernard, in her cottage at Robert's Creek, deep in the cedar forest—the scene of my happiest childhood days. It was no accident. I regarded that little house—with its tar-paper roof and robin's egg blue window frames, its neat garden of roses, fruit trees and vegetables carved from the great forest that stretched miles about and beyond—as the only possible place to go. I was a fully-fledged flower child of twenty, in tinted granny glasses and peasant clothes.

I was not so much a hippy as a failed hippy; a hippy without a cause. I had gone through the North American adolescent experience—sixties high school graduate, university with the student activists, rebellion against my parents, seven months on the hippy trail in Morocco—and come out the other end with even less idea about what was to become of me than when I had begun. It wasn't entirely my fault. I embarked on my search for mysticism and freedom because I fell in love with Yves who was the apotheosis of that world and insisted his mate should be the same. I tried. I smoked pot with the best of them and came to love it; I shed all my bourgeois belongings and came home with nothing but a small knapsack containing two pairs of jeans, and a collection of fashionable, white, embroidered cotton shirts; I frizzed my hair; I found a diet so extreme that people actually died on it—the Oshawa Zen

13

macrobiotic diet of brown rice and a few, carefully selected but none too nutritious, vegetables.

But Yves Lewis, my liberated lover, was not impressed. Returning smug and soulful I had presented myself to him at Berkeley, California—only to be turned down. I wanted to bake wholewheat bread and talk love and peace; Yves and his friends had their minds on war. He wanted to show off his arsenal of rifles and hand grenades (for the Symbionese Liberation front? I never did discover); I wanted to settle down and have babies. I had fled the tear gas and the revolutionaries of Berkeley in horror. And rejected.

Vancouver, with my healthy, sane parents was clearly out. Who could stand a father who had been a cabinet minister and was now chairman of a prospering capitalist enterprise, the Lafarge cement company? Or a doting pretty mother, who cooked roast beef and chocolate mousse? Or, come to that, four normal, obedient sisters who had the temerity to laugh at me? It was insufferable for me. I was insufferable for them. With what dignity I could muster I settled on my grandmother's peaceful home as a balm for their mockery and denseness; a sparkling escape from Vancouver with its Coca Cola advertisements and gas fumes which repelled me.

Grandma was an unwilling victim of my self obsessions, but, in her late sixties, still robust, sensible and self opinionated enough to put them down as "finicky behavior." It was a blow to my pride, but at least she left me more or less alone, once I had fulfilled my quota of daily tasks, to mope around the trees as I pleased.

Robert's Creek is a beautiful place, and perfect for self indulgence. Grandma's house stood on a bluff overlooking the Howe Sound, a wilderness of wild roses and hedge flowers. Where I could sit and day-dream, watching the endless passing of tugs towing the log booms down to Vancouver. Occasionally I stirred myself sufficiently out of my reveries to wander down the wiggling path to the sea. A profusion of lilies, nasturtiums and pansies had erupted there from the cuttings my grandmother threw over the cliff top as she worked in her garden. At the bottom, on the pebbly beach, I sat and smoked a little grass, perched on a log, waiting for the tide to come in, listening to the whining cries of the seagulls and the soothing roar of the waves on the shore. When I grew bored I poked about among the rocks for star fish and crabs. One day I watched a pod of killer whales heaving in the bay, on another a sea lion came and sat staring vacantly out to sea not fifty yards from me.

Some days I didn't feel like yearning for Yves, or dwelling on Morocco, so I basked in sentimental nostalgia for my childhood summers. I wallowed in memories: the sweet smell of grandma's loganberry pies and buns stealing into the dormitory I shared with my sisters; the shivering dawns when she harried us out of bed and we sat warming our toes by her wood stove; the nights we slept out on the veranda overlooking the bay, where the bats came whirling through the porch, sending shivers of delight down our spines as we hurled ourselves under the bedclothes.

Meanwhile grandma, unmoved by my sighs and plaintive looks, pursued her own life. Untouched by my deep scorn for all things material or "good" for me, she went right on preparing starchy, wholesome lunches, listening to the *Farmer's Report*, talking in adulatory tones about her, and Britain's, "Bonny Prince Charlie" whose yellowing photograph she had tacked up in the kitchen alongside her view of the birdbath. She was busy making herself dresses in materials of pastel colors and flowery prints and walking stoutly a mile and half through the forest every Sunday to church, shooing off the bears with a commanding flourish of her neat, respectable, schoolteacher's hat. It hid an equally neat, but to my eyes horribly unnatural, crop of tightly permed curls, tinted blue by a neighbor every six weeks.

As the days of this peaceful existence became weeks and the weeks threatened to become months, I began to wonder what would become of me. Join a commune in the wilds? Teach handicapped children? Become a nun? My wounded sensibilities could clearly stand no violent exercise or excessive noise. If there was one thing that shone out it was that never, under any circumstances, would I join the despicable bourgeois world of bridge clubs and whiskies before dinner. I would never fall to that level of "respectability." I felt ashamed and saddened for my friends who had forsaken the true path for such misguided values.

I was moping happily one day in the garden when the tele-

15

phone rang. It was a party line: three long and one short ring meant it was for us, a rare occurrence. Grandma answered: it was my mother, doubtless with some trivial and prosaic question for me. Was I eating well? Had I thought what I would *do*? I mooched ungraciously to the phone.

"Margaret," my mother was trying, and failing, to sound casual, "an old boy friend of yours has just called, someone we once met on a holiday who took you waterskiing. He wants to take you out on a date."

I was outraged.

"Mother, I don't want a date with *anyone*." My tone sounded as if she had proposed something indecent. She was suitably crestfallen. "Aren't you even interested to know who it is?"

A prickle of unseemly curiosity stirred inside me. I tried to beat it back. I failed.

"Well," it came out at last, with extreme bad grace, "who then?"

"Pierre Trudeau."

GROWING UP

MY FIRST MEMORY is of my younger sister Betsy's birth—sitting in the drawing room waiting to decide on a name, when I was four years old and used to being the baby myself. I cannot truly remember how I felt. My next image is far more revealing. My father came home from a trip—What trip? Where to? The details have gone—and he brought me a pair of blue sunglasses. Gingerly, with infinite care at handling such a precious object, I put them on. I have this vivid memory of astonishment: "These are for *me*. Just for me—all by myself." Amazed that in a family of five girls I was going to possess something that was just mine, and that my father had actually thought of buying something specially for me.

I can't have been more than five, and he was still a politician. There wasn't a lot of money at home, and my mother struggled to keep us smartly dressed and well fed, but everything was handed down from girl to girl. Being fourth in line meant I very seldom had anything new and what came my way was often scrubbed thin and faintly stained. I was also physically small, my sisters being larger and more robust, so that the clothes that should have fitted hung down loosely over my thin shoulders. That was probably the start of a lifelong obsession with clothes that fit.

My next memory comes later, though the concern is the same. I am going to school and I am extremely excited. My three elder sisters—Heather, Janet and Rosalind—attend Rockcliffe Park public school already, and now, after so much waiting, I'm at last to go with them each morning. In the playground the teachers line us up and discover that I am, by several inches,

17

the smallest. It's an honor, clearly, being the smallest in the school and I try to take it as such, but I have misgivings. Is it right to be so small?

Injustice figures next in the line of childhood reflections. My memory produces a music lesson with a redfaced teacher wearing bright purple lipstick. She is getting us to produce words to the scales. "What do these notes sound out?" she asks, and sings, "Da, *da*, da." The little girl sitting next to me puts up her hand. "I *love* you." The teacher beams. "And what about: da, da, *da*, da, da?" Trembling with my own cleverness I raise my arm and chant: "I do *not* love you." I was snatched out of my wicker chair and ordered to stand in the corner while the teacher summoned the principal to tell me what a wicked, cruel child I was. I was too upset to explain, too shocked to cry.

Until I was nine my father was a minister of fisheries in Lester B. Pearson's cabinet. A big, energetic man, he worked late into each night and we didn't see much of him. But his influence, the unmistakable stamp of his authority, was on everything we did. The childhood friends, the fads and passions of my early years, pale into a shadowy insignificance today beside this towering presence. My mother, whom we all adored, was a tall woman with hazel eyes; she was a worrier, but she seldom judged and she was never vicious.

Dad was the eldest son in a family of five, and the Sinclairs emigrated from Scotland soon after his second birthday. His father, also James, had been a schoolteacher in Granges, Banffshire, and having struggled and totally failed to make enough of a living to feed four children—the fifth was born later—decided to seek his fortune in the colonies.

He chose Canada quite simply because his passion was fishing. In Scotland he had found his freedom to enjoy the sport somewhat limited. The second time he was caught poaching on a nearby private estate, the game warden, who was an old friend, told him regretfully: "Jimmy, I hate to do it, but next time I catch you poaching it's jail for you." That would have meant the certain suspension of a teaching license. That night Jimmy and my grandmother and a fellow poacher took out the big maps and lit the kerosene lamps and made the decision to go where the fish were. Both men knew that one of the greatest salmon rivers in the world runs along the west coast of Canada; they agreed, after considerable hesitation and in total ignorance of every other aspect of Canadian life, that Vancouver was probably just the sort of place for a poor teacher with a passion for fishing to start anew. Every penny of their savings went on the boat crossing, and the first years in Vancouver, then a small fishing port filling up fast with immigrants, were a struggle.

They never regretted the move. Vancouver is green and lush with mountains running down to the water, and the fish were like no fish Jimmy had ever seen. He prospered so excellently with his teaching career—later pioneering new training colleges—that before long he had saved enough to buy a cottage up the coast, build his own smokehouse for the salmon, and indulge a passion that never dimmed. When I was a child I often sat on the steps of the cottage, listening to his stories of the move from Scotland, and of great fishing sagas, or singing sea shanties with him. When my grandmother, who disapproved of such things, was away from home, he would brew me up a special treacle from a secret recipe—in a flat pan he would melt down butter and sugar that turned as hard as stone. His accent remained strongly Scottish until the day he died.

My father inherited not just the Scottish inflections—which come back even to this day, particularly when he embarks on one of his more colorful stories—but the dour outlook of a Presbyterian Scot. An excessively strict upbringing had left its mark. There was no question but that he must excel at school, and he did, getting a place at the University of British Columbia and later becoming a Rhodes scholar at Oxford. He met my mother, Kathleen Bernard, daughter of a modest Vancouver railwayman, when like his father he became a schoolteacher; Kathleen was his brightest mathematics pupil. There were twelve years between them, and very properly he waited for her to finish school and study as a nurse before proposing.

My father doted on my mother; any bad behavior toward her on our part brought down the wrath of God on our heads. He never actually beat me, though, until I was fourteen and was supposed to be clearing up after a party. I was being lazy and clearly somewhat insolent and on being told to hurry up, shouted a careless "I hate you" in his direction. That was enough. He was out of his chair in a second, chased me all over

19

the house, and when he finally caught me, he spanked me. The one thing you can't do if you're a Scot is hate your family.

We did everything as a family: my father called us the Brawling Sinclairs and took pride in the racket and the standing of such a respectably large group, even if we *were* all girls. My sister, Betsy, was his favorite, with her blond hair and her close resemblance to my mother; she was his dream daughter and he had a joke about how when Betsy grew up he was going to turn my mother in and marry her. Betsy conformed, but retained her wonderfully dry sense of humor. Heather, seven years older than me and the eldest, was a redhead with a freckled face and blue eyes and a strong will. She went her own way. Janet, two years her junior, was a gawky and awkward child who kept lizards in jars and picked up stray dogs and was only saved from being the continual underdog herself by forming a particularly close bond with my maternal grandmother. Lin, fifteen months my senior, probably had the loneliest of childhoods. Because I was a quick learner and skipped grade three, she and I found ourselves in the same class. At one time she became fat, wore glasses and took refuge in harlequin romances. It was not to last—Lin became Miss Simon Fraser University, then Miss Radiology.

As for me, I was my father's son, the boy he never had. My sisters were all going to succeed in their own particular ways, but I was the one singled out, the one with the extra spark, the child most like my father. My mother considered me the most selfish of the family—and she was probably right.

Five girls and a domineering father: it made for competition. Between us we tacitly accepted Betsy's hold on his affection, but that didn't stop the race for favor. Very rarely was I singled out for personal attention, and when it came it wasn't always the treat I expected it to be. Dad had a grueling life; it was no surprise that a couple of Scotches in the evening helped. One night—I must have been five or six—he came home late, sat in his own particular armchair and said: "Margie, come over here, come and sit on Daddy's knee." I was overwhelmed. He drew me on to his lap. "Margie," he said, "you've got to grow up to be a very good girl because I have a bad heart and I'm going to die soon."

I wouldn't go to bed that night. My mother cajoled, bullied, threatened, and finally told me that unless I climbed under the sheets I would miss an expedition to *The King and I* planned for the following evening. I cried myself to sleep. I dreamed my father had been killed in an airplane crash, like my friend Louise's father. Next day I walked home from school: "Death means I'll never see him again. Never." I brooded. From then on I kept a close watch on him whenever I saw him doing any sort of physical work. It was a fulltime job keeping an eye on him, because he was a compulsive weekend do-it-yourself worker, building fences, moving bricks, digging out holes, re-landscaping the garden, particularly when we moved house after he came out of office in 1957 and we went back to Vancouver. He even painted a magnificent mural of fishes, copied from an encyclopedia, around the retainer wall of the pool—more than appropriate, as he said, for the minister of fisheries. Part of me was proud of this goodlooking father with a big voice; the rest of me waited for the heart attack. It never came (although at sixty-eight he underwent major heart surgery). He'll be seventy this year.

Dad was keen to turn us into healthy, vigorous children, and more than happy to leave culture to later days. The result was a curiously barren childhood—we had no ballet lessons, no serious music, no art. The only music he enjoyed was the bagpipes. Television was out—except for *The Ed Sullivan Show* on Sunday nights. The dinner table was where we were expected to learn about life, and what it means to be a family, but the noise was overpowering as everyone tried to compete for his attention. Only my mother stayed silent.

As I grew older, I found the racket quite simply insufferable. For treats my father took us all out to dinner in a nearby restaurant and it was then that I would really cringe with embarrassment. It was *so* unbelievably loud. People stared. Dad was the storyteller, the great orator, and if there were guests, he dominated. It was at these dinners that I developed my hatred of labels. "And this," he would say, pointing to me, "is number four."

"No," I wanted to yell back, "I'm not number four. I'm Margaret."

Culture for me, long into my teens, was rock music. I was fourteen when the Beatles hit Canada. Lin and I would sneak out to the garage and listen to their songs on the car radio. We weren't allowed too much music in the house. "Turn off that din," my father would yell on entering the house, guided by some sixth sense to an almost inaudibly distant tune in the attics. When the Beatles came to Vancouver in person he relented and bought us good seats. I was turning fifteen, blasé, looked older, or so I thought—but I screamed and yelled and swooned with the best of them.

If we lacked culture we got the open spaces instead. When John Diefenbaker brought the Conservatives back into power my father left politics. He bought a plot in north Vancouver and built the house he had always dreamed of, down a dead end street on the edge of a ravine with a view down the creek. Our first summer there was spent damming the water and building a path to the manmade pool. My sister Lin christened it. It was one of my father's more extreme comic fiascos. Within days she was quite ill: it was then that he discovered that the creek was one of north Vancouver's main septic tanks.

Not long after the move, he bought a second house, an old log cabin up Vancouver's most northern mountain, Hollyburn, with no running water or electricity but deep in the forest surrounded by fir trees, pines and blueberry bushes. There were mountain lakes all around and deep snow in winter which we had to gather in buckets and melt down for water. We named the cabin "High Hopes," and every weekend either took the chairlift up the mountains or, when that was out of order as it often was, we hiked up, the provisions on our back. It took two hours. During the daylight hours we built, dug and swam. At night we played cards—Hearts, Whist, Crazy Eights, Cribbage —and Monopoly. My father loved Scrabble.

My father's son, I played the part. I was a tomboy—I built forts in the woods, and had adventures on the lakes. These were happy times: a great converted dormitory for us and our cousins in the attic, an oil stove with a perpetually simmering pot of soup for the children as they came in cold from outdoors. That cabin was the best gift my father ever gave me: much later the outdoor life was the very one I tried so hard to re-create for Pierre and the children.

Looks, in a family of five girls, were more than just important. They were an obsession. We spent more time in the various bathrooms of the many houses we lived in as children than in any other single room. I can remember my sisters' preoccupations as clearly as my own: Heather was too plump; Janet too clumsy, sprouting like a beanpole at the wrong moment, with hair somehow too frizzy, and legs too skinny; Lin started fat and got fatter; Betsy didn't count so much—she was the baby. I was considered the prettiest—which led to jealousy and misery and fights, even to blows with Lin. From being so small to start with I developed a mania for making my own clothes, and spent many months in a home economics course at my Hamilton junior high school learning to sew. I believe now that I felt so determined to get nothing but the best materials, and the most beautiful clothes, principally to cover up what I felt inside: confusion, rivalry, inadequacy and an unending desire to please. I could never quite reconcile these feelings with my determined views. My sisters claim I used to sneak into their rooms and pinch their nicest sweaters.

When I was sixteen I was chosen by Delbrook Senior High to represent them on the teen fashion council of the Hudson's Bay Company store in the center of town. One girl from every school in the neighborhood came and spent Saturday mornings listening to a model talk about grooming and poise and charm; the afternoons were devoted to helping out in the different departments. The idea was to train potential managers. I loved those days; when I got to university I spent my first long summer vacation working in the store full time. It was then that the manager asked me to switch from sociology into commerce so as to prepare for a future job on the staff. I would, he told me, make an excellent manager. They even offered me a full scholarship. I was flattered, but it never really occurred to me to accept.

Leonard Cohen once described me as "every guy's great date." He meant the words kindly but he couldn't have been more misguided. The fact is I never much enjoyed dating. My mother wouldn't let us start until we reached grade ten and then, like my sisters and their friends before me, I joined the round of chaperoned Saturday night parties, hand-holding after school, intense telephone conversations, and the wearing of special badges and signs of a current steady. From the start I always seemed to get it wrong—perhaps because I had no brothers, I could never see boys as friends. My trouble was that I didn't like to disappoint anyone, so rather than fight to keep my clothes on in the back seat of someone's car I preferred to skip casual dates altogether and stick with one boy for as long as possible. I was clearly both a prude and a terrible flirt.

Dating, of course, was what my father most disapproved of. Heather had made good by finding and sticking to a boy she later married, Tom Walker. Janet was a late bloomer and never very popular as a teenager. Lin took refuge in fantasy. Betsy was too young. What boys did brave the house were rewarded by snarls and grunts from my father's deep armchair. Since I was the cutest, I gave most trouble. Dad and I fought: about the boys; about the rock music, which he refused to listen to and which I said provided the words of my rebellion; later about politics, values and money.

I graduated in the summer of 1965. A couple of years ago I saw that a television series had been made about my generation: *Whatever Happened to the Class of '65?* They had a point, treating us like a social phenomenon. We really were the last of the innocents, the end of an era—middle-class kids who never rebelled, girls who wouldn't have dreamed of wearing jeans to school, whose greatest dream on earth was to become a cheerleader.

I was given the choice of going on to the University of British Columbia, a traditional conservative university with high academic standards, or of going to the brand new university of Simon Fraser, then barely completed. I, of course, wanted Berkeley in California, but that was out of the question. My father, in his usual inimitable way, helped me make the decision: he announced that if Lin and I opted for U.B.C—both universities were some half hour's drive from my parents' house—then we could make our own way there. If on the other hand we agreed on Simon Fraser, he would buy us a car. The friendly persuasion worked, and we acquired a Volkswagen.

Simon Fraser had been built on top of a mountain overlooking Vancouver: the long, curvy road that led up to it added to a sense of isolation and remoteness. It was all concrete and glass and, because Vancouver is a rainy city, it was gray, always gray. My first year was simply an extension of my schooldays: a continuation of middle-class respectability. I was a good student; I dated a football player; I excelled in sociology and won myself a first-class scholarship.

The second year everything changed. My father's case for Simon Fraser began to make sense—but not the way he had imagined. He was dead right: as a university Simon Fraser was an exciting place to be. The classes were kept very small. And the architect of the place, Arthur Erickson, had had the ingenious idea of modeling his university on a Greek academy, with a central mall off which opened the library, the theater, the cafeteria and the lecture rooms. Staff and students were quite literally forced to mix as they moved about the campus, and so to speak and get to know each other.

Student activism in Canada was born my second year, 1966. And that mall provided a natural forum for student meetings and for spreading the word if anything happened. When a teaching assistant was fired at U.B.C. no one got to know about it for days; at Simon Fraser there wasn't a person who didn't know about the entire case within minutes. A microphone had been built into the podium in the middle of the mall—all part of Erickson's notions about communication. We made the most of it. One day we had three thousand students sitting around that podium.

I was studying political science, sociology and anthropology, and my education took place continuously both inside and outside the classroom. The dean of my department was Thomas Bottommore, a Marxist scholar who influenced me deeply. There were Maoists and Liberals, Conservatives and Trotskyists among us and we talked and talked and talked. Stuck up on that rainswept mountain arguing was a formative way in which to spend a year. It changed me.

I started to date Philip, an English teaching assistant who was in Canada to study for his Ph.D. on revolutions. A gentle, serious man, he dictated that our dates should be spent mainly studying together. A good Saturday night for us was a bottle of wine, classical music on the record player and talking politics. This was the start of a new rebellion at home. My father, never appreciative of any boyfriend, was downright rude to Philip. Somewhere along the way he had become antagonistic toward radical Englishmen, and he sensed in Philip, quite wrongly, an agitator. His hair was a bit long. He wore a beard. And he was small—he had had rickets as a baby during the war. And my father, who could perfectly well tolerate a dim football player, couldn't stand a mild revolutionary. It didn't help when Philip and five other teaching assistants—all English—supported a boy who had written a silly poem with political overtones and published it in the school paper. He had then been expelled. Philip and his friends circulated a letter of protest and when they were suspended all hell broke loose. "Riots at Simon Fraser" read every local headline. We fought, we protested, we had good times, and in the end we lost. There was a purge; the radicals, their contracts not renewed, left; those who had tenure found life so intolerable they left of their own accord.

My involvement throughout, apart from my personal battles over Philip, was a curious one: that of spectator, but never that of participant. Just as I had always turned away at the last moment from becoming cheerleader at school, so now I didn't join the students in their sit-ins. Even the Vietnam war, I now believe, was something of an abstraction for me, except when friends became draft dodgers. I, too, was devastated by the napalm bombing, and cried when I saw photographs of naked children running screaming down ruined streets. But I couldn't be swayed into becoming an activist. I didn't want to be a sheep among leftists, any more than I wanted to be a sheep among conformists. What did happen to me was that I began to question things in a way I never had before, and the form that took made my father yell at me that I was an insolent little girl. We tried a reconciliation scene at Waikiki Beach in Honolulu on a peace-offering family holiday, but that was a total failure. On our return I packed my bags and moved out.

My efforts at lodging and sharing apartments formed the next decisive step in my education. I took as little as possible in the way of allowance from my father and soon found myself installed with a professor, Michael Mulkay, his wife Lucy, who was a fashion designer, and their three-year-old daughter. I learned a lot from them. There hadn't been much laughter at home, nor touching or demonstrative love; and certainly no praise. Here I saw how nice it was to be cuddled but also how healthy it was to have real arguments and not sense the end of the world. For the first time I saw how people can and should and do fight—and survive.

26

Michael and Lucy taught me to listen to music and to look at pictures and, having heard me moan and grumble over my courses, suggested I try some English ones instead. It was through them that I came upon the Romantics, William Blake, Coleridge and Keats. I got obsessed with the idea of freedom, and choices of ways of living, with materialism and greed, with the influence of pop music and revolt. They were good months for me. In the last two semesters Marx was definitely dead. I began to listen to Timothy Leary and Buckminster Fuller; here were my new gods. (The summer after I married Pierre, Buckminster Fuller came to lunch. I asked the cook to prepare something especially delicious for my hero. He came in, sat down, refused lunch, saying he had no time to waste on food, spoke incomprehensibly and without interruption for an hour and a half, and told me that he was painting a tapestry of careful thought and I was not to interrupt. When he left I cried.)

The last two years were crowded with new emotions. A group of university friends introduced me to pot in a cottage facing the sea, where the gulls screamed at us from above our heads, and where we sat on the beach for hour after hour listening to "Penny Lane" and "Strawberry Fields for Ever" on our cassette tapes. When it rained, we retreated indoors and watched the spray hitting the window panes, and had intense conversations about cabbages and kings. Pop music meant a great deal to me— Janis Joplin and her rasping, pleading voice; the Beatles, who seemed to stand for good; and the Rolling Stones who stood for bad. Because I was the newest arrival, I cooked the meals, choosing to ignore all that Kate Millett had taught me in *Sexual Politics*, preferring a life of dependency and discovery. It was easy to get marijuana. We grew it in our gardens in the summertime or bought the grass that came up cheap and plentiful from Mexico and California. I drunk it all in—the music, the drugs, the life. I jibed only at opium, scared off by Coleridge, and though some of my friends tried L.S.D., there was no cocaine about. I did try mescaline one day, and spent eight hours sitting up a tree wishing I were a bird.

It was in this bewildered though cheerful cast of mind that I set off for what my father announced was to be our last holiday together as a family. Heather stayed behind because she had married Tom; Janet didn't come because she was in France. The rest of us packed our cases for the island of Moorea in Tahiti. It turned out to be a paradise—wild, tropical, with none of the shoddiness of Honolulu. We stayed at the Club Mediterranée.

On Christmas Eve I met a handsome Frenchman called Yves Lewis, water skiing. His father was the man who first dreamed up the Club Mediterranée, and Yves had come to Moorea to teach water skiing, at which he was the local champion. He had been on the island a year and a half, a beautiful, almost god-like man, with silvery hair bleached to the color of sunshine, with eyes as green as the water he skied on. He was also a gifted flautist and had a degree in Sociology from the Sorbonne—a yogi with astonishing humility about his own achievements. In the evenings he sang his own songs, laments about banality and greed, and danced the Tahitian national dance, the *tamourai*, with such skill and dexterity that even the Tahitians stopped to watch him. Who could have resisted him? I fell in love. But I also received a nasty shock; from my experiences with grass and sex and political activism, I thought I was quite something. Yves made me see I had a long way to go.

One hot, lazy afternoon after I had been waterskiing I stayed out on the raft, resting and gazing at the white beach and the very green palms. There was a man skiing in the bay; I followed his progress idly, more than a little impressed by the ease of his performance. When later he came over to my raft we started a "What are you doing here?" and "What do you study?" conversation, that soon, casually, led to student rebellion, and Plato and revolution.

My mother had been sitting on the beach watching. "Do you realize who that was?" she asked, as I climbed out of the water alongside her.

"Oh, Pierre someone or other," I said vaguely. She laughed.

"That's Pierre Elliott Trudeau, the justice minister—the black sheep of the Liberal party."

Oh no, not another politician, was all I thought at the time. I wasn't particularly impressed. I even stood him up one day. He was shy, almost too shy, and when he asked me politely if I would like to go deep sea fishing with him and told me to be at the dock at ten, I didn't bother to show up. I went off with Yves instead. I was young and romantic; Pierre struck me as very old and very square. Years later I discovered that he had come to Moorea to read Gibbon's *The Rise and Fall of the Roman Empire* and to decide whether to run for prime minister. That Christmas he decided; in February he announced his candidacy.

I saw Pierre only once again before our first date. That was when my father took us to the Liberal Convention when Pierre was chosen as party leader. My father was campaign manager for the west, for Turner, another leadership candidate; but after our brief acquaintance with him in Moorea, the rest of us rooted for Pierre. His most vocal supporters were young and pretty: they wore identical very short dresses and became known as the "Trudeau girls"; posters of his photograph were on every wall behind every door. The night of his election he carried the whole stadium with him, everyone shouting and stamping and calling that he was the best.

Just after his speech I was standing in the basement waiting for my family to reappear. Suddenly a great mob started approaching and I crushed myself against the wall. "Trudeau, Trudeau," they were shouting. Even then Pierre and I were naturally drawn to one another. As the mob passed, with Pierre in its center, he seemed to pause and catch my eye. Instantly he stopped the crowd, broke his way through, kissed me on both cheeks and was swept on. The reporters came dashing over. "Have you eyes for Trudeau? Are you a girlfriend?"

"No, I have eyes for him only as prime minister." And it was true. I wasn't to see him for another eighteen months.

ON
THE HIPPY TRAIL

FTER THE DISCOVERIES and the passions, the rebellion and the days in which not a moment seemed to pass without some new experience, my last months at Simon Fraser were something of an anticlimax. It was like a battery running down. Tahiti and Yves had made such an impression on me that I took a semester out of school, and spent it sleeping the time away. Yves had changed me and he had also made a mark on my soul – he had become a symbol for me, a romantic fantasy I was never to quite shake free of. When I returned to Simon Fraser my friends were all ahead of me; somehow the spark had gone. I indulged my newfound passion for the Romantics, taught for a while in a free school run in a couple of empty rooms on the campus, and moved into a hideous basement apartment in the ugliest of Vancouver's suburbs, Burnaby.

It was a lonely and frustrating time. I felt too guilty with the pot smoking to visit home much, and in any case my parents seemed to be in a perpetual state of chaos, moving from unsatisfactory apartment to even more unsatisfactory house in an effort to find the perfect solution to the simple and insoluble problem that there were now just the two of them left in what had always been an enormous family. I wasn't much fun to have around: I was preoccupied and depressed and what friends did come to visit me got snapped at. Those were my canned salmon for supper days.

Like many of the luckier middle-class Canadian students, I was offered a holiday in Europe after graduation. My parents had fixed Janet up with a family in Aix-en-Provence, and wanted to do the same for me. Typically, I wanted no plans. All I would tell them was that I would be leaving the day after Christmas, 1968. "Where will you go?" asked my mother anxiously.

"I have no idea. I will fly to Geneva–and then who knows?"

Fate, or possibly perversity, took me to Morocco. My father had fought in North Africa and told such appalling tales of white slavery, poverty and pestilence that I was probably drawn there simply to spite him. In Geneva I paired up with Ross, a friend from schooldays. He had a shiny new Ford Cortina and we bickered all the way across France and Spain and down through Morocco until we reached Agadir where we suddenly put the brakes on and stopped. We had found sun and the sea and an agreeable hippy commune of sorts, sharing showers with a tourist camp.

What the drive down had done was to convince me that my conventional Canadian upbringing was no preparation for life on the road. The first night in Morocco we had fallen in with two young Arab boys who had shown us such friendliness that I had immediately assumed I was in the clutches of the white slave trade. The generosity of strangers took me a while to get used to. Then there was the dirt. I had never regarded myself as squeamish but North Africa turned me into a cleanliness freak; washing myself and my surroundings became a fetish with me.

I was well provided with money by my anxious parents and my first action on arriving in Agadir among the hippies was to get myself a house of my own—a ten-dollar bamboo house on the beach complete with charcoal burner, cooking pots and a sleeping mat. It took me days to overcome my shyness with the other hippies; I felt square, critical and much, much too clean. But when Ross left, which he did after a couple of weeks, I had no option but to throw in my fate with the others, learn to play the guitar, eat what food there was; throw away my conventional notions of sexual morality; and live. For the first time in my life I had the sensation of peace, tranquillity and utter freedom. I wasn't lonely; in fact I reveled in the knowledge that no one from my past life had the faintest idea where I was. All I could say of myself was that I was alone on a beach looking out to the west in southern Morocco. Even my possessions had gone—all I had left from a series of thefts was a small leather suitcase with a few jeans and shirts, and a cosmetic bag in

Liberty cotton ludicrously full of face cream, scent and soap.

Finally the German tourists who shared our camp rebelled. We were a dirty, scruffy, disorganized lot to them, and what was worse, we were scroungers. They asked the police to move us on, which they duly did, very politely, to a new and far more beautiful camp north of Agadir. I took down my house and reassembled it under the trees of our new home, with the help of four Japanese boys who had become the heart of the community: four straight, industrious, inventive boys who cooked delicious Japanese meals and remained impassively polite.

Too much money rather than too little was my problem. How not to depend on it, and live like the others? After a couple of weeks I moved on again, this time totally on my own, to Essaouira, the old sea town of Mogador, up the coast, where I had heard of a Moroccan family who took in paying foreign guests. A stone wall surrounded the village and I found the streets clean, the yogurt delicious, the *hamam* spotless. I watched the Moroccan women with their purdah and their subservience and learned to inhale the mild keef smoked in long reed pipes with clay bowls. It was the only time in my life when I have ever been what my parents would certainly have considered promiscuous—though it was probably no wilder than the life of a girl of my age in Pennsylvania. There were no taboos. The only standard was to care and not to make promises for the future I knew I couldn't keep. Away from the machismo of North America I finally learned to treat men as brothers, while enjoying making love with them in a way my puritan upbringing had not allowed me to consider possible.

I soon became an established part of the North African hippy circus. Old friends from Agadir drifted through and we would exchange experiences and joints before they moved on again— only to meet up again somewhere else a few months later. There were a lot of North American boys, draft dodgers from Vietnam, dozens of French kids, some Japanese and Germans. Most of us were in our late teens or early twenties; a few had been living the life for years. It was an inexpensive and harmless existence. Occasionally, telling no one, I would sneak off for a night to an expensive hotel, with a real bathroom and a good meal in a restaurant.

After a month in Essaouira I crossed the mountains to

Marrakesh in an ancient bus, sitting next to a sheep trussed up by its four legs. I caught a bug from a shishkebab we stopped to buy on the journey, and, an antiseptic Canadian to the very roots of my stomach, never quite got rid of it again. I seemed to be a sucker for every Moroccan germ.

The bus stopped in the main square of Marrakesh, enormous, crowded, menacing after my months of subdued village life. I was terrified. This seemed an altogether new challenge. Jolted in the bustle and the dark, startled by the snake charmers and the persistent beggars, I was suddenly rescued by a young European boy who led me off silently down narrow streets into the Arab quarter. I had no time to resist.

Fate again seemed to be taking a hand. I found myself in a hostel, a halfway house run by two young Christians—Ricky, an English girl, and her Dutch husband. The house was full of foreigners like myself. Ricky organized us all with the minimum of fuss and the greatest of kindness: she allocated each of us tasks, charged a small rent, and in return fed us and gave us mats to sleep on. Only keef was tolerated. There was no sex.

One of my contributions to the household was a cheap, portable record player and eight, highly coveted, record albums—The Beatles: "White Album," The Rolling Stones: "Sympathy For The Devil," Steve Miller Band: "Sailor,"— tunes of our generation; the voices of our collective soul.

It was a peaceful, even placid life. I felt useful again: I cooked, visited the *hamam* every morning, did needlework, made clothes and got a fellow traveler to start teaching me about Buddhism.

I had been there a few weeks when one night an earthquake hit Marrakesh. It was Ramadan, and that day every family in our quarter had slaughtered a sheep for the feast. All day the streets had been thick and sticky with blood and entrails and the air heavy with their stench. Since our hostel was vegetarian the sight and the smells had been almost too much for us to bear. The tremors, when they came, were cathartic, a great wrenching of the apathy. We ran out into the open, the Moroccans shouting in terror, the memory of Agadir and its earthquake five years before still vivid. Walls cracked open around me, babies screamed, dogs howled, the ground rattled and shivered. The whole world shook. And then it stopped. We crawled back inside exhausted and bemused.

I left Marrakesh the day I could stand the lice no longer. Every morning my companions, particularly the men, would sit intently picking the nits out of each other's shoulder-length hair, grooming themselves like monkeys. The goody-goody atmosphere and the lice: I'd had enough. My Japanese quartet had turned up and I joined them for a trip into the mountains, to an orange grove and a flowing river outside a village called Eureka. There in the moonlight, among the ruins of a crusader castle, I took my first L.S.D. trip. Yves would have been proud of me. I was moving nicely up the ladder of enlightenment.

The smooth path took a bruising when, having installed myself in a hotel in Marrakesh again, I caught a terrible cold. Climbing into my *djellabah* and my long, flowered skirt I set off shakily for the local pharmacist and tried to explain in my lamentable French that I needed cough medicine. The pharmacist gave me a knowing glance and pushed a box of pills with incomprehensible instructions across the counter. I retired to bed and took two. I kept right on coughing. I took two more, and then it began . . . my entire family, one by one, Mother, Dad, Heather, Janet, Lin and Betsy, proceeded to file in through my hotel bedroom door. Each had something vital they had to tell me. They were followed by my friends who crowded vacantly around my bed, talking a jibberish I could not follow. My life passed before me, episodic and distorted. What seemed like several months later I crawled out of bed and went down to the street. There I discovered, not hard-packed dirt roads and winding alleyways, but rivers down which I had to swim, full of fish struggling in my arms. A friend found me in this sorry state and led me back to the hotel. He looked curiously into my dilated eyes, read the instructions on the pillbox and informed me that I had just taken a massive dose of belladonna. The pharmacist, assuming I was after drugs, had simply handed out what he gave anyone who came his way. This happened all the time: kids were being fed, sold, pushed, injected with drugs they had never heard of and didn't want.

I moved from the hotel to a hostel of my own, in the Jewish quarter, two blocks from the spice market, so that when the wind blew my way the air was sweet with cloves and cinnamon, myrrh and incense. I had decided to run a house like Ricky's, only without the religion. No junkies and no speed freaks—I hated the way they seemed to grow old before my eyes, their skin wrinkling, their teeth rotting. It was as well that I felt so strongly. Opposite was another hostel like mine—but this one run by a Charles Manson character called Paul who dealt in heroin, and thrived on a drug-induced hippy hypnotism, gloating over his new and often female addicts. He was about forty, older than the rest of us, with matted, filthy hair, and a maniacal look in his eye: a big man, a cheap guru. He loved what he called his "mind games" when he turned his inmates into Christs and Mary Magdalenes and ordered them around like zombies. He made a bid to get me to join the fun, but some vestiges of self-preservation and sanity remained and I became a fervent crusader against him, forbidding anyone from my own household back into the hostel if they crossed his threshold.

I became even more fanatical after Anna, my one real hippy friend, began spending hours each evening with Paul. I sometimes found her lying, sick and filthy, in the street in the morning, having forgotten who she was or where to go. Her story was just one of many tragic ones among the hippies. She had been a gentle, pretty, innocent girl from Wisconsin, a recent graduate who, like myself, had been given money by her parents to travel abroad. She left Paul eventually, and took up with three sinister figures on the Marrakesh hippy scene, three tough guys who called themselves *les trois loups* and made a big thing of their machismo superiority. They spoke only French and had the best drugs in town. Jacob, the youngest, was barely sixteen. Their favorite game was to stalk the streets in search of female prey, and having selected one, install her in a room they had rented behind a cafe, where they kept her a prisoner and played with her sexually as the fancy took them until they grew bored and threw her out. Anna fell into their clutches. Smirking like three cats with a cornered mouse, they made her walk about Marrakesh a few yards behind them. One night a young French boy whispered to her that he would get her out and take her to Rabat. *Les trois loups* beat him up and sent him on his way without their princess. That was the last I saw of her.

By now I had been in Morocco five months and was fast growing bored with the promiscuity and the emptiness of the hippy life. When a friend suggested we go back to Essaouira to meet up with Leonard Cohen and his girl friend Clare I fell in happily with the plan. I was sick of being so thin, so perpetually ill, so kicked around. Women's liberation hadn't hit the hippy kingdom: women had their place—barefoot and pregnant. As a girl you were expected to take care of the boys, sew patches on their jeans, do their marketing and make love with whomever asked you.

I wasn't out of it yet however. I joined Leonard and Clare and traveled with them to Tangier where I stopped taking drugs, rented an apartment in the European quarter and planned to work with a fashion designer friend for a couple of months while I tuned in again to normal life. My first morning in the workshops I felt a stab of pain in my left hand. A young French doctor diagnosed a break in a small bone at the back, and put it into plaster. Instead of getting better, the pain grew, throbbing jerks of agony that drove me screaming back to him a couple of days later. He was far from sympathetic. Wait, he said; give it a chance. Have a tranquilizer. That night, my entire arm by now quite numb, I wandered out into the streets of Tangier almost frantic. A Moroccan lady driving past in a car slowed down and asked me what was wrong. I showed her my hand. In a second we were on our way to the Spanish hospital, where the surgeon on duty removed the cast and discovered that far from a break I had osteomyelitis in my hand. It was already withered and a gray-blue color. I was told later that for the first forty-eight hours I spent in the hospital, much of the time delirious with pain, ripping my sheets, and quietened only by the morphine that I had so adamantly rejected in the streets of Marrakesh, the surgeon believed he would have to amputate my hand.

For two weeks I stayed in this pretty Spanish hospital, nursed by nuns with great care. Next to me was a Moroccan woman and her fat, ten-month-old baby. They shared a bed because she was nursing the child. Across was a woman of fifty who never stopped bitching, fortunately she did so in Spanish so I didn't understand her naggings. Next to her was the only member of the older generation in our mini-world—a dear lady of nearly ninety who was in her last days of a long and seemingly good life.

I couldn't seem to escape the hippy world, however hard I

tried. When I returned to my once beautiful, clean apartment from the hospital I found the place had been defiled by junkie friends using the bathroom for a clean fix. I changed the lock. Then I was introduced—no, lured is the better word—to meet Ahmed, the drug king of Tangier. I had known about him from a friend in the south, and on arriving in Tangier had refused all introductions and invitations. One day, pausing out of the sun to retie a sandal, a voice spoke out from the dark of a little shop behind me: "Come and sit down and have a rest." I went in. There was a short, stocky man, with yellow eyes and wiry hair, wearing a bright pink skirt. It was Ahmed.

I soon discovered his game. He courted me as if I were a queen, invited me to a sumptuous meal, tried to shower me with dresses, which I refused, flattered me and showed me priceless jewelry. His strategy, I assumed, was to install European girls in a villa or apartment that he paid for himself, provide her with whatever drugs she liked to take, and press her to give parties for her friends, at which they, in turn, tasted, got hooked, and ordered through Ahmed. The more I refused to become involved the more Ahmed persisted. "Would you like a house? Shall I get you a flat? A villa?" One day he appeared and threw a bunch of keys into my lap. "Here you are. It's yours. A villa. No strings attached. I won't come near you." I kept my head and threw them back. Like Paul in Marrakesh, Ahmed had to be fought. I saw it as a mission to go around warning new arrivals about him.

It took one more drug episode to convince me that I had to leave Morocco. After I had been in Tangier a couple of weeks I met a pretty young Dutch girl and her American draft dodger husband. They invited me up to their house at Chaouen, in the Rif mountains, and I accepted with pleasure, glad for somewhere to go to recuperate from my septic hand. Their house was charming, made out of stone and tiles and with lots of light. It had pleasantly furnished rooms opening off a main central courtyard. I stayed several weeks and they taught me about meditation and macrobiotic food. One day after dinner, when we were lying on cushions in the courtyard, Jeffrey said, as if on impulse: "You haven't been to India, have you? I think you'd love it. Why don't I get you a ticket? I've got friends in Bombay who'll look after you."

His wife Jenny, who was listening, rose up furiously. "Stop that," she said getting very agitated. "You're *not* to use Margaret as a carrier." Jeffrey looked a bit downcast, but it was nothing to my sense of betrayal. Jeffrey, it transpired, was a dealer in cocaine, heroin and hash. He used a whole series of girls like myself to fly around the world collecting consignments of drugs from his own dealers or delivering them back to the next man in the chain in North America. He was very pressing. He explained how he would get his contact in India to deliver two stereo speakers to my hotel the night I was due to fly home; they would be full of hash. All I had to do was hand them over to someone in Canada. There was three thousand dollars in it for me. It was tempting. But when Jenny acidly informed me that the last girl was serving a three-year sentence in a Tunisian jail for precisely the same deal I hastily turned it down.

After this episode I was convinced it was time to go home. I realized how very lucky I was not to have met the same fate as Anna or the girl in the Tunisian prison. I would leave at once, miraculously undamaged by an experience that had made victims of many other girls precisely like myself. More than that: I was not only undamaged, I had grown up. I had learned about generosity and freedom. Now was the moment to try it out on Vancouver and return to Yves to show him how truly worthy of him I had finally become.

Once again I was in for a surprise. My plane connection to Vancouver took me via Paris where I had to stay for one night. Penniless and with nowhere to sleep, miraculously I chanced upon Yves's stepfather. He welcomed me with obvious enthusiasm and we spent an enjoyable evening discussing Yves: a good omen, as I saw it, for the life to come. Reaching home I paused with my parents for no longer than it needed to convince them that an already troublesome teenager had turned into a weird, vegetarian, mystical flower child, and I was off again to find Yves in Berkeley. My relationship with Yves was like falling asleep on a train and endlessly overshooting a country station, only to have to return once more on a second train and then fall asleep and miss it again. Desperately trying to reach him, I always found I had unconsciously missed my goal. This time I had not only become liberated and relaxed: I had gone too far. Before, I had been too bourgeois. Now I was too hippy. "You're living in a hippy dream," said Yves, eying with contempt my frizzy hair and granny glasses as well as the faraway gleam in my eyes. "Come back when you've learned something about *life*." Even I realized that this was becoming a crazy exercise. Crestfallen, confused and now totally without a plan for the future, I set off for my grandmother and the Sechelt Peninsula.

A SECRET COURTSHIP

WHEN I LOOK BACK on it now I can't help being a little ashamed of the speed with which I shed my hippy certainties. One day I was staring out to sea from a clifftop near my grandmother's home, luxuriating in the romantic ideals of happy brotherhood. The next I was on my way back to Vancouver by ferry, to meet my mother for a shopping spree. Yves and flower power were relegated to the back of my heart; at the front was only one thought: "I've got nothing to wear for the prime minister."

It had been all too easy to persuade me to accept the date. I kept up my fashionable nonchalance for just the time it took to buy a dress. We trudged from shop to shop, my mother a miracle of patience, as I rejected dress after dress with the barest hint of anything synthetic. At last, in a French boutique called Armagi, I found the ideal garment—gaberdine, white, short sleeves with fine stitching around the seams. The rest of our shopping—stockings, bag, shoes, all the things I had fondly imagined I would never sully myself with again—took no time at all. I explained them away to myself as a treat not for me, but for my anxious mother.

I woke next morning to a chilly premonition that I had really let myself in for something. My sisters bounded into my room— it was like a birthday, being looked at and fêted. I had been persuaded to go to the hairdresser, and my hair was now wound up in a sleek brown knot, the jagged ends lopped off. Janet lent me makeup, and Mother pinned a diamond brooch onto my dress; Heather filled me several glasses of sherry. I was ready far too early.

At seven I heard a car in the drive. We all raced for the door, but then my sisters remembered that we had discussed who should open it, and reluctantly agreed it should be me, so they fell back. I was terrified: not only did I have then—and indeed have now—a great awe for people of importance, but Trudeau-mania was still at its height and I was part of it. What was I doing with the prime minister of Canada? Why me? And what was this formidable man really like? If I was honest all I could remember was a nice looking middle-aged man with funny old-fashioned shorts and a stripy T-shirt.

When Pierre came through the door I liked the look of him immediately. For one thing he had such an air of fun, such a charming, teasing expression that he made us all laugh. Being late summer he was tanned, which looked good against his white shirt, blue blazer and colored Ascot. He had dark glasses, and wore a flower in his buttonhole. He was confident, flying high, a good first year as prime minister behind him with the country at his feet, and the polls predicting great things for him. I liked the charm, the boyish ways, and couldn't stop myself sneaking a look at his legs: Pierre was once given the award of being the man with the most beautiful legs in the world. He, on the other hand, could hardly have been pleased with what *he* saw: what all the grooming and dressing up had done to me was to turn a flower child into a Barbie doll.

I got him out of the house as soon as I could—unable to stand the nervous gigglings of my sisters, nor the feigned relaxation of my mother. A blue Pontiac stood in the drive. The two plain clothes officers were dressed to look more like chauffeurs than policemen, but the muscles and the air of security were unmistakable. As we climbed into the back it crossed my mind suddenly that perhaps I should be wary of him: perhaps he wasn't quite the endearingly shy man I took him for, but a bit of a creep. His eyes are very blue and, when he's happy, have a way of appearing as if he is about to cry, a mildly watery look. We set off to catch the sky-ride up Grouse Mountain to what Pierre and my father had agreed was the most appropriate restaurant in town, the Grouse's Nest, perched on the mountain-top with a spectacular view over Vancouver. We made polite, stilted conversation.

The awkwardness vanished by the time we stepped into the restaurant. Within just a few minutes I had blown my cover. The little French dress was a sham, and I couldn't keep all the small talk up. We talked about student revolution and I told him about Berkeley and the tear gas, the arsenal and Morocco. It all came pouring out. I had found a friend at last.

Pierre was so obviously relieved that there was a real human being inside the Barbie doll that he gave me every encouragement. It is in his nature to be charming and complimentary to women, and, away from that sort of oldfashioned gallantry for so long, I had quite forgotten how beguiling it is. It is also in his nature to be a questioner, a listener, and that first date set the pace of our relationship. It was never really to change. I talked, chattered, explained, expounded; he asked me questions. It wasn't simply garrulousness on my part. I was genuinely embarrassed about asking him things. I knew a lot of the answers already, the public answers at least, about his trips to China, and the way he had won his first election largely on the youth vote, who saw in him a brilliant, liberal, sympathetic fellow Bohemian—more adventurer than politician.

How could I now say to him: "Tell me about how you got elected?" or "What about those canoe treks I read about in the *Toronto Star* last week?" It seemed enough of an invasion just to know that much. He doesn't welcome prying. In all the years I was married to him, I learned far more about him from his family and the old friends he made in his university days than I ever learned from him. He doesn't gossip and he never discusses people he knows. I sometimes thought I knew more about his character from the books he wrote about his travels in the Far East than I ever picked up in our conversations.

The Grouse's Nest was something of a mistake, but it served to break the ice between us. The restaurant was touristy and several of the other diners recognized Pierre as we walked through the door. They came crowding around our table for an autograph. He took it in good form, but I think it was then that we discovered a shared preference for simple meals in unpretentious places. We poked fun at the phoniness and the plastic junk: it gave us an instant bond. The photographers unsettled me, clamoring for their pictures; though today I treasure those first shots. They show an overdressed, scared rabbit out on her first date, with a huge, embarrassed smile on her face.

After a first, surprisingly close, dance we settled down to talk. I was even more in awe of him, despite the sudden intimacy, than I had expected to be. I am, in fact, somewhat frightened of him to this day. He has a quality about him that makes you want to be as pleasing to him as possible and it is hard not to sink into sycophancy. I had to keep reminding myself that had he been my age—and not, as he pointed out with self-mockery, almost thirty years older (and two years older than my mother), I would never have taken much notice of him. There was also of course the little fact that he was prime minister of Canada, and some said the most eligible and wealthy of all Canada's political bachelors.

That evening I was anxious to please. We got on to religion almost at once, and over the vichyssoise I was confessing to a confusing experience in the streets of Marrakesh where one day I had almost believed the Christian myth to be coming alive before my eyes. I had suddenly seen all the people in the street around me transformed into disciples and apostles— Jesus Christs and Virgin Marys—and had been overcome by the sensation of taking part in a religious pastoral play. Pierre is nothing if not clearheaded. He quickly put it all into perspective. He pointed out gently, and not without a certain teasing note, that with too little proper food, and, who knows, perhaps a hint of grass, visions come easily. He added: "Your Moroccan experiences are simply part of growing up, perhaps awakening spiritually. The moment of grace can be like an hallucination." I felt comforted; in some crazy sort of way I was more than ready to believe it had been the Second Coming.

I had always known that Pierre was a very devout Catholic. It was a fact often mentioned in the newspapers and by people who knew him, and it was a quality that both attracted and repelled me. I feared that, being so religious, his values might perhaps have set hard, and that nothing I could say would dent him. Had Pierre already made all the decisions and choices in his life?

I told him about my unhappiness, about my grandmother's peaceful cottage by the sea, about my shattered plans. He listened, kindly, more father than friend. Over dinner he suggested that I should leave Vancouver and get as far away as possible from the things that seemed to weigh so heavily on me: my family, my background, my friends.

"Why don't you become a writer, or a sociologist, or even an actress?" he asked. "Why don't you move east?"

The moment it was said I thought: "Aha. Now he's invited me to go and live with him in Ottawa."

As we danced again, I realized that I was feeling increasingly drawn to this intense, wiry man, the antithesis of Yves Lewis and all I thought I believed in. He didn't strike me as old. In fact it was an immediate pleasure not to be battling with a young man's ego. I never stopped to wonder what possible future there could conceivably be for two people so obviously unsuited to one another—one cerebral, clearheaded, rational, devout and almost fifty; the other confused, scatty, certain of only one thing and that was to avoid all possible formality and social responsibility, and barely twenty. "If you come to Ottawa," Pierre said, as he dropped me back at my house with a brotherly kiss, "do let me know. I'd love to have you come for dinner."

At that instant I had decided that I wanted this man for myself.

The next morning I was on the beach having a picnic on the pebbles when I saw his helicopter overhead on its way to Whistler Mountain where he was due to open the Garibaldi Park Reserve. Already, in just twelve hours, my mind was made up. I would put Yves and his unattainable ideals behind me and take up Pierre's suggestion, move to Ottawa, find a proper, serious job, and, who could say—I might even look him up.

My parents were overcome by my sudden transformation. Overnight I fell onto my mother's wholesome food with greed, and started sewing again. This time I created neat, tailored suits—just the outfits I imagined appropriate to the new city life I was going to lead. When my father mockingly inquired what I had in mind he was astounded and delighted to learn that I planned to apply for a job as a sociologist with the federal government.

I went east with some trepidation. My first sight of Ottawa was not reassuring: a busy city center full of office blocks and blue-suited businessmen. Would a lazy westerner like myself, used to open spaces and great tranquillity, ever catch up? I fell in first with a paragon family—Joan and Jack Coyne and their five children. They were old friends of my parents, and I saw through their eyes the tightknit, gossipy circle of Ottawa smart society. I didn't much care for what I saw. But I was soon swept up in my new job, as junior sociologist in a branch of the Department of Manpower and Immigration, working under a Czech called Dr. Celovsky at six hundred dollars a month. A prince's salary. I was at least rich.

It took me two weeks to build up the courage to call Pierre, two long weeks during which I kept taking his secretary's telephone number out of my bag and approaching the phone with determination, only to shrink away dejected. By the time I got through I was convinced he wouldn't even remember my name. I had signed my contract that morning, and dared myself to do it by way of celebration. Pierre's voice was warm, faintly amused. "Come over for dinner tonight," he said when he had taken in what I had done. "Be warned though. It's only spaghetti." It could have been dogfood for all I cared.

The prime minister's residence, 24 Sussex Drive, familiar to me from so many press photographs and news bulletins, is a large stone mansion set in acres of perfect lawn. It was October, a warm early autumn evening, with a few fallen leaves marring the unbroken expanses of green. I approached the door with some hesitation. It was opened instantly by a cheerful woman who welcomed me into the library. I was sad when she left me. The room itself was bleak—shelf upon shelf of art books and volumes of philosophy, political treatises and leatherbound theological tomes. "The prime minister will be down shortly," Verna had announced portentously, leaving me to browse. It was like waiting for the king. What I had seen of the hall only added to an impression of austere formality: the perfect symmetry of heavy Victorian ornaments, dour, unsmiling family portraits, gray everywhere. One thing was clear: the bachelor prime minister had done nothing to change his surroundings in his two years in office.

It needed only Pierre's voice to convince me that I had been right to come—there is no more cheery and flirtatious manner in the world than his. Dinner was the sort of meal a would-be-wife dreams of: course after course of insipid, colorless food, each more bland than the last until it became a matter of guesswork alone as to whether we were now eating cauliflower cheese or crème caramel. Always on the lookout for a task, I had an immediate picture of myself supervising delicious little snacks, under the by now miraculously smiling faces of the Trudeau ancestors.

I soon forgot the food, since the conversation seemed to progress so well. We laughed, we traded stories, we giggled at the same jokes. I like to think it was then that Pierre discovered how nice it would be to share his life, that there was something to be said for redeeming twenty-five years of adult solitude. And here was someone who felt the same way he did about a lot of things, even though she was so obviously naive and innocent.

Once again I did most of the talking, but I managed to get him to reveal something of his own past. I discovered that his father had made a small fortune by buying into service stations during and immediately after the Depression; that he had been a funny, boisterous father to have around even if highly ambitious and extremely demanding for his eldest son. Pierre was brought up in luxury, transported by chauffeur to his Jean de Brébeuf classical college in Montreal each day. He had had to overcome a shy, even gentle nature by taking boxing lessons. His mother, Grace, was Scots by origin, his father French Canadian. The Trudeaus spoke French at home, but Pierre was soon bilingual in English. He was a bright scholar, getting with no trouble a law degree at Montreal University and following this effortlessly by a master's in political economy at Harvard. After this he did a spell at the Sorbonne in Paris, and then went to the London School of Economics. Back in Canada, a group of young French Canadians, Pierre among them, started protesting within Quebec. It was sparked-off by what is referred to as the "Asbestos Strike." They published critical articles in their own magazine, *Cité Libre*, and, as a result of all this, some of them were blackballed from university teaching. Having lost his job, Pierre decided to indulge his love for travel. He crossed five continents and twenty countries with a knapsack on his back, and found he was not always welcome as a tourist. This made us laugh later when we saw the red carpet unrolled in the very cities he had been thrown out of in his traveling days.

It wasn't until 1962 that he became a teacher of constitutional law at the University of Montreal. From then on things happened very fast. Against all odds he was nominated for parliament by a principally Jewish community for saying: "If I were one of you, I wouldn't vote for me, but for one of your own." He became minister of justice in the Lester Pearson government only a couple of years later. He spent two years in that job, making a name for himself with sweeping reforms of the judicial system, championing fair play and human rights and becoming the beloved black sheep of the Liberal party. His informal approach, which included the sandals he wore in parliament on stuffy summer afternoons, was greeted with both affection and distaste, but never indifference.

I was beginning to discover that behind the silky, charming manner and the absolute confidence that had given him such a reputation for arrogance, was a curiously solitary figure. He appealed to me as a romantic who paid pretty compliments and loathed vulgarity and, as he couldn't prevent himself from saying, all the profanities of my generation. But judging by the questions he asked he was also a man of great and funny curiosity, the sort of person who can't pass a closed chest in someone's front hall and not wonder what it contains inside.

When I told him that I had just signed a six months' contract with the government a look of unmistakable panic crossed his face. "My God," I saw him thinking, "this lady's moved into town!" After dinner he proposed a stroll in the garden. I was a little cold. Across the river, in the crisp autumn air, we could just see the lights of the distant shore. Pierre gently kissed me My future looked even more promising.

Things never happen to me in moderation. Floating along next morning in a state of romantic euphoria. I was startled out of my fantasies by a letter from Yves. "I'm going to buy a sailboat," it said. "Please come and sail around the world with me. Now I have something precise to offer you." I took this to be the marriage I had pressed for. "Darling Yves," I wrote back hastily. "Your letter has come too late. I'm beached in Ottawa. I'm contracted into the very society you urged me to join— remember?" My letter wasn't entirely lacking in smugness.

I now settled down to the inflexible routine of the civil service. My job, I discovered, consisted of finding ways of helping misfits "rejoin the mainstream of Canadian economic life." The chronically poor, the hippies, the unemployed were all placed under our scrutiny as under an enormous magnifying glass. I wasn't totally happy with our way of going about things: living in our fluorescently lit, wall-to-wall carpeted offices, drawing our generous salaries, and having remarkably little contact with the people whose lives we were supposed to be magically transforming.

I soon finished what I took to be my first assignment, handed it to the director and waited to be told what to do next. Nothing. That *was* my job, they told me. The trouble was that I had done it too fast. So while they fished around for new ideas I sat at my desk with my pencils, notepads and government directories lined up neatly in front of me, reading Doris Lessing and writing timid adolescent poetry and letters covered in doodles of flowers. I was bored. I was also angry, particularly after my boss, having invited me to attend a conference on manpower with him as an observer, appeared rather shamefacedly next morning and said: "Ah, Miss Sinclair, just one thing. Would you mind wearing that little black sweater dress I've seen you in, and could you perhaps leave off the glasses?" (I wore a matronly red dress, dug out my wire-framed granny glasses and had my hair done in a neat set.)

It was just as well that I had Pierre. During these autumn months, our meetings were beginning to preoccupy me more and more. By Christmas we were confessing to each other that we were unmistakably in love, though we were both still full of doubts, Pierre far more than me. It was ludicrous, he kept saying. "I am simply *too* old. How can you take up with a man two years older than your mother?" During the moments his doubts were at their most acute he fought me off and returned to his social life of pretty ladies. I saw pictures in the papers at dinners and balls with other women—and like anyone in love suffered agonies of jealousy. One woman in particular seemed to pose a serious threat, a professor of French literature at Carleton University called Madeleine Gobeil, for Pierre frequently sought out her company. They were old, intimate friends, Pierre reassured me. No danger there. Another rival was a French Canadian actress, a sultry, pouting girl. I kept coming across pictures of her arm in arm with Pierre. None of this was quite as troubling, however, as the day he flew Barbra Streisand up to Ottawa to accompany him to a gala at the Arts Center. They had had, so my morning papers told me next day, a candlelit supper at 24 Sussex. It was romance. Every paper carried it. For the next few days my pique and jealousy was such that each time Pierre rang I slammed down the phone: "Go back to your American actresses!" I yelled at him.

The telephone was something of a problem in our lives. When things were going well Pierre either asked me to ring him at specific times, or phoned me when he had finished work. But neither of us is pushy or aggressive by nature, and on the days we were off one another, neither made a move. The telephone stayed silent. The rules for dating a prime minister are indeed tortured and complicated.

By Christmas, though, the worst was over, and we settled down to a pattern. We met for dinner once or twice a week, when Pierre's chauffeur collected me at seven, and Pierre walked me home around 10:30, when he had to get back to work. Occasionally we went to a restaurant in the more unfashionable places—what photographers did catch us simply assumed I was one of the prime minister's many pretty girl friends. Pierre continued to be the perfect listener. We did not often discuss his work—even after years of marriage I was frequently the last to know of any but the major decisions in his political career. What did happen at these dinners, however, was that I soon became convinced that Pierre, for all his reputation, was certainly no playboy. He didn't take his affairs lightly, and for that reason many of his relationships had been platonic. Though the hero of a popular cult and mobbed all over the world by glamorous women, he had seldom been intensely involved with anyone. He was too Catholic, too concerned about hurting people. If anything, it became clear to me, he was destined for eternal solitude.

The dinners were fun, but agonizingly short. But we had the weekends. Not every weekend, but many. It was then that we took off for Harrington Lake, his country residence, where we feigned great house parties and messed up all the beds for the Monday morning maids. We never in fact took anyone with us. Even better were our trips to his remote log cabin and square mile of land at Morrin Heights in the Laurentians. It was

49

on these occasions that I really came to admire his self-sufficiency, the way Pierre did things because he wanted to do them, and not for social conventions. "Choose your own life," he kept repeating to me. "Do what *you* want to do." We sat by great log fires; Pierre cooked steaks and prepared salad while I told him about "High Hopes" and my childhood holidays on the Sechelt Peninsula, my Moroccan adventures and Yves.

These were idyllic days, and the contrast between them and the rest of my life was extraordinary. Sometimes I felt completely schizophrenic. The only two people I told about our relationship were my sister Lin and Penny Royce, a friend in Toronto. It was to her that I sometimes went on the bleak weekends when Pierre was away or caught up with work. As an alternative escape I used to travel out to the airport on Friday nights with my enormous salary check and catch the first plane out of Ottawa. Sometimes I ended up in Boston or New York, where I would check into a hotel and prowl around, going to museums and the cinema. When I found myself with Penny it was as if my new life were pure imagination: in her company I soon reverted to drinking cheap red wine, eating bread and cheese, listening to pop music and getting quietly stoned.

Pierre knew I smoked marijuana but he had made it quite plain that he wasn't going to join me and that he was at least a little contemptuous of my need for it. It was an often lonely life. I had few friends in the civil service. Many evenings I wound up at a Chinese restaurant on my own. Not that I was really tempted to share my romance with Pierre with anyone else. I wanted to keep our life a secret. There is undoubtedly something inherently devious about me: I took pleasure in imagining that everyone around me thought I was leading one sort of life, while in fact the truth was so very different. I even played a game with myself: I tricked my friends into talking about Pierre, while I laughed silently to myself.

I couldn't really discuss all this with him, because I was very loath to let him see that he was fast becoming the only point to my life in Ottawa. My work was boring. I had no friends. But for him I would have packed and caught the next flight home. In any case, when I was with him my gloom miraculously vanished. I simply forgot how very lonely I was the rest of the time. As we became happier and happier in each other's company, so I lived only for our evenings and dinners alone together.

Then came the day when Pierre asked me to a costume ball at the National Gallery. It was our first public outing. We had always agreed that I would be bored at receptions at the governor general's or at diplomatic dinners, but this would be a livelier occasion. He told me that he would be going in black tie, since he hated dressing up, but pressed me to go ahead with my plans for a Juliet costume. I dug out a red velvet hippy dress, with sleeves that fell to the ground, and had my hair pinned up under a net of pearls. When I got to 24 Sussex Pierre was charmed and in good spirits; I by then was distinctly nervous. I had good reason to be.

From the instant I stepped out of the car to the flashing of photographers' cameras, to the moment I got home, I was in hell. It wasn't only that we were gawped at, shoved, and cut off from one another, but that every group we joined fell silent on our arrival; jolly laughter froze and jokes were broken off midway—"Here comes the prime minister." Wandering around in what seemed to be a lonely, aimless way I could sense people whispering, "Who *is* that dopey looking girl?" When we danced, people stopped to stare. As soon as we got into the car I burst into tears.

"I hated that and everyone was foul," I sobbed like a little girl. "I know they're nice people but why did they treat us that way? Why are they so nervous, so stilted, so *false*? I'm never going out again with you publicly that way. Let's stick to our quiet dinners."

If I had needed additional convincing that we were not cut out for public occasions I received it a few weeks later. Pierre was not going to be put off by one attempt. One evening he asked me whether I would like to accompany him to the house of some old friends of his, the Porteouses. It turned out that I had met Wendy before, and there would only be her and her husband Timothy, and a couple of other old friends of Pierre's. I was delighted and flattered. Was he perhaps finally beginning to think of me seriously?

The night of the dinner came around. I had made a special effort to look pretty. The first question that Wendy put to me was: "Do you speak French?" Pierre didn't give me a chance to reply. Unwittingly, for we had never discussed my languages, he said: "With a good old French name like 'St. Claire', what do you expect?" "*Ah bon,*" said Wendy. And, despite the fact that both she and her husband were English-speaking, and that the other guests spoke it perfectly, the whole dinner was conducted in French. The terrible thing was that I didn't understand a word—I couldn't speak French at all. The moment at which I should have told them passed by. Then the laughter and the jokes were such that all I could decently do was plaster a grin on my face and pretend to be following them. No one spoke to me. They were only interested in Pierre and in their own lives.

At 10:30 Pierre had to go back to parliament. Rudely brushing aside all offers of dessert I fled from the house after him, wailing at him in the car that I had never felt so insulted, so betrayed, in all my life. Pierre looked helpless, but it was then that we made a firm resolution: no more social experiments. Which is why, when we married eighteen months later, the event came as such a total shock to the world. "My country mistress," Pierre used to call me.

Meanwhile my life in Ottawa without Pierre remained far from satisfactory. I had moved from the Coyne's to sharing an apartment with a sympathetic middle-aged woman who worked as an interpreter in the civil service. She had lived in India and the place was crammed with pleasantly familiar bits of oriental art and ethnic material. Being so very alone in Ottawa I soon came to depend on her.

All my life I have been surprisingly naive: things that my friends know or assume immediately never occur to me at all. One early morning I walked through into our kitchen for a cup of coffee. There, in her uniform, though clearly having just got up from bed, was a policewoman. My landlady was appalled by the sight of me, and whispered apologetically in my ear: "Sometimes I get so very lonely." Shocked as I was, I pretended total calm, and the policewoman, who turned out to be no ogre, kindly dropped me at work. But it was all too much for me. I couldn't cope with Pierre *and* my rotten job *and* sharing an apartment with a lesbian. Happily an old Ottawa friend called Julie suggested we share an apartment, and within weeks we had set up an apartment together.

It was wonderful leading a normal life again, with parties and friends. But it was something of a break with Pierre. We started canceling our regular dates, and before long I had taken up with a divinity student. In my desperation at Pierre's indifference and in an attempt to bait him I even agreed to an engagement with my would-be pastor—which came to a hasty end after Pierre came west for a skiing trip to Whistler Mountain for the Easter of 1970. Joyfully, sensing a more committed relationship with Pierre, I bade farewell to my divinity student, and to the horrified astonishment of my parents proceeded to spend the most romantic, flirtatious holiday with Pierre and one of his great friends and cabinet colleagues, Jean Marchand. I also discovered that Pierre was such a strong skier that I could not begin to keep up with him. My mother was full of dire warnings: don't be the mistress of a politician twice your age, she kept repeating. Pierre will never marry you.

She might have been proved correct, but for my determination and a series of lucky events. After Easter I quit my job—I had had enough of sitting in front of an empty desk. I began to think seriously of child psychology, and was accepted as a graduate student in the psychology department of Ottawa University, to start in the fall. I had six months to fill. These changes unsettled me to the point that I realized that I no longer wanted to be Pierre's country mistress. I wanted more. I wanted to live with him. I wanted his children. And as Pierre sensed my growing closeness he seemed to shy nervously further away from me again, as if he were simply accepting the inevitable: that a dizzy, distracted girl twenty-nine years younger than he would in the very nature of things sooner or later leave him.

The end came one weekend when Pierre was holding a caucus party up at Harrington Lake. I was staying in the house, but since there were workmen around all day setting up marquees I had to stay hidden indoors. Chafing at the absurdity of it, alone, in hiding, I suddenly found that I couldn't stand the futility a moment longer. I packed and left. I saw Pierre once again as I was leaving Ottawa for the west. The airport was closed because of a major plane crash and in that rather heightened mood of fear and nostalgia for a lost love, I went to call once more at 24 Sussex Drive. I was dressed up for the part of romantic heroine, since I had decided to fill in the waiting hours by attending a garden party for Prince Charles being given by the governor general. I found Pierre in as sad and emotional a state as I was. We both cried. "I can't press you to stay," Pierre told me. "You're too young and too romantic. And in any case I don't believe you would be faithful." I went off, full of renunciation, and was immediately charmed by Prince Charles who looked at me closely and said: "Are you an actress?"

"No."

"Well, then you should be," and he moved on.

Pierre was undoubtedly right about my flightiness. I soon joined up with a group of friends about to cross the country in a twenty-dollar car; one of them seemed the perfect alternative to Pierre. He was a rock and roll guitarist, as guileless and youthful as Pierre was worldly and astute. By Winnipeg I couldn't stand the sight of him. I dialed Pierre. He was out. We pushed on. Two days later Pierre was in Winnipeg himself, and having heard of my call, scanned the crowds for a sight of me. By then I was in Vancouver.

I settled down once again with my longsuffering parents and prepared to spend the summer with old friends, forgetting Pierre. The plan worked for a while. I had fun. Then one day I realized what a charade it all was and hurried to the phone. Pierre's immediate warmth put me on my guard. "Will you come scuba-diving with some friends?" he asked, as if nothing had happened. I was furious.

"What for? More pain? I can't go on playing this sort of life." I was the one who always waited by the phone, I thought crossly. It was Pierre who played all the shots. To my surprise, he sounded confused.

"No, I've done some serious thinking. Come and we'll talk about it." He was about to pass through Vancouver on his way to the Williams Lake carnival and rodeo, so I hitched a lift with him back to Ottawa on his official plane.

We always argue about what happened next. As I see it we spent the weekend at Harrington Lake. One boiling afternoon, sitting down by the water, Pierre said reflectively: "Well, Margaret, perhaps we should talk about getting married?" It was a question. Not, says Pierre, a proposal. But I chose to take it as such. In a second I was on my feet and flinging my arms around him.

"When? Tomorrow?"

It was the first time the word had been mentioned. Pierre laughed. "Hey, take it easy." I was so excited I leaped from the rock I was perched on and into the lake where I swam around and around in circles like a frenzied dolphin. When I was calmed down, he put his conditions to me. I had to convince him, he told me, that I would be a good, faithful wife to him; that I would give up drugs, and stop being so flighty. He made it sound as stark and bald as he could.

"You must realize that you are not marrying just anybody. I am the prime minister of Canada. My job means a lot to me, and it won't be an easy life for you. It wouldn't be an easy life, even were I not prime minister. I'm fifty years old, I have never lived with any woman for long, and I'm extremely solitary by nature." I paid no attention to his words, only to his proposal.

Having made up his mind, Pierre put the days of vacillation behind him and became the most loving and attentive of suitors. He was also at pains to make it easy for me. He knew what he wanted, but he knew too that he must convince himself that it would work. Not for nothing was his motto "reason before passion," though with me reason and passion had met and clashed—and reason had lost. This period was the closest I ever came to seeing Pierre out of full control in all our time to-together. But here too reason played its part. Pierre wanted children and was saddened every time he looked around at his friends and saw them with children already grown up or even with small grandchildren around. Also we had been running the risk of my getting pregnant. Pierre objects passionately to birth control and had persuaded me to give up the pill within months of our meeting, so that the end of every month brought considerable tension between us. As for me, I didn't care where, how or when we married. I just knew I wanted to be with him.

We set off for the promised scuba diving trip in a state of considerable excitement, managing with difficulty to keep our plans from the friends who accompanied us, Joe and Debby McInnes. We went to Andros, an island close to Nassau, where the diving was superb. We lived in a derelict shack on the beach and dived all day, spending romantic and exhausted evenings pacing the sand while Pierre questioned me minutely about my past. He needed to know everything, he said, in case anyone in the future blackmailed him about me. *Everything.*

It was sometimes funny, sometimes painful telling him, but I didn't really care. Occasionally he said, almost sadly: "I know you'll leave me one day."

"Never, never," I replied passionately, furious that he could think of such a thing.

"Let's test it." he said finally. "You go back to Vancouver and keep our plans a secret. I don't want a circus of it. We'll have a quiet wedding when we think we're ready."

My family and my friends had never seen me in such a state of exuberant happiness. The worst part of it was that there was no one I could tell. I couldn't stand the loneliness and the secrecy for long, and finally broke down and confessed what was happening to my mother. She was skeptical and far from pleased. "You're making a big mistake," she kept saying, adding that on no account should I tell my father anything at this point. So the two of us, me delirious with excitement, my mother doubting and troubled, began to prepare for the day when I would become the youngest wife of any political leader in the world.

PREPARING FOR THE WEDDING

PIERRE HAD SET ME some tasks, and I was anxious not to fail him. In Vancouver, three thousand miles away from him, under the watchful eye of my mother, and my sister Lin as my other confidante, I would prove I was worthy of him. The first challenge Pierre had offered me was to demonstrate that I was capable of fidelity—particularly fidelity a long way away from him and in the company of close friends of my own age. The second was to stop smoking marijuana. Not just because it was illegal and a prime minister's wife simply cannot smoke grass and get away with it, but because Pierre was convinced that I was merely using it as an escape; a childish way of refusing to face up to reality. We had had heated arguments about it, with me begging to be allowed a few joints from time to time. Pierre was adamant. I had to give it up, or no marriage.

In a cloud of pleasure, blind and deaf to any possible danger that might lie in a marriage between a fifty-year-old prime minister and a twenty-two-year-old flower child, for so I still considered myself to be, I agreed to everything he asked. At the same time I set myself a couple of other, secret goals. I had decided to become a Catholic. Though Pierre never brought the matter up, I knew from our endless conversations how devout a believer he was. I felt that it was essential for our happiness that I should at least be able to understand and accept the rules of his faith, as well as some of its traditions. Pierre loves ritual. To this day not a Sunday goes by when he does not assemble the children solemnly around him, and read aloud to them from his leatherbound family bible, handed down from generation to generation of Trudeau sons.

I also wanted to become a first-class skier. Pierre is a remarkable all-round sportsman—though he won't play a single competitive game—and while I couldn't canoe, or play golf, or do judo, I could at least ski. I had no intention of watching Pierre hanging around impatiently at the bottom of every slope, while I picked myself out of the snowdrift above.

Then there was the little matter of the French. If there was one thing that my embarrassed and unhappy evening with the Porteouses had taught me, it was that never again in my life was I going to come across to anyone as quite so dumb. Languages, I had come to see, played a central part in his life. He was not only fluent in German, French and English, but loved speaking them whenever he got the chance, official or otherwise, taking great pleasure in his excellent accent and wide vocabulary.

One Saturday we were going up the coast to visit Grandma by ferry, Pierre having sneaked away from his work for a couple of hours unnoticed, wearing our oldest jeans and scruffy parkas, and sitting on the wooden benches on the top deck feeling as good as can be. A middle-aged man climbed the stairs and came and sat down alongside us. When Pierre looked up and smiled, he said, in heavily accented English:

"Lovely day, is it not?" Pierre picked up the accent instantly and replied in German.

"Yes, indeed. Are you a visitor from Germany?"

The man was astonished, and so delighted to find a companion with whom he could actually communicate that before long Pierre knew all about him: how he was a school inspector, traveling around Canada on his own. While they were deep in conversation, a pack of Brownies on a day's outing caught sight of Pierre and, recognizing him immediately, they flocked around him with their Brownie pencils and pads, asking for autographs. Pierre kept on talking, and as he talked, he signed away, breaking off from time to time to tease one of the little girls. Our German friend couldn't understand what was going on.

"What are you," he asked finally, "a school inspector, like myself?"

Typically, because Pierre cannot tell lies, he replied honestly. "No, I'm like your Willy Brandt." I thought the old fellow would have a heart attack. He jumped to his feet, jabbering wildly, and tried to prostrate himself on the deck at Pierre's feet.

Long after we were married, having watched him switch easily from language to language, I asked him one day: "Pierre, when you dream, do you dream in French or English?" He looked at me as though I were mad. I tried again. "When you think about something, do you think in French words or English words?"

His answer was very revealing. He said, patiently, as to a child: "I don't think in words, Margaret, I think in the abstract."

I wasn't going to be had. "Now come on, wait a minute. What is this? Of course you think in words. Everyone thinks in words. When I hear a bird singing, I hear the word 'bird' in my mind." It seems that Pierre doesn't go in for any of that. He has quite simply eliminated that stage from his thoughts. He is aware of a bird chirping, but he doesn't think of it in words. He's got beyond that—whether in French, English or German.

Arriving home in Vancouver that September I threw myself into my tasks. I found a small language school that had opened recently in the center of the city, called the Alliance Française. With considerable pride, and enjoying the deception greatly, I explained to my teacher that I needed to learn French because I was marrying a French Canadian, a young lawyer from Montreal called Pierre Mercier, and that I would be traveling constantly around Canada with him. The web of fantasy was growing.

Next I turned to the most demanding task, converting to Catholicism. It wasn't as simple as I had hoped. British Columbia is a mainly Anglican and Lutheran province and I couldn't find the sort of church I was looking for. My searches revealed just two Catholic churches in our neighborhood, a grand, social one which I shunned, and St. Stephen's, a hideous, modern building, more like a gymnasium than a church. With a sigh, I settled on that. My priest, Father Schwinkles, was obviously devout and deeply sincere, but he was an anxious, timid man and not always easy to reason with. I used the same story about marriage as I had at the Alliance Française, adding that Pierre Mercier was a practicing Catholic.

My lessons were presented as if to a child and this soon became a joke between Pierre and myself, to whom I had by now confided my intentions. When Pierre rang me each evening I would sneak off and take the call in the seclusion of an upstairs room, so no one could hear—he often suggested learned texts for me to read. Next morning I would set off to the library, take out Cardinal Newman's *Apologia,* or St. Augustine's *Confessions* or a treatise on St. Paul, and wade my way laboriously through them, storing up questions for my priest. I needn't have bothered. When I got to class I was simply presented with a manual: *What It Is to Become a Good Catholic*, with the important words underlined in heavy black ink.

One day his total disregard for deep understanding of the faith got to me. "Father, what does *this* mean?" I asked aggressively, pointing to a passage in my manual. "It seems to be saying in these heavy lines [I had of course ticked and underlined the offending words] that only Catholics go to Heaven. I have many friends about whom I care deeply and who are not Catholics. Won't I get to see *them* in Heaven?"

Father Schwinkles looked pained. "Well, Margaret, let me put it this way for you, very simply. Say you want to go to Paris from Montreal. There are several ways in which you can get there. You can row across, reach the other side and walk to Paris. You can take a train and then a steamboat and then another train. Catholicism is the jet plane to Heaven."

Without Pierre's constant help I would never have made it to conversion. A practicing Anglican childhood of Sunday School up to confirmation, a lapsed adolescence and a struggle to understand first the Moslem religion and then Zen Buddhism had left me extremely muddled. I found all the rituals of my new church both reassuring and deeply oppressive. I balked at some of the dogmatism, especially the Catholic attitude to sin, which I considered was a lot of sheepishness. It was only by reading the great Catholic theologians, and by arguing often nightly over the phone and in tears with Pierre, that I began to feel prepared for my conversion. Trying to understand what it all meant was part of my struggle to understand Pierre, so I knew I mustn't fail.

During these months I was also concentrating on the more mundane and practical side of preparing to become the wife of the prime minister of Canada. Did I look right? Was my hair cut well enough? What clothes was I going to need? I had to have a fairly extensive trousseau as I knew that soon after the wedding we would be paying an official visit to Russia for which, Pierre informed me, teasingly, I would need extremely ladylike clothes. None of my favorite shawls and beads but suits and dresses. At the same time I didn't want too many, since I planned to get pregnant as soon as I could.

Faced with this expensive and alarming demand for what amounted to a total change of style I turned to my mother for help and together we found a designer called Peter Plunkett-Norris. He ran a small shop near our house, with Isabelle Anderson, a perfectionist whose fingers were as nimble as those of Rumpelstiltskin's princess. At first Plunkett-Norris seemed the answer to my prayers: he was painstaking, friendly, and always happy for another fitting, another minute alteration. It was only later that I discovered that he was not quite as wonderful as he appeared: it was my first experience of being used. The moment our marriage was announced he held a press conference, displaying to the press the sketches of all my clothes, providing them with the measurements of my body, and telling the world lots of personal little stories: all the gossipy tidbits about how I came to him like a ragamuffin in jeans and sneakers, and how he had guessed the truth and hidden little tags with "M.T." under the labels of the clothes he made. What upset me most was the way he took credit for all the designs, when many of them were my own original ideas.

One of the dresses I had made was based on an exquisite sari Mr. Nehru had given my mother when she visited India in 1954 —white silk edged with green and gold thread. I also had a tapestry coat made, the color of rust, lined with sheepskin, with a matching hat, and trimmed with lambs' paws, as well as the essential silk day dresses and white wool coat. The cost was horrendous—my mother justified it by saying that they had spent a fortune on Heather's reception. Since I was having no proper party they would spend the same on my clothes.

During the long winter evenings, when darkness fell at four, I was learning to sew once again as I was determined to sew my own wedding dress. I went to evening classes with Mrs. Rees, certainly the best teacher of *haute couture* in Vancouver.

I had decided it was to look as little like a wedding dress as possible, yet not be so plain as to be pointless. I settled on a caftan, made out of a loosely woven white material, with angel sleeves, onto which, the last morning, so that no one but I saw it before the ceremony, I was going to stitch a hood. As I sewed I dreamed about the life to come.

It wasn't long before my friends began to ask what I was up to. Why was I refusing to go out on dates? My sisters worried that I would end up an old maid. "Margaret," said Heather as delicately as she could one morning, "Were you thinking of doing something? You can't just flit your life away without any kind of job." I saw her point. My life must have seemed strange: twenty-one years old, living at home, doing a bit of sewing, learning French, taking skiing lessons, and sneaking off to a Catholic church. I smiled; shrugged, muttered something about needing time to think.

After six weeks at home I went back east to spend Thanksgiving with Pierre in Ottawa. It was an exceptionally good visit. Pierre could see for himself that I had taken his tasks to heart, and had already made progress. I had given up marijuana and was showing no signs of a romantic fling with another lover. We had never been closer or more loving. It was then, sitting at 24 Sussex, after the turkey and the cranberry pie, that we fixed a date for the wedding. We had talked of getting married at Christmas, but Pierre had an official visit to make to India and Ceylon in January and though I would have loved to have gone with him we both knew I couldn't do it. The strain of such a dramatic switch from total privacy to the most public of public lives with no time for adjustment would have been too great. Chafing at the delay, we settled reluctantly on March 4, 1971.

Whatever doubts Pierre may have had about me as a suitable future wife were abruptly removed by a tragic incident through which I was able to support him. One of the reasons why I had wanted to be with him for Thanksgiving was that terrible things were happening in Canada. The F.L.Q., a small group of heavily armed terrorists, had launched what were all too soon seen to be the beginnings of a radical and violent separatist movement in Quebec. Until then the F.L.Q. had been going in for bombing letterboxes. In November 1970 they changed tactics.

Two cells of highly organized terrorists, among them young, educated students, kidnapped James Cross, a British diplomat, and then the Quebec minister, Pierre Laporte. Overnight a national crisis was declared. Naturally I wanted to be by Pierre's side: his loneliness in the days to come brought his position home to me in a way nothing, no pomp or glory or officialdom, had managed to before.

Pierre's reaction to those terrible days will go down in history. From the first phone call announcing the kidnappings his mind was made up: the Canadian government would not give in to terrorism. There was to be no bargaining, there would be no deals. Even though Pierre Laporte was a valued friend, no bargain was to be struck to save him. He felt this so passionately in fact, that just after we were married he told me that if I were ever kidnapped, or any baby of ours taken for ransom, there would be no deal, no amnesty. "Do you understand that?" he asked me, sternly.

"No, I don't. I can't. You mean you would let them kill me, rather than agree to terms?"

"Yes," he said. "Yes. I would."

He went on to explain that for him, as prime minister of Canada, the country would and must always come first; that whatever the circumstances he did not believe it to be morally right to give in to fanatics whose declared aim was to overthrow the system through violence and terror. "Once you do that," he said, sadly, "you're lost."

When I reached Ottawa I found him in a state of great turmoil, though his absolute unshakable conviction that he would not be blackmailed gave him tremendous strength. He needed it. When he enforced the War Measures Act, giving the police the right to pick up anybody off the streets for interrogation, the civil libertarians were up in arms. What had happened to the good liberal prime minister? He called them "bleeding hearts," scathingly, but it didn't prevent him being estranged from many close friends from university days, left wingers, who, while he had turned towards the Federalists, had joined the Separatists. The civil libertarian turned repressor; the champion of minorities turned conservative. It was a betrayal. And people said so, loudly.

63

Yet the tenacity with which he held on to his beliefs made him very popular among thinking Conservatives, and the more far-seeing Liberals, who agreed with him that what they were witnessing was a new kind of world terrorism. Pierre was one of the first leaders to take such a tough line, and over the coming years this attitude was to win him a lot of admirers, both inside Canada and all over the world. But at the time, November 1970, it heralded the end of Trudeaumania. The adulation was dying anyway: no political hero has it for long and by now he was midway through his first term in office. The sense of battle that gripped Canada only hastened its death. Accustomed as he was to public popularity, even adulation, it was hardly surprising that Pierre found the hatred and the contempt hard to take. I couldn't but feel confused myself: here were the very young people I most sympathized with, the "long-haired radicals" being persecuted, their houses broken into by police, while they were held for questioning. Only my complete trust in Pierre prevented a private battle between us.

The tragic news came suddenly. The phone rang at one o'clock on Monday morning. We were asleep. I heard Pierre say: "Oh, my God." Then: "Where did they find him?" And I knew that Laporte was dead. Pierre put down the receiver; I heard him crying. Tears pouring down my own face, I tried to comfort him. I knew that my strength for him lay in my innocence, my ignorance of politics. I couldn't understand the political implications, but I could love him. That night brought us very close together. He was a shaken man: I watched him grow old before my eyes. It was as if Laporte's death lay on his shoulders alone: *he* was the one who wouldn't negotiate, and *he* was the man who would now have to take responsibility for the murder of an innocent man. It gave him a new bitterness; a hard sadness I had never seen before.

The events in Quebec not only bound us closer than ever before; they altered, in a matter of days, our whole way of life.

Before the final blow fell there had already been some changes around Pierre. They had repelled me instantly. When I arrived in Ottawa I was met at the airport by Pierre's driver and told that we were to go straight up to the prime minister's house on Harrington Lake. It was late autumn, and a gentle mist was rolling in over the water. I looked out eagerly for the view I loved so much: the open fields, the solitude and wilderness. They had vanished. In their place were army tents, tanks, men with rifles. Before that moment Pierre had never had bodyguards. After it he was never without them. Suddenly there was around the clock security.

Pierre and I knew, although I was only there for that one weekend, that it was never going to be quite the same for us again. Our days of freedom and pure, unsullied romance were over for ever. From now on everything we did would be under police supervision. A rebel against authority anyway, I think that moment triggered in me the feeling that was later to break my spirit, when I was still struggling to remain Pierre's wife: the feeling of an omniscient police presence. It started that day, Thanksgiving 1970.

The momentousness of the discovery that we were no longer alone was briefly lightened by one comic interlude that befell us on the Sunday, while waiting for news of Cross and Laporte. We had set off as we often had in the past for a long walk by the lake, and being practiced hikers and accustomed to our freedom we had forgotten the army and the police and set off to climb alone up the mountain. It was a long trudge up and on our way we paused to watch the beavers in their ponds on the ridge, where they were busy damming the streams. Close to the top I caught sight of some very red maple leaves against a very black bough, and thought of a line in Ezra Pound's poem *In a Station of the Metro*: "Petals on a wet, black bough."

When the moment came to set off down again we discovered we were lost. Pierre was convinced it was one way, while I insisted on the other, and for a while we walked around disconsolately in circles. It was deceptive country: marshy with dozens of identical ponds and bogs. I kept repeating, somewhat petulantly: "I *know* it's this way," until Pierre got cross.

"Look, I haven't walked three times around the world for nothing. Don't tell *me* which way is right. *I* don't get lost."

At that second I recognized my red leaves and black bough, and pointed them out to him triumphantly. After a bit of a wrangle and with extremely bad grace Pierre gave in and we set off, running down the hill, leaping over hillocks and little bushes, shouting aloud with all the exuberance of relaxed tension. Before we had gone far we ran into a stranger in the woods—Pierre's guards would have been shattered to have seen him. It made a mockery of all the protection, the tanks, the tents and the armed guards. He was a hefty fellow in shorts and hiking boots and he was as astonished to see us as we were to see him. He recognized Pierre immediately. "Do something about pollution," he said in stentorian tones of outrage and strode off into the woods, out of sight.

As Pierre and I neared the bottom of the hill we were amazed to hear shots fired. It had started raining, and we were still running and leaping like mountain goats over the ridges. As we emerged into a clearing, there, before our incredulous eyes, was the most astounding sight: out in the middle of the lake, in a navy blue blazer and gray flannel pants holding an umbrella, was an absolutely bald policeman looking exactly like Kojak, with a rifle in one hand, firing shots frantically in the air to alert us. We were ashamed, and for all our uncontrollable giggles felt like a couple of naughty children in disgrace.

That weekend with Pierre should have warned me. But I was still so romantically involved with the whole notion of my dream coming true, and so much in love with Pierre, that it didn't occur to me to take stock of the life. I saw the security, and I hated it. Why didn't I listen to my own doubts, to the things I knew in my heart? It was partly because that weekend gave me a new role, a new shape for my dream. I would marry Pierre and turn his cold, lonely life into a warm, happy one. I would listen to his problems, and understand him when no one else did. The fantasy was so warm I blocked out the reality.

I got back to Vancouver in time to break the news to my father that I would be going back to Ottawa at Christmas to stay with Pierre. He was furious. "Christmas," he said, "is the time to be with your family." I realized the time had come to tell him the truth. "Dad, Pierre and I are going to get married." I have never seen a happier man, first dumbfounded then ebullient with joy. "Well, my God, how wonderful," he kept repeating, again and again. My marriage to Pierre, the prime minister of Canada, was to be the fulfillment of his own failed political dreams. He hadn't made it to 24 Sussex; I would be there in his place. He had always joked that the only thing he wanted in life was to see his five daughters all married, and what better match? I swore him to total secrecy.

I didn't tell him that I was dreading Christmas. It was to be my first real encounter with the Trudeau clan. I needn't have worried. It was such an enormous success I could see Pierre blossoming, his anxieties about me melting one by one.

Pierre and I drove down from Ottawa to Montreal together. As we were loading the car I noticed that he had packed just one suitcase. "Where are the presents?" I asked him.

"There are no presents," replied Pierre, surprised at my question. "We don't give presents at Christmas."

Coming from a family which takes its celebrations very seriously this was a nasty shock to me. When Pierre caught sight of my horrified expression he laughed. "O.K. Let's go and see what we can scrounge from the official gifts upstairs." In the attic we came upon box after box of rich spoils. I fell on them with delight: it was like Hudson's Bay Company, Eaton's and Holt Renfrew all rolled into one, and free. At first Pierre was a bit hesitant about looting these treasures, but then he joined in, and we had a marvelous morning burrowing around among the tissue paper and straw. When we set off for Montreal the car was overflowing with Christmas presents.

When we got there the first thing we did was go to tell Suzette, his sister, and Charles, his brother, the news. No, I'm wrong. We didn't actually tell them we were getting married. We didn't have to. It was absolutely apparent. Never in his life before had Pierre brought a girl home for Christmas, and never had he treated a woman so attentively in their presence. He rarely left my side.

Pierre's sister, with whom we were spending the holiday, lived just down the street from his mother. It was from Suzette, a docile but stubborn woman some three years older than Pierre, whom I liked immediately, that I learned something of Pierre's childhood, and the very powerful part his mother had played in it. As Suzette made ready for Christmas, she and I chatted, and I started putting together a picture of this happy, prosperous family struck down tragically by Pierre's father's death when he was just fifteen.

The only sadness that Christmas was that Pierre's mother, Grace, was already very frail and her behavior almost childlike, but with rare moments of lucidity. She appeared as a fragile, birdlike figure, bearing little trace of the elegant woman she had been in her heyday. Only a certain fastidiousness remained, a love of good clothes and things correctly done, and the piercing blue eyes of a young girl. She conveyed her approval of me silently, clasping my hand tightly as I sat by her bed.

Grace Trudeau, I learned, had taken her husband's sudden death courageously. For all her oldfashioned style she had become strongly independent, and she traveled, often with Pierre, all around the world. She was a woman of exquisite taste, decided judgment and great generosity. In the forties she had become a patron to many young artists in Montreal. She kept an extra bed in the house for starving young artists (particularly ones with talent), and she went to great lengths to get their work shown. After the war she became a close friend of Georges Braque, having met him first with her brother who had a villa in Provence, and their house in Montreal was hung with his paintings.

Pierre was a devoted son to Grace and lived with her much of the year long after he was grown up. On her insistence Pierre went to the best universities, and it was because of her enthusiasm and encouragement that he set off on his many travels. Because Pierre is the way he is, and not spoiled as he might have been, he traveled frugally. He invariably stayed in small, cheap hotels, but then once in a while, rather as I did in Morocco, he would splash out and treat himself to the very best. That was exactly his mother's attitude. When together they traveled not as tourists, simply gazing, but as Victorian travelers did, trying to absorb and understand everything they encountered. She had always encouraged Pierre to read, to argue, to develop his mind, and I believe that it was largely because of her that Pierre has turned out as generous, tolerant and understanding as he is. She achieved it by never putting any pressures on him to conform, or to hurry. It was never: "Pierre, you must get a job. You must start practicing law, or what will people think?" She didn't give a damn what people thought, nor does Pierre.

The Trudeau family home in which Grace lived and, soon after I met her, died, had been bought by Pierre's father at the end of the twenties. It was a wellbuilt, solid, very comfortable house in the center of Montreal; but it was not beautiful. It was Victorian down to the minutest detail and not a corner had been altered since Pierre, as a little boy, had fled in terror from a surrealist painting of a skeleton holding a skull which hung in what the Trudeaus called the "family room." The parlor was, of course, kept formally for best: a dark, oppressive, front room, full of browns and lace, with a mahogany grand piano and *petit point* upholstered chairs. Pierre and I escaped whenever we could to the shabbier comfort of the rest of the house.

Grace Trudeau was the kind of woman who has beautiful, expensive possessions. One of her most cherished *objets* was a nineteenth-century Dresden teaset, white with pink flowers. As a hostess, she was famous for her tea parties. Montreal ladies were invited for four o'clock and sat around the drawing room, perched on the *petit point* chairs, sipping their tea and fingering their *petits fours*, with their latest hats on their heads. They drank not from the best teaset, nor from the second best— the seashell Lalique, green leaves on white—but from the third best, the Wedgwood with the pink daisies. Then came the invariable ritual. When the last drop was drunk, one of the ladies would lean forward and say in a hushed and respectful voice: "Grace, show us *the* teaset." Mrs Trudeau would feign surprise, go to the cupboard, and then reverently lift out the Dresden cups one by one, just to admire, to touch and hold up to the light.

When she died the sad task came of distributing among the family her possessions, and making sure that every one of them had those things they best remembered. We discovered hidden away in one of her bureaus a complete handmade trousseau of the finest silk, embroidered in Paris, wrapped in blue tissue and never used. On top concealing it lay a second set, rather like the teacups, of well-used, sensible lingerie. I like to imagine her from time to time putting the mundane daily set to one side, lifting the silk trousseau from its blue wrappings, simply to gaze at the fineness of the lace, run her fingers through the silk, look lovingly upon the hand stitching, and taking pleasure in the simple ownership of such perfection.

Being the only member of the Trudeau family small enough, I acquired the trousseau. I hope she would consider that I have used it well. When I had time to examine the chest's contents more fully I found that I had inherited the most delicate of silk slips bordered with lace, exquisite nightdresses in georgette satin and chiffon, and gossamer fine handkerchiefs. My instinctive feeling was that it was far better to use them, rather than to leave them unadmired in a forgotten drawer. So I wore them for occasions which mattered, like the days I lunched with the Queen, or the nights I hoped to conceive a child. And once used they would be lovingly handwashed at 24 Sussex, so that they are in as fine condition today as when I first acquired them.

Pierre also inherited his mother's puritanism and frugality. I used to laugh at him when we were first married because, with the well-stocked linen cupboards that we had at 24 Sussex, he nonetheless chose to dry himself with the smallest and meanest towel he could lay hands on. He's a big, thickset man and the towel would barely reach around his middle. It made no difference pointing out to him, that, big or small, the towel would have to be washed just the same. "It's the training," he used to reply. By years of virtual brainwashing something of this rubbed off on me—something, but not much: frugality doesn't come naturally to me.

As March 4 grew nearer so Pierre became increasingly agitated. Every night our phone in Vancouver rang. "Are you quite *sure* you want to go ahead with this?" came his anxious voice down the line. If anything, as the weeks crawled by, my certainty grew.

In January came the day to make the wedding cake. By now, through dint of hints and guesses, like an elaborate parlor game of innuendo and forfeit, most of my family knew what was about to happen to me. Everyone that is, except for Betsy, who was away, and Janet, whom I dared not tell: I love her dearly, but she is the wickedest gossip alive. She was not living at home when Mother and I set to work on the cake. We were all in the kitchen giggling, having a stir for luck, when Janet flounced in.

"What in heaven's name are you making Christmas cakes for at this time of year?" she asked suspiciously.

Fear made me glib. "I'm going to wrap up all these separate layers in cheesecloth, soak them in brandy, and put them in the freezer for next Christmas," I burbled on. "I went to that sale at Safeway last week and found a lot of cheap candy and fruit." To my own ears it sounded insane. Luckily she didn't seem to notice.

70

I chose that moment to break the news to my grandmother, who came down from her cottage on the cliff to spend a few weeks with us. Her first reaction was one of total horror. "Oh, no, no, good lord no, you can't mean that," she said, without pausing to think how much it would upset me. I had made a point of preparing her because I wanted to give her time to go shopping with my mother and buy something new to wear for the wedding, but my mother had warned me that with her anti-Liberal, anti-marriage, anti-playboy views, there was bound to be trouble. She was a devout Protestant, to boot.

Being a basically kind woman, she got mother to take her off shopping and she bought a traditional wedding card in which she placed a handsome check. "I know I can't change your mind," she said, handing it to me, "but I'm not going to treat you any different from any of my other granddaughters, even though you're marrying *that* man." She went on: "I won't say another word. I just want you to be happy."

Pierre won the day. He could charm anyone. I warned him over the phone that grandma wasn't too happy. "Leave it to me," he said. When he arrived at the church for our wedding he saw my grandmother standing drawn up near the steps. "Hey, Mrs. Bernard," he called out. "What are *you* doing here? Don't you know Protestants can't come into a Catholic church?" She frowned, then her face creased with laughter. From that day on they were firm friends, with grandma flirting with my husband in the most outrageous way.

Just one curious, and not wholly pleasant, incident came to break the quiet pattern of those last few weeks. Among my trousseau I had made myself a blue coat, from a Dior pattern, and by good luck had found the perfect dress to match. I liked the outfit, and was dying to show it off. Toward the end of February I was invited to go to the wedding of two close friends just across the United States border at Blaine.

I rang around my friends, and four of us decided to drive together, in a battered old van: Ross, my friend from Morocco days, with his woolly beard and long hair; Barbie, who was to be bridesmaid but had decided to make the journey in jeans; and another Barbie who wasn't planning on dressing up. Of the four I was the only one dressed for an occasion. It wasn't entirely a coincidence: I was delighted for the excuse to see all my friends gathered together at once, particularly at a wedding, because knowing that none of them would be at mine, I was going to pretend that it was *my* wedding, and that they were raising their glasses to *me*. Hence the new outfit.

At Blaine we were curtly stopped and ordered out of the car by a couple of arrogant customs officers. Ross wasn't going to put up with it; he answered back, giving as good as he got. That was enough for them: they dragged us all to the station and began frisking us for drugs.

As it so happened Charles Trudeau, Pierre's brother, and his wife Andrée had been to India the previous autumn where they had come across a Swami who had told them that he "materialized" things in his hands. On falling into conversation with him, he had "materialized" some ashes for them and told them to give them to someone about to enter their family. That had been my Christmas present: a little sack of ashes, which I carried around in my wallet, with a picture of the Swami on the front.

The police seized on it with delight. "And what is *this*?" asked the inspector with a sneer of triumph.

"Those are sacred ashes," I replied indignantly.

"Sure. Sure thing."

"No, you're making a mistake," I told him, growing alarmed. "They're important to me. Just take a look at them. Do any test you want. But I promise you they're not drugs. They are the ashes Swami Babi materialized for me."

Hardly surprisingly they didn't believe a word, and took off a pinch of ashes to analyze. Meanwhile they had discovered a few grains of a substance that seemed to them to look distinctly like hashish hidden in a locket belonging to one of the Barbies. There wasn't enough there for them to take to the laboratory, but the find gave them the privilege, the singular honor, of marching us down to the cells for a complete body search. I was ordered to take off my smart new outfit. "Spread your cheeks, honey," said the woman officer in charge. I was outraged. To make matters worse, hanging on the wall of the cell was a picture of Nixon, leering.

They kept us there for four hours, and never did let us into the States. They told us they would impound the car unless we could produce a hundred dollars in American currency. It was

Saturday, and we made a few vain attempts to try and find a friend at home willing to drive down to us at the border with some American money, but after ten useless phone calls we gave up. Meanwhile the police kept up the harassment, interrogating each of us one by one. When my turn came, the red-faced cop, who seemed to me at that instant to personify all that I had rebelled against all my life, said to me, with an ingratiating smile: "What is a lovely girl like you doing with a bunch of bums?"

"Fuck off," I shouted at him. "Those are my friends."

He was suitably shocked, but said that I could go. I only hope he read the papers two weeks later, saw the photographs and that the connection clicked.

There was an ironic side to it all that he never did know. The truth of the matter was that one of the Barbies *did* have some drugs on her. She had had a lump of hash concealed in that locket around her neck. As we walked into the customs shed she emptied the locket behind a radiator—unfortunately leaving a few grains behind that the police picked up. Ross, with his wonderful impudence, threw down his car keys near the radiator after our four-hour ordeal had ended. Leaning down, ostensibly to pick up his keys, he retrieved the hash, which was smoked merrily within sight of the border.

Years later, at a White House dinner, President Carter asked me about the rebellions of my youth. "What happened," he said, "to the student activists of your generation, and the great hippy push?" I told him my story about Blaine and the customs officers, as just one example of the hostility that we met with every day—the way kids from good homes were constantly harassed simply because of the way they were dressed.

When they finally let us go we had to turn around and drive back the way we had come. In some ways I wasn't sorry about the experience. When I told Pierre about it, I added that nothing in the world would make me cross that border as his wife on a red carpet if they wouldn't let me in as an ordinary person in my own right. The first and only time I went to the United States on an official visit, as the wife of the prime minister, was in 1976, six years later.

As February wore on Pierre became, if anything, still more

nervous and jittery. Some days I even thought he might have called the whole thing off if it hadn't been for my rock-hard determination. Even his friends began to see that something was wrong, but when they questioned him he brushed them off brusquely; he made it much harder for himself by telling no one, locking himself up with a secret and worrying. His excuse was that he wanted a sacred marriage, not a circus.

It wasn't long, however, before his jumpiness exploded in public. In all fairness I have to take the blame for it; I was the one who used coarse language, not Pierre. One night, a couple of weeks before the wedding, Pierre was in the House of Commons in an unusually distraught and distracted mood. As the session wore on tempers became heated and one Opposition member in particular seemed to be directing needling cracks at him. Suddenly he could bear it no longer. Leaning over the bench, he mouthed, extremely distinctly, "Fuck off." There was an uproar. Instantly Pierre, very red in the face, explained that he had been saying "Fuddle duddle" to the honorable member.

No one was fooled. Within hours it had become a *cause célèbre* in Canada, and "fuddle duddle" a national slogan. It started a mania for T-shirts printed with the words, and cartoons in all the papers and magazines. It was even raised as a question of privilege in the House. Does a prime minister have the right to tell a member of the Opposition to fuck off/fuddle duddle?

Those last few weeks were full of private jokes, half truths and minor deceptions. I didn't enjoy them any the less for being so secret, but I was finding it harder and harder not to tease my friends about my new life. I set a guessing game for Betsy when she got back home to Vancouver. Riding up in the ski lift one day, she leaned across and said, in deeply serious and concerned tones: "Margaret, what are you going to *do* with your life? You can't waste all your education just sewing. Your relationship with Pierre is obviously going nowhere. Why don't you go out on dates anymore? What are you going to do?"

"Well, I don't know. Maybe I'll go back east. I've been thinking about going into domestic service. I'd like to be around children, and I really want to be in a home. I'm not cut out for the nine to five job." She looked at me speculatively and thought me quite mad.

Throughout this period I had been working toward my Catholicism. The final conversion took place just one week before my marriage. I knew then that I had to come clean with my priest because he would be officiating at the wedding.

I went through a quiet service with two close Catholic friends and afterward approached Father Schwinkles very earnestly. "Now I'm a Catholic I would like to confess," I told him. "I want to get all my past misdeeds out and be forgiven." Father Schwinkles was somewhat surprised by my sudden religious zeal but gave me an appointment for the next morning. I had realized that, being the timid man he was, he would never be able to stand the shock if, instead of Pierre Mercier, Pierre Trudeau had appeared before an altar on March 4. I also suspected he was a bit of a gossip, so confessional, with its oath of secrecy, was the place to warn him.

Next morning, suppressing my laughter, I knelt down behind the red curtain. "Father, I have disobeyed my parents. I have had premarital sex. And I have occasionally told lies." I could see his head nodding, scarcely attentive to my words. "I'm afraid I have lied to you." I sensed a sudden keenness in his attention. "I'm not marrying Pierre Mercier. I'm marrying Pierre Trudeau." There was a long silence. I started giggling on the other side.

Finally there came a low gasp, and in a strangled voice Father Schwinkles pronounced: "Go down on your knees, and say the Lord's prayer. Do three Hail Marys for your sins."

When we emerged from our adjoining booths I found Father Schwinkles white and shaking, saying in a quavering voice that he must go and talk to the bishop. His pretext was that he considered himself to be too humble a priest to marry the prime minister of Canada, and that we should have none other than the archbishop officiate at our wedding. Before he scurried off, muttering to himself, I stopped him. "Father we want *you* to officiate. We want a quiet and very simple wedding."

March 4 dawned clear and chilly, with bright sun and early spring flowers pushing up through the snow that still lay deep on the lawn. The wedding was fixed for 5 P.M. Given the time difference, we had planned that a late afternoon wedding would give Pierre time to leave Ottawa at 2 P.M., still do a morning's work, yet also give us enough leeway to get away to the mountains that night.

Like all wedding days mine started with a series of minor mishaps. Early in the morning I drove down into town to the hairdressing appointment my mother had insisted on. For all my couturier clothes much of me still clung to my hippy past, so I went reluctantly. How right I was. When I got there I found that the hairdresser I had been practicing with over the previous few weeks was away with flu. His replacement made a terrible mess of me. I came out almost in tears, looking like a fuzzy poodle.

Then the cake, my beautiful cake that I had planned with such care, was ruined by the shop where I had sent it to be iced. When I took it in I had begged them to leave it absolutely plain, since I planned to cover it with fresh violets and freesias. Disregarding all pleas, the pastrycook had spent hours covering it laboriously with little figures of bride and groom, and it appeared cascading with bees and doves leaping off into the air. I got it home with just enough time to strip them all off and start again.

Dad had explained the big event that night by cooking up a story that it was sixty years to the day since the Sinclairs had emigrated from Scotland, and that he was going to celebrate the occasion with a family dinner. In an unusual fit of generosity he had told each of my sisters to buy herself a special new outfit. I went along to help them, being considered in the family as the one who knew about clothes. Lin, as my maid of honor, was in a dress exactly like mine, only blue, and without the wide sleeves. Mother wore blue silk.

During the morning the phone rang. It was our local radio station. "I don't quite know how to put this," the reporter on the line said to my mother, "but we've heard a rumor that some wedding rings have been made for one of your daughters. Marrying a diplomat or something. Is there any truth in it?"

"Certainly not," replied my mother, quaking. He seemed satisfied, but it was a close shave.

Just after lunch our photographer appeared. My father had insisted on a family picture taken before the event, so we were all decked out ready in our wedding clothes. (The photographer, who seemed very nice at the time, later made a fortune from selling the pictures to *Time* and *Life*; he even had the nerve to send my mother a bill for our copies.) Only Janet was missing. She and Betsy were the only ones who knew nothing. She arrived late and, when she saw us all dressed up, her face fell. Looking at me in particular, her vicious tongue unchecked by any sense of occasion, she said "What kind of an outfit is *that*? You aren't wearing that dress *tonight* are you?" I looked at her. "Janet, I'm a bride. I'm going to be married today." She fell on my neck with a great hug. (That didn't stop her sneaking off out of the house to a payphone and contacting a friend, so that later he was the first to take a picture of us leaving the church.) Betsy just couldn't stop her tears of amazed joy.

Then, as I was putting the last touches to my dress, and packing up the suitcase I was taking with me into the mountains, disaster struck. Without warning, the worst snowstorm in recent Canadian history hit the east. Ottawa airport was closed. When Pierre asked them to keep it open for him he met firm resistance. What was the point in the prime minister risking his life for a skiing holiday? For such, officially, was his plan.

For an hour things looked bleak. A white blanket of snow settled over Ottawa, and the weather forecast promised more. Then, by one of those miraculous twists of fortune, the sky lightened, just long enough for Pierre to dash to the airport and take off. We had been listening to the forecast from Vancouver with horror. Then came his call: "Don't worry. We're off. Wait till I call you from the airport." And he was gone. (He fared better than his family. Suzette never got further than downtown Montreal, where their car was completely snowed in. "Oh well, we'll get to the wedding," said her husband comfortingly, having been told this was our engagement party. "No," she replied, sobbing, "this *is* the wedding.")

Even on board the plane Pierre was too cautious to break the news. Just before landing, he disappeared to the lavatory and came back in his morning suit. "Oh, I forgot to mention it sooner," he told his astonished aides, "but before we go skiing I have to go to a funeral in north Vancouver." So unsuspecting were they that even Pierre's executive assistant, Gordon Gibson, who had been a close family friend for years, had no clue. He turned up at the church in jeans and a windbreaker, grinning from ear to ear.

The call came at 5:30. Pierre had made it. It was a beautiful clear early spring evening, with the light just fading. There had been a soft fall of snow in the morning but through it you could see the crocuses and daffodils. We drove up to the church, my father at the wheel, Lin and I in the back. There was a car blocking the way. A policeman stepped out from behind it and said rather haughtily to my father: "I'm sorry sir, no one can come in here." "Get that car out of the way," replied my father, laughing, "I have the bride in here."

We had done it. No one but our families knew anything. There were no crowds, no reporters. Pierre had achieved his sacred ceremony, even if it was held in a church that looked more Protestant than Catholic and was so shabby that it even lacked real pews. To make up for it we had splashed out on the flowers: freesias, daffodils, tulips and cornflowers, nothing but spring flowers, banked up in all the bays and window sills and on the altar, and with sprigs of wheat in the posies (the Virgo sign for fertility). It looked more like a flower shop than a church.

The ceremony was very simple and I had chosen the words with care. Nothing about worshiping each other; just texts to do with love and peace. There were fourteen people in the wedding party: Father Schwinkles, an organist, my family, with my grandmother, came to seven; Pierre's side, since Suzette was stuck in the snow, consisted of Charles, his brother and best man, and Charles's wife Andrée. Gordon Gibson was drawn in to avoid the unlucky thirteen. My carefully planned service was followed exactly, even if I did break with orthodox behavior by throwing myself into Pierre's arms in the nave, without waiting for the ceremony to begin.

After the wedding service we drove off to the Capilano Golf Club, where my father had booked a private room for his six-tieth anniversary celebrations. The food was superb: smoked salmon, *filet de boeuf* with Béarnaise sauce, wedding cake and champagne. We were almost too excited to enjoy it: the tensions and secrecy of the past months bubbled up in all of us, and we drank and laughed and joked on the verge of hysteria. Even my sisters shared in my euphoria. Pierre and I had not seen each other for nearly two months and we were in an agony of impatience to be alone. On the flimsiest of pretexts we met in

78

the cloakroom to steal a quick kiss. But then we had to join the party once more.

That dinner was the first inkling of what was to come, the first realization that I had done a truly incredible thing. I hadn't just married the man of my dreams: I had married the prime minister. The waiters were all shaking with nerves because they had not been prepared for this. Even my parents were almost respectful. "That's the way it's going to be," I thought. "People are in awe of him. In time they will be in awe of me."

Weeks before we had planned that, at 9:30 precisely, Gordon Gibson would make the press announcement because by that time we would be well on our way up the mountains to my parents' log cabin. As it turned out we were having such a good time, and I was so carried away just being with Pierre, let alone married to him, that we were still at table at 9:30. So by the time we set forth from the club the first reports had arrived, and by the time we got to my parents' house where they had invited a few friends for their "anniversary" it was indeed a circus. The drive and entrance were lit up by television lights and crammed with reporters, stamping their feet in the snow and yelling their congratulations. I was too happy to care. We were married. We'd had our sacred service.

In the carnival atmosphere of the house, still almost breathless with excitement, I went off upstairs to my room and changed into tweed culottes and a yellow pea jacket. Father was still so dazed by the day's events that he tried to put Pierre into a separate room to change.

As we left for the mountains we were pelted with buckets of rice, our eyes blinking in the crisp air and the yellow glare of the arc lights set out in a fan all around the drive. We were driven up to our honeymoon in the back of the police car, the driver and his fellow officer in front, tactfully chattering away to each other, their eyes fixed firmly in front of them, while Pierre and I held hands and whispered in the back. I was happy and proud to be the prime minister's wife. My blues were over. I had never believed I could feel such devotion, adoration or commitment for anyone. I knew that the crisis was now behind me, and that everything that was good, all the happiness in the world, lay ahead.

Because of the difference between eastern and western time,

it was very late for Pierre by the time we reached the cabin after a two-hour drive. Then, at 6:30 A.M. next morning the telephone rang. It jarred us out of a dead sleep. Pierre leaped out of bed in a frenzy as this was an unlisted number, and he had told his switchboard to put no calls through except in an extreme emergency.

"Hello, hello," I heard him say urgently into the receiver.

"Oh hello," came the laconic reply, "I called to congratulate you." It was President Nixon, calling mid-morning from Washington to tell us how happy he and Pat were.

Later that morning we went out skiing. It was a brilliant sunny morning and I was looking forward to the day. I soon discovered that in the long months during which I had been preparing myself so diligently for marriage, in one field at least I had overprepared. We set off from the top of the mountain and within seconds I was out-skiing Pierre completely. He spent the next few years catching up with me.

My father had this family shot taken for one of his political campaigns—even at four, I had an eye for the camera.

This charm school fashion parade shows why The Hudson Bay Company is famous for furs and blankets, not swimwear. I was sixteen.

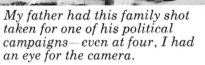

Right in the center and unable to smile with my mouth open—the orthodontist had not yet begun—but I was learning charm.

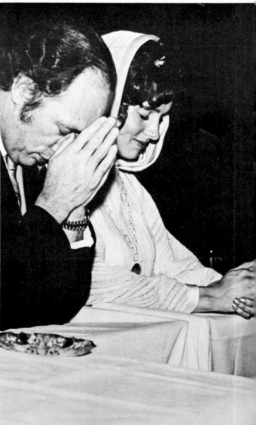

My sister Betsy (left) always claimed that Pierre asked her to marry him first—but I'd got him!

While prayer for a catholic is a serious affair, I couldn't help but reveal my happiness with a smile.

It was skiing for four hours straight on our first day of marriage, but then I did marry un sportif.

The bright lights are on me and so is my organic brown rice (always in large supply). It was put to good use by my sister Lin who pelted us as we left the reception.

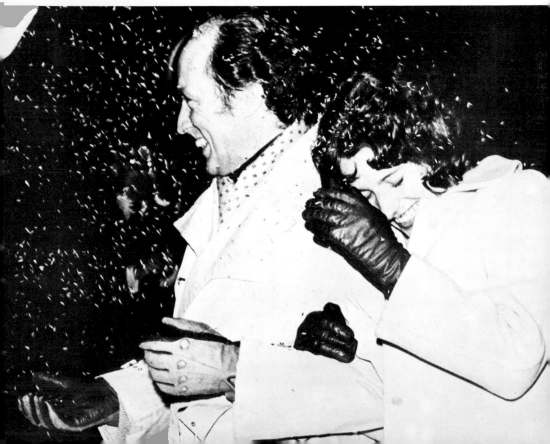

Justin, my perfect Christmas son, three days old and already wide-eyed and curious.

During our first summer vacation we visited an island belonging to the Republic of France. My peasant skirt, handmade from material I bought in Moscow, and Pierre's T-shirt did not match the official elegance of our hosts.

May 1971 in the Soviet Union— the opening moments of my first state visit. I will always remember Mr. Kosygin for his kindness and warmth.

Mommy is back from China and Justin is as eager to reach me as I am to hug him.

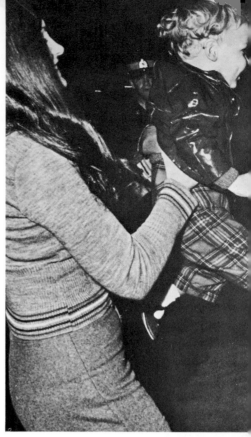

BELOW, LEFT TO RIGHT: *Three moments of joy for a mother: the homecomings of Sacha Justin, and Micha.*

Sacha hangs on to his pregnant Mom while we open a new play center. Like Justin, he was almost bald and his chagrin is a direct result of being deprived of the conductor's hat which he wore everywhere.

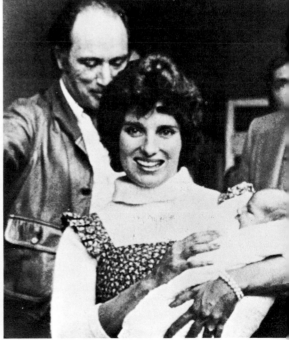

Leaving Boston Airport with Micha, our angel. We were there to see my parents and help them understand why I was leaving Pierre.

Micha and I both snug in hand knits from my mother.

A happy moment in the Rocky Mountains—Pierre carried Justin and I carried Sacha.

A happy family at Harrington Lake.

Justin greets the Queen and Prince Philip but seems more interested in the camera—does he not realize who is coming to dinner?

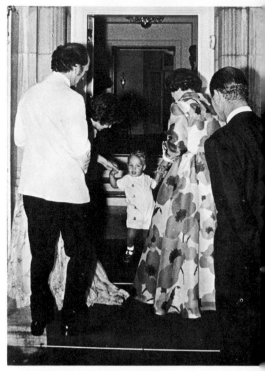

BELOW LEFT: *I always had the pleasure of escorting Prince Philip during royal visits and so was able to enjoy his extraordinary wit and charm.*

BELOW RIGHT: *Pierre and I join Anne and Mark, happy newly-weds, at a disco party. We found both to be honest, warm people.*

While Pierre admires his impeccably coutured wife, I am lifted from a near fall by my gracious Queen.

Prince Charles with an "older woman" (by two months). I have only met him officially yet I feel we share a common spirit.

The table at 24 Sussex Drive is set for an official dinner.

The Prime Minister of Luxembourg and Mme. Thorn chose to share our wilderness retreat at Harrington when they came to Canada in 1975.

My visit to the Louvre with Mme. D'Estaing and Mme. Chirac—it frightened me so much that I passed out cold in front of a great French masterpiece.

It was a great honor to meet such a woman as Golda Meir.

ABOVE LEFT: *President Nixon's charm is known—we were obviously enjoying our only meeting.*

ABOVE RIGHT: *Arriving in China, October 1973. We are met by Chou en Lai, a truly remarkable man whose friendship toward me I will always cherish.*

OPPOSITE: *With my new Parisien hairstyle but lacking the* haute couture *I should have been wearing, my discomfort at the Elysee Palace was lifted only by the humor of President D'Estaing.*

LEFT: *Liberated Margarets of the world unite! Mrs. Whitlam of Australia and I enjoyed airing our views on women's rights in Jamaica.*

Being eight months pregnant could not deter me from climbing the Great Wall of China.

ON BECOMING CHATELAINE

O N MARCH 7, our absurdly short three-day honeymoon in the mountains already over, Pierre and I flew to Ottawa. I had been dreading our arrival at the airport. I knew that there to meet us would be cabinet ministers and their wives, as well as close friends and relations of Pierre's who had heard the news over the radio and wanted to be the first to welcome us back. We stepped through the glass doors into pandemonium: congratulations, embraces, warm handshakes—all eyes on us, beaming smiles everywhere. Photographers, reporters and curious onlookers thronged the hall, pressing in on us until I felt dazed. Dazed, but not unhappy. It was a wonderfully warm welcome, and I longed to tell them all how happy I was and what a success I was going to make of it. The pictures taken that day show a shy but eager girl; a brand new blushing bride.

For six months of the year Ottawa is under snow. The winter of 1971 was one of the worst in living memory, and the weekend we married six feet of snow fell, laying a great cold hand over the city. Driving down the street from the airport was like finding our way down a tunnel. The snow had piled up on the pavements in towering mountains of ice, soon, with the gravel they had laid, to turn into great filthy piles of gritty slush. But the day we came home to 24 Sussex Drive there had just been a fresh fall and an air of stillness and magic lay over the scene—the immense white garden, the big windows lit up cheerfully to welcome us. In the back of the car I hugged Pierre: this was to be my home.

We turned into the gates, the guards came to attention and

saluted, and we swept up the drive to the front door. I found the whole household waiting to greet me in the hall, a long file of smiling people eager to say hello. I already knew most of them, of course, because of my eighteen months of surreptitious calls on Pierre. But my arrival at 24 Sussex as his bride was quite a shock to them, particularly since only three days before they had no idea that Pierre was even planning to marry. Now here he was with his bride. This was a very different matter from a casual, eager-to-please girlfriend. They finally had a mistress of the house, a twenty-two-year-old girl whose reputation as a hippy and a flower child was known to every one of them.

Clustered around in the hall in their uniforms and most formal clothes, laughing and joking with Pierre about the suddenness of the event, they made me feel enormously welcome, hiding whatever doubts they may have felt under pleasant words and wide grins. There were seven women, and one man, Tom MacDonald, the steward of the household, making it rather like a convent with a father confessor. There was Hildegard, a middle-aged German woman, the senior maid who later was to make me happiest at 24 Sussex. There was Verna, the maid who had shown me into the library the night of my first date with Pierre, who for my homecoming had arranged flowers in the form of messages all over the house. "Welcome home, Mrs. Trudeau," said the roses and carnations all the way up the big winding staircases to the first floor.

My married life had begun, and with it the long, arduous task of learning to be chatelaine of 24 Sussex Drive. There was so much to learn. Not merely the protocol, how to receive guests and what to talk about to important visitors, but the entire organization of an enormous household, which had been running well for years without me. There was the new and cramping formality to get used to; the invitations and presents from total strangers; and, perhaps most overwhelming of all, the fact that, from now on, I would always be on show. A goldfish in a glass bowl.

My immediate problem was not so much the space and grandeur, as simply getting used to having so many servants, so many strangers bustling around my house. I kept waking up in the early morning and wondering what all the noise below was, and whether someone had broken in. It was an effort to stop doing things for myself and accept being waited on.

The first morning I threw a pair of panty hose with a hole in the toe thoughtlessly down onto the chair in my bedroom instead of putting them into the waste basket. That evening I found that they had been painstakingly darned—a pair of cheap, ordinary panty hose. The maids couldn't do enough for me to make me feel at ease.

The halcyon days didn't last terribly long. The effusiveness and warmth that I basked in during my first weeks as the prime minister's wife didn't survive the long Canadian winter. Before the snows had melted it was clear that there would be friction between me and almost everything I touched. The glossy façade began to crumble. The rot started with the servants and it provided me with a sour, if symbolic, taste of things to come.

It was hardly surprising that my new staff resented me. I was younger than almost all of them by many years and totally inexperienced in the household affairs in which they excelled. Who was I to pronounce on dirty silver or inept waiting at table? For one thing they had been looking after a bachelor prime minister of modest, even austere, tastes for over three years and had had relatively little to do. For another I was a fussy perfectionist, and determined to turn Pierre's gray existence into something luxurious. I wanted 24 Sussex Drive to be a much praised establishment. And I was dreadfully impatient; twenty-two and in a hurry.

My first battle was with the cooks. There were two of them, Margaret and Rita, when I arrived, neither one with any gourmet pretensions, but both of the plain, oldfashioned, English school. Given my taste for brown rice, and my fastidiousness, I wasn't going to put up with the extraordinarily drab and unvaried meals that I had eaten during my earlier evenings with Pierre—one long round of steak pie, chicken pie, meat loaf and chocolate chip cookies. Two days after the honeymoon was over I started work on the menus.

I was made more courageous in my forays into the kitchen by hearing the story of Golda Meir's recent meal at 24 Sussex. Pierre told me how on leaving for work the day she was due to come to lunch, he had explained to Rita and Margaret that the food must be kosher. They beamed their acceptance. The menu said *sole au gratin.* It went first to Mrs. Meir, who seemed taken aback and then to Pierre, who saw to his horror that the fish had been piled unceremoniously into an earthenware oven casserole, with greasy marks down the sides, and that it hadn't been deboned. The guests fished in vain among a great bony mess lying in a bed of sauce and cheese.

I set to work, fired by a crusading zeal to get Pierre eating a proper balanced diet. I couldn't see how all the needless excess sugar and cream and sauces could be doing him any good at all. I hadn't been there a week before I had been out and bought a dozen cook books and begun to make lists and study recipes, comparing fourteen ways of cooking chicken or eleven sauces for fish. From these I drew up a series of healthy, nutritional and, to my mind, delicious menus.

Then, braving the wrath of the cooks, I insisted on being present when a new dish was tried out, and refused to order anything for a formal dinner party until it had been well tasted among ourselves. It wasn't easy. Rita was charming and gentle, and eager to please me, but I soon discovered that Margaret was a tyrant, the kind of woman who was as sweet as cloying sugar to my face, yet harried and tormented the other servants behind my back.

One morning I slipped unheard into the kitchen and heard her nagging, grating tones. She was an enormously fat woman, weighing some three hundred pounds, and she was chopping away at something on the board with an ominous thud, thud, thud. It wasn't the sound that alarmed me as much as her words.

"You get the hell out of my kitchen or I'll throw this knife at you," she was snarling at one of the maids.

I said quietly, not raising my voice, "Margaret." She wheeled round.

"Oh Mrs. Trudeau, how very nice to see you. I didn't realize *you* were here."

Verna, from the start, tried to protect me. She was an engagingly cheerful woman, with children of her own, and she treated me just like one of them. "Don't get involved," she said when she saw me witnessing these scenes. "You are the *lady* of the house. It's not your job to sort it out." But I felt that I had to. Morocco had left me with a feeling that a community of people have to work harmoniously together, in order to survive. This became all the more important to me later as the children came.

Margaret and I just couldn't hit it off. It was hardly surprising: it would be hard to imagine two women less alike. I was slight, thin, determined and in a position of authority; she was fat, lazy and domineering. One of us had to go. But it took me ages to find a replacement. Pierre wanted a French chef; I secretly longed for a Chinese one. I wrote to cooking schools in France, talked to the French ambassador, advertised widely. Margaret eventually left of her own accord, and for a while we put up with Rita, who was deeply insecure with the gourmet menus I asked her to produce. The wonderful day came—but this was much later—when I found Yannick Vincent, a burly, thick-shouldered French immigrant who had trained in France and was executive chef at the National Arts Center. He was the ideal answer, a superb chef, and a comfortable family man who raises sledge dogs and paints landscapes in his spare time.

The fact that I was so immediately engrossed by the details of our food and servants gives some idea of how lonely those first months of marriage were. After the dry, mild weather of Vancouver even the climate was alien to me.

Throughout April it thawed. Layer upon layer of salt, sand, garbage, dog dirt—day after day something new and vile was exposed, until finally the sun and rain got rid of every last patch and dirty smell. In Vancouver spring starts at the beginning of March; here I found I had to wait until May. Night fell almost as soon as lunch was over. Luckily Ottawa is so cold that most days there was a crisp blue sky, and until the thaw began in earnest the snow was crunchy underfoot. On those pearly mornings I would put on my high fur boots and stride around the gardens. Then would come a week of ferocious blizzards, when an icy wind came roaring up the river, and I languished indoors, chafing at the restrictions and niggling away at the staff.

I had few real friends in Ottawa. I found myself to be a spectacle of ceaseless curiosity, often perfectly friendly curiosity, but I soon sensed that everything I did, or wore, was instantly repeated around the town.

My isolation was increased by the fact that Pierre had decided that there was no need for me to get involved in politics.

He put an embargo on me. I was absolutely taboo, not only for his office, but for everybody. No one was to come near me, no one was to pester me, or ask me questions. I was to give no interviews. No one dropped in: who does drop in on a prime minister? I had grown up in a house full of busy, gregarious people, where friends came and went all the time, and at first I begged my friends to do the same at 24 Sussex. But they were daunted by the police checks, however friendly, and that distinct aura of formality that lay like a shroud over the house.

During those first months I also had a hard time transforming myself from a peasant-skirted, Indian-shirted hippy into a gracious lady. None of it seemed to come very naturally to me, though I did find that being hostess at parties, where I was often the youngest person in the room by twenty years, was aging me with frightening speed. At the tea parties and luncheons for the wives of visiting heads of states I sometimes felt more like their youngest daughter than their host's wife.

They put me down continuously, nicely but continuously. It was as if they couldn't help it, but I felt very small. And I soon found that I didn't have much in common with most of the wives of Pierre's colleagues; partly because they were all so much older than I was, and partly because I am, by nature, indiscreet and I had to protect myself by not becoming involved.

My closest friend was Nancy Pitfield, wife of the head of the civil service, whom I had met while she and Michael were courting and Pierre and I were starting to go out together. She was moral but with a great sense of fun, absolutely my opposite in that she was always calm and unflustered whatever happened. I made few other close friends, though my relations with Pierre's cabinet were very genial. It was as if I had become the sympathetic ear—I remembered their children's birthdays and their wives' names and I did my best to create an aura of friendliness. But it was often hard. Several of the women I found very ambitious and very bitchy, quick to hit out at me if I made the slightest mistake. The few exceptions came about by luck; like the day I helped Jane Faulkner, wife of one of Pierre's ministers and a recent arrival in Ottawa, paper her nursery before the birth of her second baby. I was happy to help; I had nothing else to do.

102

The one political wife who was immensely kind to me from the day I moved to Ottawa was Mrs. Michener, wife of the governor general. She was a perceptive, if somewhat regal, woman, and once I had become accustomed to her formal airs and astonishingly high standards I grew to love her dearly. Soon after we were married she gave a party for us in the governor general's residence: it was to be the wedding reception we had never had, and Pierre invited all his close friends. (The dress I wore that night was the one that later got me into such trouble in Washington on my last official engagement as the prime minister's wife. It had been made especially for the party, a fine white wool dress studded with pearls and fitting like a glove, which to my romantic eyes seemed more like the real wedding dress than my caftan ever did. Washington accused me of slumming.)

A few days after the ball my phone went again. It was Mrs. Michener; would I care to take tea with her? Somewhat fluster-ed I made my way across the street, and then proceeded to be given my first lesson in How To Be The Perfect Prime Minister's Wife. Mrs. Michener, who knew about these things, had a favorite expression, "a woman in her own right," which she used all the time. In 1971 that meant something. When her husband was the Speaker of the House she had written a little book on protocol, as well as another on Rideau Hall, the governor general's residence, and on the functions and protocol of his job. So she was a master of the art of protocol, a petite, trim, immaculately groomed woman, with an intelligent, crisp voice.

She wasted no time. No sooner were we sitting around her immaculately laid tea tray with its bone china and thinly sliced cucumber sandwiches, than she started listing some of the things that I must do.

"If you have a president's wife, or someone who ranks higher than you do—and this applies particularly to royalty—and you see them pick up a cigarette, then you must pick up a cigarette yourself to make her feel comfortable."

Since I didn't smoke, I laughed. Naively, I explained why it was such a joke—how could I possibly light up a cigarette when I don't smoke? She frowned.

"That, my dear, is just the point," she said succinctly.

"Protocol is learning all the things that you have to do however much you find them unnatural and trying."

I felt suitably chastened, but my heart sank at what was in store for me.

This was the first of many such teas. Mrs. Michener tried very hard to make me good, and for all our differences I adored her and listened hard to her lessons. I fear I wasn't a very good pupil.

But I took her lessons to heart, and would hurry home from the teas with lists of advice, full of good resolutions. In this I was helped by my character. I'm a perfectionist and all my life I have worked very hard at details. So to protect myself from the endless petty chivvying at home, I set to work to become not just the Perfect Prime Minister's Wife, but the *most* perfect wife in the world.

It was at the Micheners' ball that I had my first hint of a wonderful development in my life. Halfway through the evening the head of her household had asked me to dance; he had all the poise and skill of a ballroom dancer and he whirled me around the room in a mad, gay waltz. Suddenly I thought I would be sick. My immediate instinct was that it must be the anxiety or overexcitement. Trying so hard to learn so many new things at once, who wouldn't feel sick at times? I put it out of my mind. Then at Easter when we had a real honeymoon, skin diving with two other couples in the Caribbean, the strange queasiness struck again. With it came a heat rash which spread over my skin every time I went into the sun. One of our friends was a doctor, and he looked at me in a funny way; the only cause he could think of was, he said, some metabolic change. And what could *that* come from?

The day my pregnancy was confirmed there was not a happier lady in Canada. I've done it, I thought, I've done it. The doctor took my dates, worked it all out on his plastic calendar, looked up and said laughing: "Your baby is due on December 25." Overnight, none of the little things that had once been niggling at me seemed to matter any more. I stopped fighting against being locked away in an ivory tower. An ivory tower that wasn't an ivory tower at all. It was just an awful load of daily responsibilities of a kind I had never expected to find myself coping with.

Shortly after we got home from the Caribbean, I went off on my first official visit as wife of the prime minister, and a pregnant one at that. It was to Russia, a grueling program of seven cities to visit, as well as a couple of days in Siberia. Pierre was to discuss technology and trade and the laws of the sea that we shared. I was almost childishly excited, and extremely anxious to do well: now had come the moment to show off the results of Mrs. Michener's lessons.

Before our departure no one had taken any notice of me at all: since Pierre had placed this strict embargo on me, no one from his office came near me to brief me about what lay ahead. On top of it all his staff were used to dealing with a bachelor prime minister and probably gave little thought to the added complication of a young and ignorant wife. As our itinerary kept changing up to the last day of our departure I wasn't even told how many long or afternoon dresses I would need. Was there anything I needed to know? I asked everyone I met. No, no, they all replied comfortingly. Everything will be taken care of. The ambassador's wife will look after you. Just go along and have a nice time.

We shared our plane with some hundred reporters, and for many of them this was their first glimpse of Pierre's wife. I shifted about uneasily, uncomfortable in this blinding glare of eager curiosity. There was one journalist in particular, Christina Newman, who had come to Canada especially for *Macleans* magazine to get a story on me, and she made my life a misery. The government press office in Ottawa had told her before she joined us that there would be no point in trying to get an interview with me—Pierre wasn't having it. She came anyway and as the days went by her frustration grew; I had my first taste of bitter journalism from her.

The only person who knew I was pregnant was Mr. Kosygin's daughter, Mrs. Gvyshiani, a gentle, tactful, very educated woman whom I grew very fond of. I had confided in her because I didn't want to appear rude at official banquets by not eating or drinking vast amounts, and also to explain why I wasn't as eager as I might be to start out at 8:45 every morning with a full day's schedule of hospitals and factories to visit. I begged her to keep it a secret. If the baby was announced too early it would be a long wait for the Canadian people. She was touchingly kind and considerate, and found a marvelous way of stopping my morning sickness by carrying lemon around in her bag and giving me slices to suck in the car between visits.

She couldn't do much for me at the official banquets though, as I usually found myself stranded miles away down the table from her. One night I was placed next to an important gentleman who, peering around at me said gallantly: "We like our women *big*," and proceeded to pile another huge mound of dumplings onto my plate, while helping me lavishly from a passing dish of meat. I found all the food heavy and rich, and there was much too much of it. I struggled away at my task, trying to look on each mouthful swallowed as another mark in Mrs. Michener's book. Then came the day when I was presented with the great Russian speciality: horse. That was nearly the end of me.

So intent was I on swallowing the food that it was several banquets before I noticed a curious fact about Russian protocol: at every official meal I found myself seated next to the same man, the minister for science. The only possible explanation was that he must have ranked precisely as I did. Nice as he was, and hard as he tried to keep me amused on stories of Russian life, our conversation could hardly have failed to have flagged: most meals consisted of seven courses and they were spun out interminably. What was more, every word we exchanged had to go through our interpreter, who sat on a stool just behind my shoulder. It was hardly surprising that we didn't rise to many jokes. We smiled, we grinned, we exchanged grimaces of amusement and self-mockery, but there our relationship ended.

As if the loaded platters of food were not enough, I also had to contend with the seven glasses lined up in a neat row in front of my place, each intended to accompany a course, and each full to the brim with vodka. The first night I discovered that my neighbor suffered from a liver complaint—who could wonder with so many official banquets? He had solved the problem by asking that each of his glasses be filled with water, not vodka, at the start of the meal, so that at least he could go through the semblance of toasting and yet not fall under the table in agony. I welcomed his solution with joy. The waiters obligingly filled my glasses with water. When the toast came around I took my first swig, with a sideways smirk of triumph at

Pierre, who I could just see out of the corner of my eye struggling with his vodka. The smirk froze on my face. I hadn't reckoned with Russian water. It was without doubt the most foul-tasting brew that I have ever swallowed. High in sodium content, salty, hard and so frothy it might have been a glass of liquid detergent. From then on I stuck to pretended sips of vodka.

Before we left for Moscow we had been warned by Pierre's office that we would undoubtedly be bugged the entire time, and to behave therefore with some caution. "Oh come on," I said laughing to the man who told us. "What's all this cloak-and-dagger stuff? Don't tell me they bug the prime minister of Canada." He looked patronizing. "Just you wait and see."

Our second day in Moscow his point was proved. We were installed in our suite in the official guest house, an austere, dark set of rooms with plain, almost drab furniture relieved only by touches of luxury all the more remarkable for being so rare: gold silk bedspreads and carved headboards. I decided to test out the bugging story. We had been walking around the city looking at the sights and I was exhausted. As we shut the bedroom door behind us, I said loudly and distinctly to Pierre: "Oh Pierre, what wouldn't I give for an ORANGE! My kingdom for an ORANGE, one fresh orange." Five minutes later came a knock at the door. Outside stood an expressionless waiter, holding a tray in his hands. On it sat a banana, an apple and, in the middle, occupying pride of place, an orange. He placed the tray ceremoniously on a side table and started carving up the orange, which he then presented to me with a low bow. Not a word was said.

I came to respect the technology of their bugging greatly. On the day we went to St. Peter's summer palace in Leningrad, it was perfect summer weather, clear, still and very hot. Pierre and I strolled off on our own, down the avenues of gardens with their gold fountains and splashing dolphins, hand in hand. Soon I was dying of thirst. "Water, water everywhere and not a drop to drink," I complained to Pierre. When we got back to our car the driver was waiting for me with a plastic bottle and a glass.

"Madam, I was just wondering if you were thirsty?"

It was absurd. Long-range transmitters to pick up every word.

Before long the charms of our permanent eavesdropper began to pall, and Pierre and I found ourselves retiring constantly to our bathroom, where—both taps running so that we wouldn't be overheard—we engaged in furious arguments about Russia. I complained that it was all so incredibly drab and dingy, while Pierre defended it. When the eavesdropper took the form of my interpreter Tanya, a dumpy, white-shirted, black-skirted lady who stalked so close to my side that she was always bumping into me, my irritation grew. Her unreasoning patriotism also drove me mad. Her lines were quite something. One day we visited a park with three decrepit benches, a moth-eaten patch of grass and one solitary tree. This, so Tanya informed me, was no ordinary park. It was a rest-and-recreation area donated by the all-loving government, so that the People of Russia could relax. Another day she took me to the Tretyakov Gallery in Moscow, hurrying me past the masterpieces of pre-revolutionary Russian art and coming to rest with a reverential sigh of admiration before a row of paintings of great buxom ladies with their sickles and vast haymaking machines. "These are the *great* paintings," she informed me. "But it ain't art," I replied.

But I did try very hard to be pleasant. I made friends with Premier Kosygin, whom I found gentle, considerate and grace-ful—a man whose soft eyes had a charming twinkle to them. Obviously a family man, he talked to me for hours on end about his family and his grandchildren, what they had studied and where they worked. He spoke English to me because he knew how much I hated going through an interpreter. I was struck by his well-tailored clothes, his manicured hands and rather austere good looks. Mr. Brezhnev was quite a different proposition. From the moment I set eyes on him I was reminded of faceless civil servants and politicians the world over, in their navy suits, preferably pinstriped, their light blue shirts and ties, like insurance salesmen at conferences. He gave the im-pression of being a hard, brusque man—burly like a great, sleek bear. Neither of us could think of anything beyond banalities to say to the other. To him I was just a wife. (I wasn't the only person who found Brezhnev hard. Several years later Rostropovich, a close friend of Pierre's, whispered to me at a concert between acts: "I luff your husband. I luff Willy Brandt. Brezhnev is a shit.")

Perhaps our most extraordinary visit was to Siberia, to see something of Russian technological developments in the permafrost—something we Canadians might one day have to copy. Both Pierre and I, after the rather formal reception in Moscow, were immediately charmed by the warmth and friendliness of everyone we met. The warmest people in Russia inhabit the coldest place on earth. The Russians appeared simply to have accepted that Norilsk was the most freezing, miserable town to spend one's days, and made the best of it by building the best-equipped leisure centers I saw anywhere in the world, and by spending their summer holidays in Georgia.

I shouldn't have been all that sorry to leave Russia. My complete lack of briefing had made me an ill-equipped and ignorant visitor, my morning sickness had spoiled my sight-seeing, and for young lovers hating to be apart, the protocol was terribly confining. It was my first taste of enforced segregation. Every time the official cortège cot off, Pierre traveled in front with Brezhnev and Kosygin in one car, while I was stowed away in the second surrounded by ambassadresses and their incessant "quack, quack, quack" of small talk.

The official "goodbyes" were said on the red carpet at the bottom of the steps to our plane but for me the visit did not end there. Mr. Kosygin broke with protocol and followed us up the steps to our own territory. He understood my emotional state—saying goodbye is never easy. Dismissing his entourage of aides, K.G.B. and ambassadors, he boarded our plane and in the crammed quarters provided for the Canadian Air Force men who traveled with us, he hugged me farewell. Both of us wept openly. In a world so full of divisions, political manoeuvering and protocol, I felt our tears were an unspoken prayer for peace and friendship: please, no more borders!

If there was one thing that I learned faster than anything else, it was that a prime minister's wife has an extraordinarily varied life. One minute I was firing a cook, the next discussing icefloes with strange, non-English-speaking geologists; one day sitting at home watching television, the next, in full regalia, waltzing with a head of state. There is no studying for the part, no under-study to take over when confidence fails. In the first year I had a taste of almost everything that would come my way during my marriage to Pierre: a state visit abroad, a number of receptions at home, a household to reorganize, official and formal clothes to buy, a style of life to master, even a pregnancy. It had two other major events: a journey inside our own country and along our borders, which gave me a chance to see something of Canada, and a visit from Queen Elizabeth, certainly for the wife of a Commonwealth prime minister the most daunting and fearsome of engagements.

When we married, Pierre promised me a visit to Newfoundland, part work, part fun, and I was delighted when, not long after Russia, the day arrived to embark on our naval icebreaker at Lunenberg. I went on board laden down with a great sack of licorice, for which I had developed an insatiable craving during the first months of pregnancy.

An icebreaker is not exactly the most comfortable and luxurious vessel afloat, particularly when the fog comes down and the sea gets rough, but the Navy did their best for us, providing us with the Captain's mahogany-lined cabin, and Pierre and I were very happy. After several days at sea, by which time we were very relaxed and even quite tanned, we reached the French island of St. Pierre et Micquelon in the Gulf of St. Lawrence, just down the coast from Newfoundland and a haven for bootleggers.

The governor of the island and his wife were very French and, oh, how protocol conscious! Being pregnant and, as I had foolishly imagined, on vacation, I was wearing a loose peasant skirt that I had made myself, and a cotton shirt, a happy throwback to my flower child days. When we docked I saw to my horror that the governor's wife was in a Chanel suit with hat and white gloves. Neither Pierre nor I had quite realized the official status of our visit to this, the Republic of France.

It turned out to be protocol gone mad. From the dock we climbed into a vast, gleaming open car to head a motorcade on a tour of the island, some ten to fifteen miles across. "You will see," said the governor's wife to me very graciously, "our extremely unique and beautiful coastline." The cars purred off, one behind the other, dignified and slow. There was just one little problem: thick fog. We couldn't see the famous rocks, let alone a coastline. Our hosts kept saying, without the shadow of a smile: "And over there is one of the most beautiful bays in the whole island." What could I say? It was all I could do not to giggle. Pierre made everything bearable. On occasions like this he sat by my side and clutched my hand and I felt I could handle anything.

It needed all Pierre's understanding and sympathy and many rehearsals of Mrs Michener's lessons to prepare me for my first encounter with the Queen. It came in July when she visited Vancouver for the British Columbia centenary celebrations, an occasion I had been both dreading and longing for. It was my first really frightening social engagement, and my first visit to my home town as the prime minister's wife.

My immediate reaction on seeing Queen Elizabeth on the steps of her private airplane was one of shock and incredulity: her dress and coat were simple, even dreary. Where was the regal aura I had been dreading? As she came down the steps toward me my terror began to fade; her expression was genuinely friendly and as I curtsied she gave my hand a warm squeeze. As we stood talking, a gust of wind swept the hat I had so carefully chosen from my head. I caught it as it flew off. A lady in waiting appeared as if by magic at her side with a hat pin, and the Queen showed me how to secure my wretched hat firmly to my hair, her very blue eyes gleaming with amusement.

The three days of her visit passed smoothly, professionally and without incident, a tribute to the extraordinary polish of her official machinery. I did my bit, a cog that gave no trouble. I felt I had been simply swept up, carried along on a sea of goodwill and exemplary manners and deposited gently down again at the other end, before the magic carpet whirled up and away on its next engagement. I was delighted and very pleased when Pierre told me that she had seemed pleased with his choice of wife. When it was all over I received a letter from my Aunt Jessie in England, who had seen some of the official reception on television. "I'm proud of you," she wrote. "You did that like a lady."

OFFICIAL
RESIDENCES

THE PRIME MINISTER of Canada has two official residences: a town house in Ottawa at 24 Sussex Drive, and a rambling country house at Harrington Lake, some twenty minutes' drive from the center of the city. In time Harrington Lake became my proper home, the place where I felt happiest and most at ease, but not before I had inherited the large, cold, gray mansion in the city, assessed its many drawbacks, and done my best to turn the place into an acceptable home, not only for us, but for the servants who shared it with us. It was a long, often nerve-racking process.

I knew 24 Sussex Drive already, of course, as a rather cold, blandly furnished residence. From the outside it looks precisely what it is: a large, gray mansion built by a lumber baron at the turn of the century. He was the boss of a wood company who liked to sit and watch his lumber being carried up the Ottawa river. He had positioned the house with genius, so that the main sitting room has a spectacular view over the river toward Quebec, possibly the most beautiful and historic view in the entire city: Ontario looking into Quebec.

The house had first been bought for the prime minister's residence in 1954 and was then completely gutted so that just the outer shell remained. The poky little rooms and winding staircases were torn down and replaced with spacious, airy rooms. They are magnificent, with an awesome splendor about them, but they are not calculated to seem cosy to a young bride. The two main rooms, which open off a large central hall, share the same view down the river, but, being large enough to seat and feed some twenty-four people they are somewhat chilly for two.

112

From the day I first set eyes on the house, long before I married Pierre, I had an overwhelming itch to get at it, tear down its somber decorations. It was hideous, it was shabby and it didn't begin to reflect our taste. There was nothing to be proud of in this dim, gloomy establishment.

When Pierre had been elected three years before our marriage, he had been too busy and insecure of his future to alter the home he inherited: his bedroom in fact had the same figurines, the same pink and blue painted reproduction furniture of his predecessors. Every piece in the house was reproduction something: there wasn't a genuine item in the place. It had all been done up by one of our department stores for Lester B. Pearson's wife, a woman by then far older than I was, and set in her ways. In any case, 24 Sussex wasn't her real home, simply a house that they were temporarily perched in, like long-stay visitors in a seaside hotel. You could smell it in the air.

The servants' quarters were shocking: bare lightbulbs hanging down from pea green ceilings, and monstrously ugly furniture. An atmosphere of unrelenting melancholy, as of perpetual winter.

The carpet throughout was gray broadloom which over the years had worn thin in patches like a moulting terrier. Where it had frayed away altogether someone had stapled-in, not sewn, little ill-assorted squares of different colored carpet.

The curtains in the living room had faded almost to white where the sun fell on them. Everything was supposed to be a shade of gray: the walls were gray, the ceiling was gray, the carpets were gray. The entire living room was cluttered with dozens of little tables and chairs that appeared to be in preparation for a convention of the I.O.D.E. (International Order of the Daughters of the Empire) at a country hotel, and yet there was nowhere to sit in comfort. Quite simply, I hated it. It depressed me.

It was eighteen months before I was finally let loose on the house, because Pierre wanted to win the election before spending the nation's money. I was still chafing under the restriction when a chore came my way that few brides will ever have to face: re-equipping a prime minister's official residence. The Minister of Public Works let it be known to me that if I were to buy new linen, china and glass they would be most grateful.

They couldn't have realized how, with nothing else tangible to do, and hating my surroundings as I did, I fell on this one positive task with utter delight.

The job of keeping up the equipment and furnishings of the house had fallen before my arrival to Tom MacDonald, our steward, and some of the sad decay I now discovered around me came from his somewhat haphazard and indifferent touch. He had been a valet in the army, and was an efficient, archetypal Scot, but not a man temperamentally suited to running a large house entirely staffed by women, nor imaginative or artistic enough to do so with much taste. He was superb when Pierre's shoes needed mending, or a cocktail party for 150 guests had to be organized, but his rather haughty manner made him seem callous and dictatorial with people's everyday problems. Pierre had simply never noticed the hideous towels, nor the dreary soap, had never taken in the power struggles, the jealousies, the petty intrigues that went on in the servants' quarters. But I did notice, and my coming battles with Tom MacDonald made my relationship with Margaret, the cook, look all sweetness and love.

Surveying the linen cupboard in my first few weeks I had seen nothing but institutional quality sheets, thin, frayed towels, and table mats and napkins so bleached that they had long lost any vestiges of elegance. I set off resolutely for the best linen shop in Montreal, Heaney's, and between there and a shop in London, called the White House, had soon furnished us with embroidered Madeira linen sheets for our kingsize bed (our *private* kingsize bed, for I had refused to sleep a night in the People's bed), with handstitched birds in blue and pink and yellow, and a scalloped twenty-four place set of natural linen, with muslin insets, and enough soft, luxurious towels to keep the place stocked for many years.

From linen I turned to china. The Pearsons had been eating off quite pretty blue Wedgwood plates; I decided to do away with them as they did not match my color scheme for the house, and replaced them with a white, gold and orange Ginori service for fifty and a modern Thomas Clunes breakfast set which we could also use for lunches in the garden. The gold service, also for fifty, was set aside carefully for formal parties.

Everything that, bit by bit, was replaced at 24 Sussex found a home, much of it up at our country house by the lake. Though the budget was open ended we were always attacked. In parliament Tom Cossitt, member for Leeds, accused us of living like kings; so every corkscrew and table napkin I bought was listed and read out in the House. Cossitt got a red face one day. He had demanded to know exactly what the prime minister spent on liquor and wine. He wasn't to know it, but Pierre is not a drinker himself and does not encourage it in others. Guests are offered just one glass before a meal, and then not a very generous amount of wine with the food. He was only too happy to give the honorable member his bills. They came to rather less than those of an average Canadian family, despite the numbers of people we had to entertain formally.

Hardly surprisingly these changes brought me into immediate conflict with Tom MacDonald. It started the day I discovered that as each Val St. Lambert crystal glass was chipped, so he had the rim ground down; this way the red claret glasses became relegated to white wine, the white wine to sherry and so on as they shrank down the scale. The only trouble was that the original soft edge became sharp and cutting to the lips. When I remonstrated, Tom MacDonald dug his heels in. It was the first of many such battles. It wasn't long before I found that he kept all the store cupboards locked, so that when the maids needed to put out another roll of toilet paper or box of tissues they had to go to him for the keys. I found the suggestion that they were stealing very degrading, and told him so. Ever afterward the cupboards were kept open.

Then I discovered that he was a terrible planner and shopper and that the house was crammed to overflowing with unwanted tins. Hardly a day went by without a dispute of some kind. I took it out on him by refusing to acknowledge his authority.

He got his own back. He nagged me constantly for the menus and the lists, and refused to order anything unless I asked for it. When I did our marketing on Fridays he would hand me an envelope with twenty-five dollars in it—he kept all the household accounts, and tried to charge us separately for the diaper service, and for anything other than the most functional soap.

He even fell out with Pierre one day, and then my spirits rose because I began to see that he needn't necessarily be my life sentence. Count Rossini, who owns the Château Yquem vineyards, had sent Pierre a present of a dozen bottles of his wine. Mr. MacDonald, who fancied himself as knowledgeable about wine, slipped up and uncorked three precious bottles for a perfectly ordinary working lunch.

It took me five years to get rid of him, five years of growing torture, and during the last two we never spoke to one another. He wasn't easy to replace, and before long people had managed to convince me that it was my fault and not his. It was only when I promoted Mary Alice Conlon—a nun who came to us first as a simple maid—to housekeeper, a job in which she proved splendid, that he got the message and left.

The day after he won the 1972 election, Pierre gave me a hug: "O.K. You're off. Now get going with that house decoration."

I took him at his word, and set to work instantly, in case he had second thoughts. Within hours I had found a woman who knew a tremendous amount about beautiful homes, Louise Beveridge.

First I had the servants' quarters redecorated. Then Mrs. Beveridge and I embarked on the main rooms. Together we discussed color schemes, and a couple of days later Louise, who is the sort of tireless worker who is prepared to travel all the way to Boston for a single light fixture, would reappear with a vast selection of samples to choose from.

It was hard work but the greatest fun. Within months I could begin to see the house turning into somewhere I actually wanted to live. The living room we painted in soft neutral colors, with beige, thick pile carpets, modern comfortable sofas and Georgian furniture. I felt that what was needed was extreme simplicity in a room intended for receiving large numbers of people. We papered the dining room in a Fortuny print, an orange-red Italian cloth, in order to show off the splendid moulded ceiling with its hand-sculpted white plaster swirls and ovals. It became a room that was cheerful by day and elegant by night. And so we went through the house, Louise and I, very carefully, taking our time, room by room. She was a practiced bargainer, and she managed to convince antique dealers that because the cost for the prime minister's residence was coming out of the people's pockets they should keep their profits down. It was unscrupulous but effective: we got fantastic bargains.

Louise and I had just one disaster: Pierre's study. Louise talked me into painting it light green, with thin venetian blinds and orange and rust-colored furniture. Despite the open fire we kept lit most of the winter—all the rooms have open fireplaces—it is a cold, formal place, more like the waiting room of a hospital than a prime minister's den.

Pierre liked to have photographs of heads of state—every head of state brings a signed photograph in a beautiful frame—on show. By the time I got there the grand piano in the living room was groaning under their weight. I begged him to give the living room over to the Royal Family, and relegate the others to the library. My feeling was that people love to see the Queen and Prince Charles, but that they don't give a damn for all these mugs from around the world, particularly when heads of state change with the speed of a merry-go-round. Visitors kept arriving and saying:

"You know *he's* no longer our head of state. There have been two since him."

We were able to hang excellent paintings in the house, by borrowing them from the National Gallery, and changing them every year. Pierre had his own collection of paintings, which we kept for ourselves, upstairs. My new living room was the very place to show pictures off: pale, plain colors and good furniture meant that I could let my fantasies run wild. In the middle of winter when everything outside was white and deadly and immense, I'd hang outrageous modern paintings and turn the room, like switching on a light, into somewhere warm and gay. In summer, when there were bright colors from the flowers outside, I chose softer landscapes.

Of course, the National Gallery kept pressing Canadian landscape artists like A. Y. Jackson and Tom Thompson on me. When the dining room was finally ready I had a furious argument with them: they wanted dreary pines perched on the edge of cliffs; I demanded French masterpieces. In a fit of bad humor just before I left Pierre I hung one of the ugliest ladies I have ever seen in the dining room: a stern harridan with glasses slipping down her nose peering balefully down at the table with a reproachful glare. Pierre thought it was vicious of me.

We were very lucky with the timing when decorating 24 Sussex. There is nothing like a visit from royalty to galvanize people into action. The Queen had planned to come in 1973, in August, to coincide with the Commonwealth Conference. We declared that the due date for the house to be finished.

And we made it. We had just one dry run for the house in June. It was virtually finished by then: the walls were painted and the carpets laid, but we had not a stick of furniture, when Mrs. Gandhi arrived on her first official visit to Canada.

Traditionally the governor general gives a big formal dinner in honor of a visiting head of state. That is on the first night and for about 150 people: the entire diplomatic corps, with full protocol and decorations. I found those evenings tense and unhappy. The next night, by the same custom, Pierre and I would give the prime minister's dinner, for just twenty-four carefully chosen people which was all we could (and all I was prepared to) seat round our table. We had long lists of possible guests to choose from and we pored over them for hours, selecting someone from business, someone from the arts, someone from the law. At first I couldn't imagine who was going to come all the way from the other end of Canada just for our dinner, but then I discovered that everyone was flattered and our real problem was not getting them to come but to go home. Before they got used to my ways the Department of External Affairs used to send me over the table plan in all innocence, and if I saw that a subtle, interesting man had been put next to the biggest frump in the whole country, whom I had failed to have scratched from the list, I would simply juggle them about. I knew it was making me enemies; my defense was that I simply wanted things to be more fun. And they were.

We explained to Mrs. Gandhi very regretfully that we couldn't hold a dinner at 24 Sussex for her because we had no living room furniture. Her answer came back immediately: "I'll come anyway." What could I do but accept?

By three o'clock on the day of her visit we were still without a single dining room chair. I was in a panic. It's one thing to have no sofas, another for guests to have to stand for an entire evening. Yet they arrived, in the nick of time, minutes before Mrs Gandhi; the moving van rolled up our drive, the staff tore backwards and forwards like an army of ants and the chairs were in place. The combination of our brand new house and the inevitable informality in fact made for the best party we ever gave. There was a good deal of laughter and Mrs. Gandhi looked marvelous. She and Pierre had one tense, tough conversation over nuclear technology when in a flash she shed all the shyness and charm like an actor swapping masks. It was back again just as fast.

The day the Queen arrived everything was in place. For royal visits houses simply do get painted, furniture repaired, and streets cleaned. I took immense pains with the preparation, cooking part of the dinner myself. After much thought and consultation with Pierre—I very rarely discussed the house with him but on this occasion I felt I had to—I had decided to make a most ambitious duck pâté. The recipe made it sound rare and very tempting, with Cointreau and Grand Marnier, little pieces of chicken liver floating on top, and jelly all around. Then the jelly didn't gel. It tasted good, but it looked like a collapsed sand castle. I hid it as best I could with festoons of herbs and angelica. All the vegetables were fresh from the garden, and we had *filet de boeuf*, new potatoes, and crêpes stuffed with cream cheese, orange rind and Cointreau, served with a sauce of fresh raspberries.

I had asked Toronto's answer to Constance Spry to come and do the flowers. The flowers at 24 Sussex had always been a source of irritation to me. Mrs. Michener had a curious passion for pinky orange roses and anything gold, and had turned over the entire greenhouse to these two colors. I wanted bright colors to match my new house: cornflowers and daisies and lots of red. But never did I manage to eradicate the lingering golds and pinks. It was as if she had cast a spell on the greenhouse: flowers that started a perfectly honest shade soon reverted to dowdy pastel. This was an area where I was fast becoming a little bitch: I was lucky enough to have fresh flowers every day, and here I was carping about what they were.

The Queen's dinner was a complete triumph. The flowers, the new house, the furniture, the singer Colette Bokey, who entertained between courses—everything worked. I felt immensely proud. I even had a good time myself. Because of protocol the Queen and Pierre sat at one end of the table while I sat at the other with Prince Philip on my right. We had a marvelous hour swapping jokes. When Colette Bokey reached the high notes in an aria from *La Bohème* Prince Philip whispered to me that he was afraid the chandelier would shatter. Pierre, hearing my laughter, kept giving me stony looks. It was very stuffy at his end, not because of the Queen who tried her best, but because of all the ex-prime ministers and their wives we had had to invite and who were all clustered around Pierre.

I was silently congratulating myself on the evening as we showed our guests out. Then suddenly a huge black spider, walking slowly and with a sense of purpose, stepped out in front of the Queen. "Ah, Margaret," she said, her eyes twinkling, "Is *this* part of your decorations?"

It's good to have a due date for a house. After the Queen's visit we started to enjoy it, and then for the first time 24 Sussex became home. I loved it when people who had known it in its previous incarnation came to see it, and I basked in their admiration.

None of the same restrictions or worries contaminated my love for our country home at Harrington Lake. No prime minister before Pierre had ever really used the house, so we found it run down and dilapidated. For me that only added to its charm. It was a warm, happy place and I didn't much care what it looked like, though gradually, as I spent more time up there, I came to change almost everything about it, until I had turned it into the sort of informal country house any normal ordinary Canadian couple might have owned.

I spent my happiest married days in that house, and when the babies started coming I migrated up there from the city for the entire summer every year.

The old, two-storey house is big, rambling and wooden. It stands alone in a wildlife sanctuary, perched on the top of a hill surrounded by a vegetable garden and a massive fence to keep the deer at bay. Rough gardens stretch all the way down to the edge of the lake, where there is a narrow shingle beach. Pierre anchored a raft some way from the shore, where we could lie and sunbathe in total privacy. Harrington Lake was a perfect contrast to the bustle of 24 Sussex. All was calm and wilderness: no people, no noise, no formalities, no telephone pealing or cook coming to discuss menus. I will always associate that house with two things—utter tranquillity and the good, unique smell of countryside.

120

I had decided not to touch the upstairs of the house except where it was essential. It is very simple, with white wood walls, and all the bedrooms have big fluffy quilts.

Downstairs there is one large area which served as both living room and dining room, separated by glass doors which we kept open most of the summer. Huge stone fireplaces stand at either end. They burn whole chunks of tree trunk.

I brought up furniture we didn't want in Ottawa. I added a few inexpensive pine tables and chairs and had curtains made in rustic material.

All the floors are wood and, I discovered, in very good condition. I had them waxed and I laid rugs down. Then I turned the warren of servants' quarters into a children's playroom, which doubled as sitting room for any nanny or maid who came up to the lake with us, though in the early days I rarely took anyone. I was the chief cook and bottlewasher.

The kitchen was wonderful. Nothing had been done to it for years so I was given a free hand. I made it all natural wood and stainless steel, with a wooden work table on wheels which had deep drawers for all the cooking implements. Then I did something I had been longing to do ever since we married: I got all my old kitchen equipment sent up from Vancouver—bright colored cooking pots, baskets with spices, dishes I had brought back from Morocco—and hung them in my new kitchen. The result was friendly and homely: a big, warm, romantic kitchen, the sort of room any Canadian family might have, with a huge pine table in the middle at which we ate all our family meals.

Often I did my own shopping for Harrington Lake, at the charming local market. I was learning Japanese and Chinese cookery, because I liked to eat small portions of delicious things, and also because Pierre loves Oriental food. When the children were old enough, they helped me stuff the wonton with meat and spices at the kitchen table, their tiny fingers fumbling over the little doughy packages. When *Chatelaine* magazine asked me whether I would like to write something about my life, I described my summer up at the lake, and how I cooked and marketed and grew all our vegetables. Loud jeers went up. "What a lot of hogwash," people wrote in. "Don't kid us. You wouldn't catch Mrs. Trudeau doing her own baking and freezing."

How wrong they were. I not only cooked and froze vegetables but I supervised the creating and planting of a vegetable garden, a patch of land that had been part fallow, part given over to a nearby farmer who used it to grow turnips for his cows. Since racoons and deer menace the garden we had to have the section wired off so heavily that from a helicopter it now looks like a prison compound with high meshing and barbed wire. I then had it organically sown with every kind of vegetable and fruit, from wild strawberry to marrow, and as they ripened, so I set to work picking and freezing my harvest.

That was the point of Harrington Lake, to be able to do this kind of thing. I must admit that I carried it to absurdity. As our life in Ottawa became more formal and austere, with regular lunch parties and a staff of eight to handle every menial chore, so I actually yearned to do some housework for myself. Monday to Friday I was a princess, waited on hand and foot. Saturday and Sunday I turned into a parody of the harassed suburban housewife, yelling at Pierre to come and help me with the dishes, while I struggled to cook a meal and look after first one, then two, then three babies.

FAMILY LIFE

BEHIND THE OFFICIALDOM and the formality, the show and the façade, Pierre and I led a very quiet life. Anyone reading the stories published in the newspapers and magazines about our glamorous high life, our exotic parties and expensive tastes would have been amazed if they had seen what really went on at home. Pierre is a shy, unsociable man by nature, and I spent much of the first few years either pregnant or nursing a new baby. Apart from the glittering official receptions, when I scrambled out of my jeans and hurried off to the hairdresser, and my afternoons with old girlfriends, we saw very few people. That was the way we wanted it: ours was a private affair. Shared jokes and a same way of looking at the world were an important aspect of our marriage. There wasn't really room for strangers. And as the children started to come, we turned ever more inward, protecting our cosy, sheltered intimacy from all outsiders.

From the day I entered 24 Sussex as Pierre's wife I knew I had to establish one room that I could call my very own. I told Pierre that I needed a corner that was out of bounds to everyone else in the house, a place where I wouldn't be disturbed by domestic problems or put on show. Pierre understood perfectly. "Take one of the attic rooms, then you'll be really out of the way," he said at once. He had asked me whether I would like a piece of jewelry as his wedding present. I thought long and hard about it. A diamond necklace? An antique ring? Some emerald earrings? Finally it dawned on me. I went hurrying down to his study. "What I would *really* like," I told him, "is a sewing machine." It may sound funny but that's the way it was: in those days I simply couldn't imagine anything in the world that I wanted more.

The sanctuary I chose was on the third floor, a charming, sloping attic room, with a fine view that allowed me to gaze out over the gardens and down to the river. It was the room into which Pierre had unceremoniously bundled all the presents he had received from official visitors. The bulk of it was real junk; expensive, ornate objects, but junk nonetheless, the sort of acquisitions you can never find a use for, yet are just too valuable to throw into the garbage.

It was packed solid with gold statuettes, engraved carvings and brass bric-à-brac, among them some beautiful objects. The Thais had presented him with a set of wooden dolls, as big as small children, dressed in the dancers' costume of the old courts, rod puppets whose hands and feet could be made to move. Exquisite, but what can you do with things like that? Then there were the obviously expensive solid gold and silver engraved boxes. Unfortunately none of the Canadian museums would have been interested in showing them. There were crates of plaques with university crests on them: "To Prime Minister Trudeau from the University of. . . ." Pierre had an idea that we might hang them on our own land as trail markers, so we put the plaques on one side. But there were also piles of hand-knitted polyester socks, Czechoslovakian glass goblets, Eskimo handcrafts, an almost lifesize cast iron horse from Italy, something in fact from every single visitor who had passed through 24 Sussex in Pierre's three and a half years as prime minister.

Once I had chosen the attic room for my own exclusive territory, I worked on it for a couple of hours every day, reveling in the privacy but aware that my behavior was slightly absurd. I enjoyed trying to imagine the people who had brought all these curios and treasures and what the countries they came from were really like. It was like a private junkshop, opening boxes and chests and cupboards, not knowing quite what I would find inside, but that if I liked it, it was mine to have. When I had taken stock of what was there, I started racking my brains for where to send it all, trying to decide what to keep, what might be useful now, what any children I might have could conceivably enjoy, what to offer to a museum, what simply to throw away. Would Ottawa Museum be interested in a scaly stuffed gray pike? Or Toronto in the cast iron horse? Or the nearby hospital in sixty-two pairs of socks?

It took weeks until the day came when my room was bare. I looked round with pleasure: now what? Should it be basically a sitting room, with squashy chairs and a hi-fi set? A little study, where I could work? I settled on a sewing room, and gave my Ferrari of a machine pride of place. It stood on a plain pine table which I had made in the government workshops. I splashed out on the walls, and had them painted a bright canary yellow, a color I love, with white, lacy curtains. Here I was to spend many happy and tranquil hours. (Eighteen months later, when I was unleashed on the rest of the house, I took a renowned decorator, whom I was considering employing, on a tour of the rooms. He looked glumly about him as I threw open doors and cupboards. As he left he said, to my delight: "There is only one pretty room in this house, only one really *nice* room, and that's the yellow attic room at the top of the house.")

The sewing room was invaluable, not simply because it provided me with a sanctuary: it was the room in which my growing wardrobe took shape. My parents had given me a start in my married life with a handsome and generous trousseau. It served me well on official occasions, but my problem was the sheer amount of clothes I was expected to have for official functions both at home and abroad. As newspaper articles were beginning to teach me, it was no use buying one superb dress and wearing it again and again. "Mrs. Trudeau, wearing her pink flowered dress *again* . . ." the fashion writers took delight in writing. It seemed particularly sad and wasteful when, having found a dress I really liked and felt good in, I had to part with it after just a few wearings. Yet I dared not put it on again for fear of criticism. And how people noticed. I couldn't get away with a thing: a laddered stocking, an ill-matching hat, a linen skirt when it should have been silk. . . .

Since I wore jeans and sweaters about the house, spending so much on a formal wardrobe seemed a shocking extravagance. But here Mrs. Michener took a hand. At one of our early teas she intimated that I didn't have *quite* the right afternoon gown, or quite the number of long evening dresses required. And what about hats? And gloves? Having youth on my side, she said sternly when I protested that no one would notice because I was so young, was not enough. Wasn't it a challenge to become one of Canada's best dressed women?

Soon my cupboards were overflowing with morning suits, tea dresses, cocktail dresses and ball gowns. The situation wasn't helped by my growing family. One month I was size eight; six weeks later I could barely scrape into a ten. I became a local lending boutique for all my friends. A size twelve ball dress? I had one in pink tulle or one in flowered silk. A size six tennis dress? I owned just the thing. Size ten ski pants? In navy and beige. I had so many unwanted clothes that I soon started dressing our maids from my cupboards. I laughed when I saw them waiting at table or opening the door in dresses that I could remember myself wearing at the Elysée in Paris or on the Great Wall of China.

When I first arrived at 24 Sussex the weather prevented me from exploring the grounds. After a couple of months a thaw set in and the tunnels of ice slowly shrank with the drip, drip, drip, of a burst pipe. The skies cleared and seemed to recede from their lowering presence over the city, and I began to appreciate more clearly what the house and its gardens were really like. As soon as I could I roamed around every corner of our magnificent gardens, up and down the drives, across the road and into the governor general's enormous park. The outside of the house, as I had always known, was squat, solid and unpretentious, like some great stone toad. Nothing could change that.

So I turned my attention to the gardens. 24 Sussex, as Pierre soon informed me, comes under the National Capital Commission. The job of planting out the formal beds, and keeping the flowers in full bloom, falls to them. As the snow thawed a team of government gardeners appeared in their heavy aprons and leather gloves like purposeful gnomes and set to work. Within hours platoons of bulbs were in place, then, just as I was getting used to them, the gnomes would be back. With military precision, the beds were stripped and replanted with something else. There would be rows of tulips, serried ranks of stems, six inches apart, same height, same color, same shape; the next week there would be beds and beds of pink impatiens, same height, same color, same shape. And so it went on. I started a campaign against the system, begging for a little spontaneity, a little mixture. The gnomes eyed me warily but the next time they came I found more color, a few lupins and dahlias, some snapdragons and stocks, injected into the platoons of regulation buds.

Though the house from the outside appears enormous it had curiously few habitable rooms. For a nursery I had to take one of the guest rooms on the second floor. I turned it into the most charming baby's room imaginable. I bought an antique rocking chair and table, scoured the handcraft shops for a patchwork quilt, and had a plain pine crib carved and upholstered. Everything was in the palest robin's egg blue.

During my first pregnancy I felt wonderful. My morning sickness soon disappeared. I didn't smoke, I didn't drink and I refused even an aspirin. However, I have never yearned more for modern medicine than when I caught the worst cold I had ever had during that pregnancy. But the baby's wellbeing came first, and I did nothing without thinking about its effects on the child. After all, this was what I had been waiting for, and I wasn't going to take any risks. Pierre seemed as happy about it as I was and we spent idle, gloating hours discussing the future.

When I went to the hospital for my five-month checkup I discovered to my outrage that fathers were not allowed to be present at the birth. I protested and threatened to move to another hospital. There was no question of going through it all without Pierre. Finally the doctor relented, and applied for permission from the directors of the hospital, particularly when I told him stubbornly that if he did not agree I would have my baby at home. The rules were changed for all fathers-to-be at the Civic Hospital and a promise given that Pierre would be with me.

Just before Christmas the phone rang late one evening. It was Jill Turner, the wife of a minister in Pierre's cabinet.

"John and I know that you're not going to be able to join your family at Christmas because the baby is due so soon. Would you like to come and have Christmas dinner with us?"

"How kind," I said, touched by her thoughtfulness. "But I'm afraid there's no question of that. I'm having my baby on Christmas Day."

She laughed. "Margaret, honestly. I've had four babies and they never arrive the day they're due. It just doesn't happen. Don't be absurd."

But I knew it would. Pierre and I had worked it all out. We'd go to mass at midnight on Christmas Eve; sleep in on Christmas morning; open our presents; have lunch; then go and have the baby. It all went according to plan. When I woke on Christmas morning something was definitely happening. We opened our presents, had lunch and called the doctor. Like Jill Turner he laughed increduously, but to humor us came over to check. He didn't laugh so much when he had examined me.

"Take that labrador for a walk," he suggested, "and bring the baby on a bit."

Pierre had given me the puppy months before on the doctor's advice that I should take constant exercise, and I had walked miles with him, cutting paths through the deep banks of snow right up until the last day. So we set out, Pierre with his stop-watch to time the contractions, me hanging on to the leash with one hand and Pierre with the other. I was perfectly calm: I felt fit and happy and confident. It was Pierre who was getting increasingly agitated—particularly when he put down the stop-watch somewhere and couldn't find it—despite the fact that he and I had discussed the event at length, and Pierre had even attended the fathers' pre-natal class.

Justin's arrival was as uncomplicated as the nine months he had spent inside me. Pierre, who is a fanatic about drugs, had convinced me after reading every book on the subject he could find to go through natural childbirth with no artificial help at all. To please him I agreed, despite the reluctance of my doctor. My midwife was a sensible, reassuring woman, and I had no more than twenty minutes of what could be described as real pain. I didn't even have to ask what sex he was. I had known it was going to be a boy. Pierre and I hugged each other. Justin had come, and it was Christmas Day.

He couldn't have been given a warmer welcome. The people of Canada seemed to rejoice as much as we did over his birth, the first to a serving Canadian prime minister in 102 years. There were announcements on television, telegrams and phone calls, thousands and thousands of letters of congratulation. I must have received many hundreds of handknitted sweaters, bonnets, bibs and bootees. My collection of bootees was soon crowding me out of my room. Every woman in Canada seemed to have knitted her appreciation of the event.

I was overwhelmed. They were all lovely, but there were just too many of them. In the end I had to pack them up by the barrel to load and send them off to orphanages and hospitals. And as soon as it was known that I was breastfeeding Justin, thousands more letters poured in congratulating me for my decision, and holding me up as an example to the other mothers of Canada. This friendliness and warmth happened each time I had a baby—there can be no happier feeling in the world than basking in such universal affection.

Just seven days after Justin's birth I was invited to an official reception. It was something I could well have refused on grounds of exhaustion, but I felt so happy and so well that I longed to get out and start enjoying myself again. We took him along in a rush basket. It was the first of dozens of public appearances complete with baby: Justin spent many solitary hours tucked away in one corner of the Speaker's office in the House of Commons, or bawling his head off in spare offices, while I had to leave many a dinner table halfway through a course to go to him. It wasn't made easier by my stubbornness over feeding. I refused to follow the four-hour hospital routine. Justin had food when he asked for it. It made me the joke of all my friends, the way I would give him breakfast, and then elevenses, then a little lunch, then perhaps a little afternoon snack, followed by teatime. Then came supper, and not long after the big meal, and then of course milk and cookies before bed. During the night he would need a few snacks. I never stopped. I wanted to feed him for a whole year, but as he grew older and more curious he got bored with me. I shall never forget the last morning I fed him. He was just six months. I brought him into our bed, as I always did. He took one look at my nipple and made an awful spitting sound of disgust, crawled hurriedly over to Pierre's side of the bed and snuggled up to him.

The funny thing was that within days of giving up breast-feeding I too was feeling restless, eager for the first time to emerge from the happy but claustrophobic cocoon of mother-hood. I hadn't yet had anyone to help me with Justin, but now I felt the moment had come to enlist a little support from among the maids. Rather than employ someone from outside I offered the job to Diane Lavergne, a young, jolly, rather wild country girl who had come to us as a maid. She was rather awkward and inept when it came to waiting at table or letting in guests. But she adored Justin and she accepted my offer with joy. She was my helpmate with the children for over five years.

The fact that Pierre and I divided our time between two so very different establishments—the rigidity of 24 Sussex and the heady freedom of Harrington Lake—was yet another incentive to split myself up into separate people. Since the security and the formality effectively screened off most of my friends at 24 Sussex, I took advantage of the lake to have fun: colleagues of Pierre's who came to stay there were astonished to find us living frugally and having such an ordinary good time. Gradually we made a set of friends who lived near Harrington all the year round and we joined in their weekend activities.

During the winter months we skied, played broomball on a hockey rink and met at each other's houses, bringing cakes and homebaked pies. In the early spring we gathered maple sap from the trees and boiled it up in enormous copper vats over wood fires. In the summer there were picnics and barbecues. Pierre shot the rapids in full flood while I waited at the bottom with the other wives and children, armed with hampers of good food. It was a wonderful life, but there was all too little of it. It certainly wasn't the glamorous existence the Canadian public imagined me to be leading.

Because Harrington Lake was becoming so important for my peace of mind, I felt even more strongly than I did in Ottawa about preserving its privacy and intimacy. No one was going to ruin it for me.

"Mrs. Trudeau, we understand you and your husband are going away for a couple of weeks," the man in charge of keeping up the property said to me one day. "We'll seize the chance to replace all this hideous old clapboarding on the house, and put up a nice new smooth façade."

I was appalled: "The hell you will," I replied, without pausing to be tactful. "Over my dead body."

He retired, crestfallen. A few months later he was back: "I've been looking at the wooden windowframes and I think they must be very draughty. I'm going to replace them with some aluminum ones."

Again, I was incensed, "Oh, no you're not," I yelled. I won the day.

The funniest battle—it became something of a *cause célèbre* in Ottawa—happened one day when I was baking bread in the kitchen. Jarring hideously with the silence came a noise that sounded like an invading army. I hurried to the window. Down by the lakeside was a huddle of men, with bulldozers and a concrete mixer. They were about to lay a concrete road and loading platform: the previous winter, bringing their boats out of the water, their cars had got bogged down in the mud. I dropped my dough and, without pausing to wash my hands, I grabbed a rolling pin and raced down the hill. "Stop it," I shouted. "Go away."

One by one their heads turned and their mouths dropped open as I approached, flailing my arms and yelling my head off. The foreman ordered them to switch off the motors. An almost eerie silence, made all the sharper by the previous din, descended on the scene. I begged, I cajoled, I threatened. They scowled and muttered. In the end, seeing that I would rather lie down in the mud and let the bulldozer ride over me than give them permission to ruin our precious wilderness, they went away. It would indeed have ruined it; concrete roads would have put an end to our tame deer and our choir of birds.

Another day I came down from my bedroom to find a thin, angular machine, rather like an enormous spider, puffing out clouds of dense, white smoke: insecticide to kill the mosquitoes which plagued us all June and July. I let out a screech of anguish: "You're poisoning my babies." Pierre was angry when I had sent the machine on its way.

"Wait till you get really bitten," he warned. He had a point, as I soon discovered.

When I learned that I was expecting Sacha we converted a second spare room alongside Justin's room, creating a new guest room in the attic. At the same time we decided to have a private sitting room for the family on the second floor, a room that would be absolutely out of bounds to all strangers. Justin saw it for the first time when he was nearly two, and the room still without any furniture. A cheerful, bright, manically energetic little boy, he peered around the door, broke into shouts of pleasure, and started racing around and around it in circles, yelling at the top of his voice: "Freedom, freedom." He had picked up the lines of a song by Richie Haven which I often sang for him at bedtime: "Sometimes I feel like a motherless child. A mighty long way from home. Freedom! Freedom! Freedom!" From that day on, our sitting room was the "freedom room."

I count that room as the greatest success at interior decorating, not least because it became my family refuge, a domestic haven. By covering the walls in beige raw silk, by hanging beige curtains and laying a thick beige pile carpet, and furnishing it with modern Italian furniture—marble tables, leather chairs, sunken stereo and television—I transformed what was a dreary, depressing hole into somewhere friendly and comfortable. It was also exceedingly luxurious, something we were instantly criticized for by our friends in parliament. Pierre's response was immediate: "We'll pay for the freedom room ourselves and we'll take it with us when we go." And he means it.

In the autumn of 1973 I was in the last months of my second pregnancy. I had had a lot of trouble with the baby, who was lying in a slightly awkward position giving me twinges of agonizing pain. I was also far larger than I had been with Justin, and could scarcely heave myself about the house. As Christmas approached, my efforts to give Justin a special day on the twenty-fifth, for after all it combined his second birthday with the first Christmas he was really conscious of, redoubled. I combed every department store in Ottawa to find the plastic motorcycle he had been begging for.

We ate Christmas dinner on Christmas Eve, so that the staff could spend the holiday with their families. My mother was staying with us, as was my sister Janet. Just as I raised my glass of wine to Pierre's toast I felt a strange, familiar twinge. It went away. After dinner I stretched out on a sofa to watch television. The pains started again. This time there was no mistaking what they were: contractions.

Soon after ten, Pierre came to take me to midnight mass and was amazed to find me lying down. "Pierre," I said, laughing, "I don't think I'd better come with you. This baby's coming."

He roared with laughter. "Trust you to imagine yourself into a second Christmas baby," he teased me. "You couldn't *possibly* have two babies on Christmas Day. Come on, get your coat on. It's just false labor."

I dragged myself up and called Tara, the Jamaican maid we had brought back with us from our vacation there. She was a Catholic and had decided to come to midnight mass. I told her what I thought was happening. It made the service a somewhat comic event, particularly when a procession of choirboys filed past. One of them was bearing a plastic bread basket with a plastic doll to represent the baby Jesus. "If they don't watch out," I whispered to Tara, "they're going to have live entertainment soon." We giggled again at "Hark the Herald Angels Sing," for by then I was really in labor, clasping the seat to suppress a groan when the contractions came.

Still Pierre wouldn't take me seriously. When we arrived home he put me firmly to bed and wished me goodnight. He needn't have bothered; less than an hour later I woke him to summon Dr. Gluck. "Merry Christmas," was all the doctor said, on answering the phone. "I just knew this would be bound to happen to *you*."

Sacha's birth was a long and painful one. It took all the rest of the night. Again, prompted by Pierre, I refused to take all analgesics and in the end I was proud I held on. He was born as dawn came, a rather weary and angry baby. I fell in love with him at once, and our shared painful night was the start of a special bond between us which exists to this day. There was also something quite uncanny about the date; not just one Christmas baby but two. And Yves Lewis was born on Christmas Day as well.

With two children in just under three years of marriage Pierre and I found that our basically strong earlier physical attraction for one another was being seriously undermined. I got fat and preoccupied and was soon unrecognizable from the carefree, sexy, twenty-two-year-old he had married. Pierre couldn't have been kinder or more understanding: the early domination of all passion by intellect that he so prided himself on had turned him into something of an aesthete, and a man with considerable discipline of mind and body. Confronted with his cheerful domesticity, I found all the stories about Trudeau the playboy more and more absurd. Pierre and I would now laugh about them.

The honeymoon had by now vanished in any case under a blanket of diapers and small babies, and Pierre and I settled down to an untroubled domestic life, broken only by the trips abroad we absolutely could not avoid making. We spent what time we could up at the lake, and even in the city saw as few people as possible. It was a way of life that suited Pierre as much as it did me; he is a conscientious and loving father and much given to routine. The days sped by, scarcely altering.

At five to eight each morning a maid would knock on the door, wait for a muffled groan, then come to draw back the blinds and close the windows. Pierre is a fresh air maniac. Whatever the weather—snow, hurricane or sleet—he insisted on having both windows open at night. Sometimes it was so cold that the glass of water by my bedside was frozen solid, and then the maids would wear their coats when they came in to us, bringing whichever baby was currently being fed by me muffled up in several layers of bonnet and shawls.

Pierre got up at once, while I lingered on under the covers for another hour. We had agreed early in our married life that he should rise first. When I did leap out of bed to have breakfast with him, I simply sat at the table like a blob, struggling but failing to make conversation. This was a strain for both of us: he preferred to read the papers on his own, before leaving for the office at nine. Now that the children are bigger, he always has at least one of them with him while he eats breakfast.

As I heard the door slam behind him, and his cheery greeting of the security guards patrolling outside, I climbed out of bed and went down to my own breakfast. I could have had it in bed, but Pierre's sense of discipline, and some lingering inner puritanism of my own, forbade me to be so idle. Between nine and ten I read the papers, discussed menus and household matters with the staff and planned my day. Then I telephoned my assistant and together we organized the day's schedule: who had to be rung up, and who invited to some coming charity ball, or official reception. When I was first married to Pierre, I shared his personal secretary; later, when more and more letters started to pour in for me, I was given my own assistant, Marie-Hélène Fox. She divided her time between me and a political job in Pierre's office.

Lunch was the one meal I made for myself. Around one o'clock I would wander into the kitchen, putting the cooks into a dither—would I like an omelette? some fish? they would ask solicitously. Every day I refused. A quick look in the refrigerator and the pantry and I would make myself a toasted sandwich of crab, tuna or salmon, or even just an apple and some cheese. Very occasionally I would get a craving for a hamburger, and then I would walk down to the local store and buy myself half a pound of ground beef.

During the afternoon the babies slept and I tried to deal with my responsibilities: I'd write thank you letters, sort out gifts, dream up new menus. Even now that they are bigger, the boys know that the afternoons are silent times at 24 Sussex—they can do whatever they want, but they have to do it on their own, and quietly. Tea was really the best part of the day. Often I took them around to friends for a moan and a gossip, the most ordinary and unexceptional afternoons in the world.

Punctually at a quarter to seven Pierre would arrive home. Before we had the indoor swimming pool built he would merely pass through the house to see how we all were, and then go straight out jogging. Now he swims forty-four laps, never more, never less, every evening. Seventeen minutes later the little boys would begin their fifteen-minute swimming session with him. Most evenings there were just the two of us, and that continued throughout our marriage. The other political families would have been annoyed to hear us: we talked about ideas and ideals, never whether Pierre should put more money into the health program. We always thought that once the babies grew up a bit it would change, and we would become sociable, but somehow it never did. In the early days we didn't want anyone breaking in on our loving solitude. Later, when I started kicking against the quiet life, it was too late to change.

The nanny left at seven, so the evening was our time with the children. Pierre insisted on it. First one and then the other would come wriggling out of his bed and wheedle his way to the dining table and sit on our laps eating our bread and butter. Pierre and I had dinner precisely at eight, waited on by a maid. When the babies were small and fretful I kept them on my knee, with my napkin laid over their bald heads to stop them being scalded by spilled food or covered in sauce. Sometimes I would

let them nurse as I ate. With Justin, Pierre was always embarrassed to see me do it in public or even in front of our staff,
so I covered myself and the baby discreetly in cumbersome
shawls. By the time Sacha and Micha came he took it all as a
matter of course.

Dinner was usually a four-course meal but neither of us have
big appetites. We both share one passion though—caviar. At
each of the babies' christenings we made certain there were
generous helpings of caviar and champagne. Sometimes late at
night Pierre and I would creep down to the kitchen and sneak
a can from the fridge. We were very lucky: we always seemed to
have an inexhaustible supply of it from Russian and Iranian
friends who knew how much we loved it. Pierre is such a fanatic
about it that he won't let the staff open the can and serve the
eggs on a dish because he claims that loses too many of them.
He has to get every single last egg, and at the end he'll spend
another five minutes scraping down in the bottom of the can
to make quite certain every last shred has been eaten. Caviar
and vodka became a symbol for us, a celebration of good times.
Justin seems to share our greed: at Sacha's christening we
found him with his fists deep in a pot, his face smeared in the
slimy gray eggs, his jaws munching happily on an enormous
mouthful.

Pierre is almost obsessively health conscious. After a meal
he will do nothing requiring deep thought for up to three-
quarters of an hour while, as he puts it, he digests. This period
was given over to hanging paintings, fixing up and mending
little things for me, and listening to music. The forty-five
minutes up, Pierre would start working again. Time with Wifey
was over. That's when the loneliness really hit me. I had been
on my own all day waiting for Pierre and then, within minutes
of seeing him, he seemed to be back working. I was absolutely
forbidden to interrupt him as he worked. Occasionally I felt
rebellious and went off in a huff to visit friends. Usually I
sewed and nursed the babies and waited for Pierre to stop
working at about midnight.

Even Pierre sometimes permitted himself a night off. If it was
a Friday it took the form of sitting at home watching *all* the
late night movies at once. Pierre handled the remote control
buttons masterfully, switching to one scene from a dreadful

horror movie, to a bit of a great drama, to a long look at a western shoot out and even to the soft porn movie that was always showing. He regarded each of them with equal curiosity and interest.

Sometimes we would have dinner in a Chinese, Greek or even Lebanese restaurant in Rideau Street. Never a French one though. What was the point? We had the best French chef in town. Afterward we went to movies, or to plays, always very secretively, taking care not to be recognized.

Our third son, Micha, arrived on October 2, 1975. Throughout my pregnancy I had been convinced my new baby would be a girl. By now I was getting into the knack of childbirth: no more ridiculous inhibitions. As he popped out I gave a bloodcurdling yell; you could have heard me down on the parking lot. My immediate reaction on seeing another boy was bitter disappointment. I wanted nothing to do with him. It was a wily nurse, who remembered me from Sacha and Justin, who got round my rage. She brought him to me to feed when I had relegated him to the nursery: as he started sucking so I fell in love.

It was an ordinary Thursday. I was delighted. Two babies on Christmas Day had made me feel something of a freak. My relief was shortlived. Ten days after the birth I received a letter from an Indian living in the east. "Congratulations. Your son was born on Mahatma Gandhi's birthday and the Archangel's Feast day. He is specially blessed."

Having expected a girl, Pierre and I had no boys' names ready. Pierre wanted to call him Raphael or Serge (after Sergio Leone, the spaghetti western movie director, who came to dinner just after he was born). I objected that Raphael would be shortened to Raf. Meanwhile he remained "Baby." Finally, as a compromise, we hit on Michel. Even that sounded wrong and irked me until a Vancouver friend unwittingly said "Micha" over the phone. He was christened on the spot.

It was our children who really broke down the barriers between us and the servants. After they arrived the big house became less divided, even though Pierre was always trying to keep the kitchen smells away from the rest of the house. From the start I was very conscious of how hard it was going to be bringing up children in a house full of servants. So we made certain rules. The children are not allowed cookies or candies from anyone. Nor are they allowed to be punished by the staff: I had this image of them, particularly when they were being especially wicked and racing up and down stairs, spending the day getting hit by everyone they came across. Discipline was kept to the nannies, Pierre and myself. We made constant efforts to prevent the children exploiting the servants. We didn't want them to expect to be waited on, so they had to get their own glasses of water and clean up their own toys, and most importantly show respect. If I ever caught a Little Lord Fauntleroy in the act, there was big trouble.

When Justin and Sacha graduated to eating proper meals they lunched in the staff room, until I found they weren't eating properly, overexcited by too many people barking out orders at them. So I moved them down to a room of their own in the basement, having converted Mrs. Pearson's Canadiana museum into a playroom. My decision proved extremely successful. It not only gave the children a nursery of their own, but it gave visitors a chance to see some of the fine collection of Canadian furniture which I now scattered among our things throughout the rest of the house.

The basement looks out at a cement wall which used to be gray; I had it painted white to make the room lighter, and filled the playroom with furniture scaled down to child size. It was here that Diane, who by now looked after both Justin and Sacha, ran a playgroup for our children and four others, a marvelously inventive little school in which she used some of the more exotic trophies we brought home with us from official visits.

When Micha was born I asked Tara, the Jamaican maid, to become his nanny. Eventually Diane left us. We were all sad. Finding her replacement must have been the most publicized advertisement in the history of Canadian small ads: absurdly and meanly hoping to get a reduction on their usual exorbitant fee, I asked the *Globe* and *Mail* whether they would give us a special price? Certainly, they replied. The advertisement made the front page as a news story and was picked up by every other newspaper, television station and radio program in the country: "Want a job? Mrs. Trudeau needs a nanny...."

Pierre and myself and the babies: we were a happy, intimate family when we were allowed to be. There was also something very cloistered about my existence, particularly when Pierre was away on a trip, and the chef, the only man in the house, had gone home for the night. Eight women and three small children living together, retiring to our own cells at night, like a secluded nunnery. It was then that I felt more like a mother superior than a prime minister's wife, doing the rounds of my postulants and worrying about their souls.

SAVED BY PROTOCOL

HERE WAS NO ESCAPING official life—it was there all the time, lurking. It emerged in frenetic bursts of entertaining and dressing up; catching planes to new places and talking to strangers through interpreters, only to be switched off again just as suddenly, leaving me washed up in my privacy and peace.

It wasn't long before my childhood habit to be secretive, to split myself into separate isolated parts, each carefully locked away from the other, began again with a vengeance. I became two different people. In the background at 24 Sussex and up at the lake I was Mrs. Trudeau, an ordinary suburban Canadian housewife who liked to bake bread and cross-country ski. The moment officialdom struck I was transformed into the wife of the Prime Minister; it was all rather like Cinderella and her pumpkin. And how does a twenty-two-year-old girl, with no experience of protocol, formality or procedure, learn the rules? One thing was clear; I had to learn them, and I had to learn them fast.

"Protocol will protect you," Mrs. Michener, my mentor, kept repeating. "If you get that right, you won't have to put *yourself* on the line. You will be judged by your manners."

I believed every word. The problem was how to absorb it all. By keeping his staff away from me, and not thinking to provide me with an assistant, or even an experienced social secretary who could have guided me along, Pierre effectively kept me in the dark far longer than I need have been. He meant it kindly, but it was a mistake.

I learned the hard way, by watching and listening to the other wives when they came to visit us, or I went to them, and imitating those whom I judged masters of the art. Everywhere I went I kept muttering rules and advice to myself: "Remember to offer Mrs. So and So orange juice, because she doesn't drink alcohol. Remember to carry the carnations sent by the principal's wife when you visit the school. Talk to General X about sailing. Don't mention religion to Mrs. Y. . . ." And so it went on. To my astonishment it soon dawned on me that I wasn't alone in my revulsion against the tedium of official life. Almost everyone seemed to loathe it, and some were driven nearly insane by it. And this realization, in a sense, was to prove my downfall, for I now set out, singlehanded, to change it all. I had a mission, a crusade. I was going to make official life fun.

Pierre had told me on several occasions that he believed that Canada as a peaceful neutral nation should do its best to have an effect on international relations and in bringing opposing countries together. Fine, I said, for that we must have sincerity, not stuffy protocol. Couldn't we start by putting a bomb under all our chiefs of protocol—as alike as Siamese twins whether in Peking, London or Belgrade—blow up that separate culture called protocol? No, said Pierre, we couldn't. So I chose my own way to beat the system. I decided to master it to perfection, so that there was no wife better than I at the details and the niceties, the small talk and the correct titles. Then, and only then, properly briefed, immaculately dressed and at ease wherever I went, would I emerge from behind the protective coloring and be a real, honest person. I kept repeating to myself the words that first Mrs. Michener and then Prince Philip had both said to me: "It is your duty. It's a vocation. Get it perfect."

There was a lot to learn first, and I tackled the job with a mixture of impatience and dedication, getting into trouble more times than I care to remember. My first official visit as Pierre's wife, to Russia two months after we married, had left a scar on my soul and it was to that that I returned in my thoughts when deciding what to tackle next.

First there was the issue of the presents. From the day Pierre and I arrived in Moscow I was showered with presents. One day Mr. Kosygin gave me a magnificent amber necklace; the next, the government presented me with a bone china teaset. Then the foreign minister's wife, Mrs. Gromyko, produced an interlocking set of Russian dolls and lacquered boxes. Mrs. Gvyshiani gave me boxes and pins and ornaments. Then came the day for our return present giving; I had been counting the hours until I could return some of their generosity.

I asked the external affairs secretary to send over my present for Mrs. Gvyshiani so that I could wrap it up beautifully before presenting it. To my consternation, and total disbelief, there appeared a meager plate silver maple leaf, costing probably no more than thirty-five dollars. "But this," I moaned to Pierre, "is what I ought to give Tanya, my interpreter, *not* the prime minister's daughter."

Mrs. Teresa Ford, our ambassador's wife, overheard my squeaks of outrage. She hurried over and offered me the gold maple leaf, encrusted with emeralds, that the governor general's wife had lately presented her with. It was an incredibly generous gesture and I was very touched, but I refused her brooch, and got round my dilemma by telling Mrs. Gvyshiani that by some oversight in the packing, her present had got left behind. The day I returned to Ottawa I went to our best furrier's and bought a Mackenzie mink stole. It was sent off in the diplomatic pouch to Moscow. That, I thought, was a more suitable present of thanks for all the warmth and hospitality.

Then I asked external affairs for their policy over official gifts. None, it transpired. A few months before I married Pierre a woman civil servant had simply been asked to stock a cupboard in the ministry with all the presents she could think of that might do for an official visit. The result was a pile of worthless rubbish, greatly inferior to almost every item I had thrown out of our junk room. It had led to some scandalous mistakes. On a recent official visit to London the Canadian presents had all been blankets. Not a bad idea. But when the day for presentation arrived it was discovered from the labels that they had all been made in Birmingham.

From that day on I made presents *my* business. First I used to try to learn something about the people we were giving presents to. Were they young? Frivolous? Interested in crafts? Books? Then I enquired about good Canadian artists and craftsmen and went to visit their studios. I didn't feel the gifts had to be expensive, as long as they were suitable and reflected Pierre's personal taste rather than government charity.

My searches took me to the government warehouse which handles all Eskimo and Indian art on its way into the galleries and shops, and this proved an invaluable source for my better presents. There were always so many to plan—up to twelve on any major foreign visit, ranging from something of obvious value for the prime minister's wife, to something modest but distinctive for an interpreter.

The presents were, of course, a two-way business. In the United States all official presents belong to the state; in Canada they belong to the recipients. I soon found myself showered with things of immense value and beauty. Just after we were married the governor of Newfoundland offered me an otter coat, and the Commissioner of the North West Territories a Mackenzie mink —Pierre made me refuse them, saying they were too costly. But there was little he could do about the sunburst gold Andrew Grima brooch covered in diamonds given me by the Queen, nor the Inca pink clay adobe with tiny carved figures given me by Mrs. Perez nor the four crates of Japanese tableware, nor Mrs. Gandhi's silk saris, nor Mrs. Nixon's Bartlett print, nor Mme. Giscard d'Estaing's marble jewelry box—24 Sussex was filled to bursting with the teasets, boxes and lacquered trays, though Pierre put his foot down at a sealskin kayak and presented it to the Museum of Man. My attitude to the presents didn't always make me popular. When I met Mrs. Perez I was so charmed by her that impulsively I unpinned a carved gold killer whale brooch engraved by Bill Reid from my own dress and pinned it onto hers; the trouble was that I had been presented with it by the Aquarium of Vancouver when I opened their new section, and not long after my return to Ottawa I was asked to lend it for an exhibition of Haida Indian art.

I discovered very early on that it was impossible to match the hospitality and generosity that Pierre and I were shown on official visits. The smaller and poorer countries in particular gave the most lavish and expensive of gifts, almost it seemed, as a form of bribery. I felt the irony of it keenly especially when Sheikh Mujibur Rahman, the President of Bangladesh, came to Canada in what was principally a search for aid, and brought with him an entire trunk of silks and an exquisite necklace of seed pearls.

The gifts under control, I now turned to the more awkward question of briefing. Having been humiliated in Russia by the full depth of my ignorance of everything from simple geography to the identity of the people to whom I was introduced, I begged Pierre to make certain I had written notes in good time before a visit. In the early days this would merely consist of another copy of the collection of notes that went out to the press. Later on, after I had seen how thorough and elaborate the American briefing books are, with photographs of all the people you are likely to meet, and a brief resumé of their tastes, I became more demanding. Sometimes I even got my hands on Pierre's notes, which were far more amusing. . . . "Perhaps you should not get too heavily involved with X," they would read, "because having evaded tax for six years, he is about to be impeached."

Gradually I started to exercise some control over my program, mixing obligations I could not get out of with visits to places that genuinely interested me. In Japan I accepted a morning's flower arranging, but then I also made sure that I paid a visit to the Nikon factory to see how the cameras are made. I discovered that I was free to choose, and that if I ever suggested anything my hosts seemed only too delighted to lay it on. It was also one positive way of escaping the interminable cups of tea with the dreary diplomats' wives trying hard to look pretty and think up inanities to say to one another.

Of all the official visits I paid, the one to France in the autumn of 1974 was the most difficult and the most redolent of protocol. It wasn't made easier by the fact that I wasn't long out of the hospital following serious emotional stress. By then the contradictions of my life were really beginning to tell on me.

There is no doubt that the French can be the rudest, most arrogant people in the world. This was our first state visit to France since De Gaulle had made his "*Vive Québec Libre*" statement in Montreal during Expo '67 and so effectively cut off relations between France and Canada for almost a decade. We simply had to do well. It wasn't going to be easy: we had to open the door of good relations again, yet at the same time assert that France could not treat Quebec as a separate, independent country.

My first function without Pierre (he was at an official, men

144

only, lunch) was a reception given by Mme. Chirac, the prime minister's wife, a chic woman with a sharp nose. The food was superb. The guests were all women, the wives of cabinet ministers, diplomats and members of parliament, and, oh boy, did. they condescend to me. I was the youngest by twenty-five years, and they made me feel like a stupid, ill-informed, clumsy, illiterate child. Outwardly all was civility and good breeding; inside I was seething. I had Marie-Hélène Fox with me, Pierre's political secretary, a professional career girl. The conversation soon came around to how very selfish career women are, and how very arrogant it is of them not to marry and have children. I did my best to support Marie-Hélène but with lamentable French and, as a wife raising her children being in a weak position myself, there wasn't much I could do.

The hostility oozing out of these French women toward me grew more intense as the days went by. I had one afternoon off. Savoring every minute of it I decided to go to a fashion show. It was at the time when St. Laurent was changing his neat, tailored look and presenting wild Russian peasant costumes in his collections. I was eager to see them. Mme. Chirac, on hearing my plans, pressed me to go to an *haute couture* fashion parade by a more conservative designer. I protested: "No. I really want to see St. Laurent." They demurred. Finally, with sighs and considerable bad grace, Mme. Chirac insisted on accompanying me to St. Laurent. Behind us during the show sat an entire row of *Paris Match* reporters listening to our conversation and chattering gaily among themselves. I longed to join them. Instead here I was, trapped, condemned by association, blushing with embarrassment while Mme. Chirac kept up a long tirade in a clear, carrying voice, about how appalling the clothes were. I was barely polite. In the end I was as rude as she was.

Clothes were so immensely important: if I felt correctly dressed it gave me that initial boost in confidence that enabled me to cope. If my shoes were even slightly scuffed I felt distracted and selfconscious. I had begged to be able to take a maid to France with me, but my request had been turned down as pretentious. On the night of our grandest dinner during the tour, held at the Elysée, I had a pink silk organdie Valentino dress with painted peonies to wear. It was a very low cut dress which I kept for only the grandest occasions. To show it off at its best I decided to have my hair done by Alexandre, who opened his salon especially for me. His makeup man took three-quarters of an hour on my mouth alone. I came out radiant: my hair cut severely across in bangs, the "mandarin look," white and black and impassive. But it was not the hairstyle nor the face to go with a fluffy pink decolleté dress, as I soon discovered back before my own mirror. I scrubbed most of the lipstick off my mouth, but had no time left to do much about my eyes which had almost totally disappeared under more layers of greens and grays than even Elizabeth Taylor puts on. In despair I realized I would have to abandon the fluff for something far plainer; something stark: I settled on a white silk shirt and a long black evening skirt. No sooner had I stepped inside the Elysée than I saw my terrible error: there was not a woman present who was not wearing *haute couture*. Alone, I looked out of place.

The formal dinner started in agony. If anything, it got worse. I sat next to President Giscard d'Estaing, who, with a slightly flirtatious manner that always reminded me of Pierre, did his best to put me at ease. On my other side was Prime Minister Chirac, a heavy, somber figure like a successful French lawyer or a big American mid-Westerner. At least, I thought, if all else is a disaster, the conversation will be memorable.

Indeed it was. All Giscard d'Estaing wanted to talk about was hippies, as if I were a rather curious specimen from the sub-culture.

"Tell me all about marijuana. What do you young people really feel about drugs?"

I was somewhat taken back, but then thought: "Perhaps he really does want to know," and opened my mouth to reply.

Before I could speak, M. Chirac waded in. "Talking about marijuana," he said ponderously, "we had that problem in my family. One of my nephews started smoking it." I felt indignation rising inside me at the sound of his authoritative, self-righteous tone. "We just made it perfectly clear to him that if he carried on with it he would be disowned, his family fortune taken away, and he would never be allowed in the house again."

I looked at him aghast. "Has he ever smoked marijuana again?"

"Certainly not," replied Chirac, both surprised and indignant, as if the boy could not conceivably have made any other choice.

My worst gaffe in France happened on the day that Mme. Giscard d'Estaing took me to the Louvre. I was with a crowd of French ladies and we passed in front of what seemed to me to be every single picture in the building, pausing for a few seconds, while the ladies kept their eyes riveted upon me to check my reaction. My French was still atrocious (adequate accent but horrendous grammar) and I felt that they were testing me. I took a cowardly if unpremeditated way out. I passed out cold on the floor. The dear wife of the French Ambassador to Canada, Mme. Viau, threw herself forward to break my fall, but I collapsed all the same in a heap on the stone floor, I now believe entirely under the pressure of feeling myself on the defensive and sneered at.

Fainting was an unconscious escape I often took on formal occasions, particularly when very nervous or pregnant. When the Queen spoke in Charlottetown and was halfway through her address I disappeared under my chair on the podium. On another occasion I was sitting next to Mr. Michener and across the table from President Tito during his state visit to Canada, toward the end of a seemingly week-long meal of interpreters, cigars and goodwill. Just as Mr. Michener rose to his feet to offer the official welcome toast, I had to stumble out of the room before fainting.

We stayed in Paris four days, then went on to Belgium where the N.A.T.O. summit on nuclear de-escalation was to take place. These were tricky and tense talks for Pierre who was trying to formulate a special relationship between Canada and the E.E.C., while hinting that we were also considering a series of defense cuts. I did my best to keep my deep sense of unease from him. It was in Brussels that I got my first real inkling of my exact social rank in terms of world protocol. One night, while King Baudouin held a working dinner for the N.A.T.O. heads, Queen Fabiola gave a dinner for the wives, and then took us on to a concert. At the dinner, I found myself on her left, because though many of the wives, like Frau Helmut Schmidt and Mrs. Harold Wilson were senior to me in age, my husband had served longer as prime minister. On Queen

Fabiola's other side sat Mrs. Gerald Ford. I learned that Mrs. Ford and Mme. Giscard d'Estaing rank the same, so that, had she been there, Mme. d'Estaing would have been in my place.

The dinner was held at the queen's palace and the food was, if possible, even more delicious than that at the Elysée. It was a full dress affair with tiaras and decorations. This time I was correctly dressed in my Valentino pink dress and felt in control —all the more so as I had noticed that I was not the only wife who blundered. At a lunch given by Mrs. Luns, the wife of the head of N.A.T.O., the wives were asked to assemble by 12:45 P.M. All were there at the appointed time, except for Mrs. Ford. We drank one glass of sherry, then another, and then a third. Still no Mrs. Ford. At 1:15 she strolled casually through the door, without the hint of an apology, saying she had been at the hairdresser. By then a definite sense of schoolgirlish camaraderie had grown among the rest of us, particularly after Mrs. Luns had somewhat maliciously regaled us with stories about how early that morning the American secret service had arrived to ask if they could stand in the kitchens. They wanted to watch while the meal was prepared—to be certain no poison crept into the meal. Mrs. Luns refused.

At its best, the dressing up was like some magical fantasy world, a reward for all the boredom and stuffiness of the long social occasions. I knew I could make myself look lovely, and that if I did throw myself into the part, I could quite easily be transformed from a jeans and sneakers girl into a sophisticated woman. With the pomp and the grandeur of these evenings I sometimes pretended I was in a fairy tale. It was made more romantic by the fact that each time Pierre put on his black tie and tails I fell in love with him all over again. I don't know what it was about him dressed up, but we made the most of the romance. We were on show, the "flower child who married a prime minister." We acted the part.

Possibly the most successful and certainly the most unusual trip we made was to China in the autumn of 1973, a "getting-to-know-you visit" of the oldfashioned sort made more important by the fact that we were the first western nation to visit China officially. I was seven and a half months pregnant with Sacha. I went to my doctor for my monthly visit in October, bewailing the fact that I was going to have to miss this trip. I was astonished to hear him say: "Why ever don't you go? There's absolutely no reason not to." All he insisted was that I take along someone to help (which was a godsend for it set a precedent and in future, especially when ill or pregnant, I was allowed a companion). I chose Joyce Fairburn, Pierre's parliamentary assistant, and was especially pleased when Pierre chose one of his British Columbian M.P.s, Len Marchand, and his wife Donna to accompany us. As it turned out I couldn't have been looked after better: one of the men on our plane, the deputy minister from the Department of Health and Welfare, Maurice Leclerc, was a doctor himself, and the Chinese were so anxious that all would go well that they had a doctor waiting at the airport who wanted to rush me off and examine me the moment the plane touched ground.

It was mid-October when we arrived in Peking. The weather was perfect, warm by day and cool at night, which was just as well since I had had very little time to prepare suitable clothes for the trip, and was in any case a very awkward shape. I was amazed by the beauty of Peking and the way that the capital of the most populated country in the world still looks like a sprawling country town, with single-story buildings made of sticks, clay and bamboo poles. Everywhere there was green. Mao's order that for every Chinese born a tree should be planted had taken fruit by the time of our visit: huge trees lined every street, turning Peking into a restful, gentle city. When we went south we found orange blossom out, jasmine trees smelling sweetly, and cassis flowers everywhere.

The beauty of the country was only the first thing that surprised me. I found myself unsuspectingly riddled with western prejudices about China, absurd notions that I had never thought to check, and only now saw for the first time in their full absurdity. I had assumed I needed vaccinations for every illness under the sun—not so, China is virtually free of disease. I had simply accepted that it would be hideous—not a bit of it, it was magnificent. I had images of a country of thin and sickly people—I found them all very healthy, and caught up in a cult of physical fitness. Their energy extended itself to me: when we went to the Great Wall not only Pierre and the Canadian delegation but our entire party of Chinese hosts and journalists, expressed concern about me. But I felt absurdly well, so when they tried to prevent me from climbing the Wall, I turned to a journalist alongside me and said: "Race you to the top." I beat him.

My most appropriate visit while in China was to Peking's one maternity hospital. It was a very comic occasion. I went surrounded by a great gang of journalists and at the door we were enveloped in big white coats, and sterilized masks, hats and slippers. There was lots of laughter and jokes. The first ward we visited contained an extremely sad-looking woman lying dejectedly on her bed. "Why is she so sad?" I asked the chief obstetrician. Through our interpreter I learned that she had given birth the previous day by Caesarian and that she had wanted natural childbirth. "Did she have acupuncture?" I asked.

"Yes," came back through the interpreter. Simply to make conversation, having no doubts at all that the answer would be no, of course not, I asked whether the woman had felt any pain. To my amazement the patient perked up.

"Yes," she replied in clearly resentful tones. "Indeed I did. It hurt very much indeed." So much for painless acupuncture.

From the ward we went on to the case room, which, to my Canadian eyes, looked like a relic from one of our history museums. Forceps, a bucket and a rickety old table. Mischieviously I asked the doctor where the mirrors were to let the women watch their babies being born. He looked shocked. "Oh yes," I insisted, "you know, mirrors where Mommy and Daddy. . . ."

"Daddy," came a horrified cry, "Daddy in here . . . ?"

Since I had myself had a blood problem with Justin I asked my interpreter to find out what this hospital did with cases of RH incompatibility. The doctor in charge looked puzzled:

"What do you mean? The babies die, of course."

It was my turn to be astonished. "They don't need to die. That's a disease of the past. There's an injection you can give within two hours of the birth of the first baby." And I described the inoculation that had been discovered in Winnipeg at the RH Disease Center and what it had done for me. The Chinese doctors were very interested and when I saw our deputy minister of health that night at the hotel he agreed to

150

put the Winnipeg center in touch with the Peking hospital, and get them to send vaccine and information. Even Pierre was impressed. And it was uphill work impressing Pierre.

We traveled all over China. Pierre had been there a couple of times before, so he wanted to avoid the obvious cities like Shanghai and Canton. Our best trip, and certainly the most romantic, was to Kweilin, a seven-hour boat ride down the most beautiful river. A charming guide insisted on describing in detail every boat, factory, bird and person we floated past. Pierre and I were in fits of giggles and I thought I would choke to death. These shared jokes, the way we could laugh with each other, were undoubtedly our best times.

Kweilin is one of China's most famous beauty spots with remarkable caves of stalactites which we explored for an entire afternoon, and tropical, totally deserted mountainous countryside. Sadly, it was here that we met with our first example of Chinese pollution. There is a soap factory at the foot of the mountain, and as we rounded the final bend in the river, Pierre and I saw smoke rings of dense gray cloud rising and settling over the top peak in the mountain range. It was clear that no one had given it a thought. "You have one of the finest sights in the world here," I said severely to Vice-President Teng through our guide. "Why don't you move the factory up the river?" He looked surprised, since we were some of the first westerners to visit Kweilin, but he also seemed impressed.

That day Pierre and I made a private vow that has stayed with me ever since: to revisit China one day, and make our way along its rivers and canals by boat, finishing up in the Yellow Sea.

At every stop in China we were met by a vast, enthusiastic crowd. To my western eyes they were all identical. I became convinced that the crowds plus costumes and bands were moving with us, because wherever we were, they were—the same little girls doing the same dances in the same clothes with their faces painted, tassels in their hands, and little black shoes on their feet. And they always chanted the same song, a verse which, roughly translated, means "Long Live Friendship between Canada and China." Unfortunately it sounded exactly like "God-damn Whistle: Canada–Peking." Once I had told Pierre, neither of us could hear it any other way, so our paths were lined with little girls leaping into the air singing "God-damn Whistle: Canada–Peking."

For all our marvelous travels, I did miss one encounter I had much looked forward to: a meeting with Mao. By then Mao was already weak. No appointments could be made to see him; it was simply a question of waiting and seizing the good moment. That moment came just at the time I was visiting a kindergarten, so Pierre went alone. Later he described how impressed he had been by Mao: an old, old man, who looked utterly frail, yet had a mind that was perfectly lucid. Instead of repeating questions as other men of his age often did, Mao moved the conversation around the world, one step at a time, never repeating anything and displaying a keen intellect with provocative questions of policy and international relations, especially about the Middle East and Africa.

Missing Chairman Mao was a terrible disappointment but compensated for by a fascinating encounter with Premier Chou en Lai. The year we visited China he was seventy-six, a handsome, thin, elegant man with prominent cheekbones and warm brown eyes. I had had several unremarkable conversations with him in the course of our many receptions. Then came the day we were due to leave Peking. Pierre and I had a free lunch to ourselves. Since, despite the series of delicious meals we had eaten, we seemed to have missed out altogether on Peking duck, I asked our Chinese guide whether there was a restaurant in the city we could visit to eat it? Then I thought no more about it.

That morning we were in the Great Hall where Pierre and the premier were signing documents. When the formal ceremony was over, and we were preparing to take our leave of him, Chou en Lai took my hand and said, with oldfashioned courtesy: "I have heard you want Peking duck. It will be my privilege to have a Peking duck lunch for you and your party."

The feast was prepared as by a magic genie. No more than what seemed like minutes later we were summoned back into the dining room at the Great Hall. At the door the Chinese maître d'hôtel started, Chinese fashion, sifting the men from the women, so that all the women in the party were directed to sit at one side of one huge round table, and the men at the other. Chou en Lai stopped him and my translator told me what he had said: "Mrs. Trudeau doesn't like protocol of this kind. As it is her lunch she is sitting next to me."

What followed was undoubtedly the most curious and fascinating discussion in all my five years of official banquets. Our entire talk was conducted in English, despite the fact that Chou en Lai usually makes a point never to speak anything but Chinese in case his words are misinterpreted. He broke his rule for me, I think, because I was just Pierre's pregnant wife.

We began by talking about my coming child. "I have very strong views about illegitimacy," the Premier began. "I think it is a terrible thing for women to have to give up their babies, or have abortions, because they aren't married." He paused. "I have been thinking about this for many years, and I'll tell you why. Just after the Revolution a woman got on a train with her baby. When she got off at the next station, she left her child in a basket on the seat with a note which said: 'Please take this baby to Chou en Lai and let him bring up my beautiful boy. The social stigma against me having this baby because I am not married is too great to bear.' "

"Did you keep the baby?" I asked immediately. "What happened to him?"

Chou en Lai replied: "My wife and I already had a family of our own, so we couldn't adopt him. But we put him with good people."

"And have you followed his progress?"

"Yes," he replied, smiling with obvious pride, "indeed we have. He's turned into a fine boy."

His next topic was even more unexpected. "I imagine you think Chinese women are liberated?" he asked me.

"Well," I said cautiously, "they appear to be working side by side with the men. Economically they seem to be liberated. They're a main part of the working force."

"Ah," he said. "You're wrong. They are not liberated. You are liberated."

I was astonished. "Me? I'm pregnant. I don't work. I am a mother and a housewife."

"Yes," he said. "But the Chinese women are extremely embarrassed by their femininity and you are not. Let me give you an example. I had what you call [this gives some idea of how excellent his English was] a Girl Friday in my office, a girl who was really indispensable to me. I also liked her very much. Then one day she didn't appear. I assumed she was ill. After a week of embarrassed silence from everyone it finally emerged that she had transferred jobs—because she was pregnant. She had left word that she would return when this embarrassing state was over. She couldn't stand the thought of facing me in so humiliating a state." I was immediately conscious of my huge belly. I grabbed a napkin off the table and covered it. Chou en Lai laughed. "Oh dear, no, no, you have come to terms with your self as a woman. You are proud. To watch you walking as proud as a queen with your big belly is the happiest sight to see because you are so proud of it. Chinese women are still feudal in their attitudes toward their own femininity, their own bodies, their own sexuality. They have just become versions of men." I was so astonished by his words that I managed to swallow down the only course in the entire meal that I found repellent: snippets of the ducks' intestines floating around in broth. In a true Peking duck dinner you eat the whole bird.

During my six years with Pierre we paid one or two major visits abroad each year, and we traveled around inside Canada almost continuously—Pierre was usually away from home for a trip at least every couple of weeks. The Canadians, I soon found, don't really like their prime minister traveling despite the fact that internationally Pierre has put Canada on the map. The picture I got of these trips from reading the newspapers was a slightly malicious one, as if they hoped to catch him being absurd, or on a joyride at the taxpayers' expense.

Our staff, on the other hand, loved them. All seven women and the chef would be lined up on the steps of 24 Sussex when we set off on a visit, and the maids in particular reveled in the new clothes and the tales I brought home. It demeaned them to have a prime minister's wife in jeans; they hadn't joined the staff for that. They were much more respectful to me when I put on my silk dresses and floppy hats.

God knows I did so often enough. For every trip abroad, we hosted at least six at home. The whole world comes to Canada; everyone wants wheat. The staff rallied round, and I began to come into my own. Pierre is terrible at names. Since we had to give receptions and dinners and mingle in crowds with our guests I would stick closely to him and then if a guest appeared before us and said, "Hello Pierre, I bet you don't remember *me*," the chances were that Pierre certainly did not. However, usually the name would pop into my mind, and I could say: "Oh hello Dick, of course we do. How is Monique?" Pierre would then continue. (It didn't always work. One of my worst gaffes was to mistake a lady-in-waiting for the wife of a head of N.A.T.O. I spent an hour and a half questioning her laboriously about her country and seated her on my right at lunch, while the true wife was put down the table next to my assistant.)

Of the dozens of official visits I hosted, a few stand out with particular vividness; they are usually those which ended in disasters, or near disasters. President Bhutto's visit in 1976 is such a one.

We were scarcely settled after returning from a visit to Mexico where rosepetals had cascaded daily on our heads, little girls had dressed up in peasant costumes and serenaded us everywhere, and there had been endless singing and laughing—a warm, delightful visit. It was midwinter in Canada when we got home and the morning we met President Bhutto and his wife it was bitterly cold. The reception took place in an icy military hangar, where the president was to review the guard. As we went to leave the hangar and climb into waiting cars, the huge doors slid open and a massive shower of huge icicles came crashing down, denting the tops of the cars. It was a miracle that President Bhutto wasn't killed.

While all the crashing, shouting and chaos was going on I felt a terrible giggle rising up in my throat. I clamped my hand over my mouth. As we left the hangar, a journalist came up to me. "Mrs. Trudeau," he said slyly, "I couldn't help noticing that you found it very amusing that there was nearly a terrible accident."

"No, no," I said hastily. "I didn't find it a bit amusing. It was just that I couldn't help thinking of the contrast between Canadian hospitality and Mexican hospitality. When we arrived in Mexico we were showered with rose petals. When guests come here they're showered with icicles."

The Bhuttos' visit was much improved for me by the good relations I soon established with his wife, who is a sweet-tempered and gentle woman, very quiet, unexpectedly tall, with sad eyes and an expressive face. I had taken pains to find her a present I thought she would really treasure: a sculptured candle snuff with gold nuggets that had been cast from the moss of the nearby Gatinean hills. She and Pinto—her ambassador's wife, a dear old friend of mine—and I had three marvelous days together.

It is, however, my conversation with President Bhutto that sticks in my mind; it was to have a sad irony about it later. He struck me as an arrogant, rather haughty man, with a slightly disdainful manner. "What," he asked me as we sat down to our formal dinner, "is the most important and controversial issue for your people and your country at the moment?"

There was no doubt at all in my mind about what to reply. We were in the middle of an extremely traumatic debate about the abolition of capital punishment, with the issue about to come before parliament as a free vote, and passions raging high throughout the country. I described the situation to the president, and went on to tell him about the man who had recently admitted to the murder of five little girls. President Bhutto looked incredulous. "You mean you're not even going to hang *him*?"

"Well, we haven't hanged anyone in Canada for eleven years, so it's nothing new."

"But what do you do with your country's enemies?" he asked. "People who steal land and water supplies? People who threaten the government?"

I told him that the only people who could possibly be executed in Canada, even if the pro-capital punishment lobby won, would be those who murdered policemen. He was horrified. "We have 350–400 executions every year in Pakistan," he told me, almost cheerfully.

I find it hard not to be blasé about conversations such as this one—there were many more like it. Pierre, as prime minister of a prosperous country, eager to forge strong international relations, was continually meeting world leaders, and during those years I was almost always at his side. However charmed I was by the people I met, I could never quite forget that what they said reflected on whole nations and many millions of people. Some of the leaders failed to live up to my expectations;

others, like Chou en Lai and Giscard d'Estaing, were not only impressive, but open and approachable. I wish I could tell of some fascinating encounter with President Nixon, which would shed some new light on his character. Alas, we had but one, and then an all too brief, exchange of words.

In Ottawa one night I was sitting between the president and the U.S. secretary of state, Bill Rogers. Bill Rogers asked me whether this was my first meeting with the president. "Yes," I told him. "And I'm pretty in awe of him." To my embarrassment, Bill Rogers leaned across me.

"Hey, Dick," he called. "Mrs. Trudeau doesn't know what to say to you."

President Nixon gave me a baleful look. Sighing deeply, he embarked on a long and tedious story about how his pandas had never mated. Then he turned quickly back to Pierre. I turned back to Bill Rogers.

"How did you find him?"

"Quite frankly, I'm still in awe. The only conversation that I have now had with the president of the United States is on the sex life of pandas."

My official chore at home, once the prime minister's dinner was over, was entertaining the wives. I usually gave a luncheon, generally for eight women, chosen, like our official guests, from different professions and parts of Canada. These lunches weren't always much of a success. I sometimes found myself surveying the table with loathing and irritation: what in the world can I possibly find to talk to these crows about?

After lunch was over, I would dream up ways of entertaining them—take them to day centers or a city school, or simply for a drive into the countryside. I soon discovered on my own travels, getting to know the wives and the official circuit, how very little any of us actually wanted a heavy official program of visits to places in which we had not the slightest interest. Frankly, I just wasn't interested in dental hospitals, or zoos, or centers for adult education. They bored me almost to tears. They bored all the other wives too. I cannot see a picture of a prime minister's wife opening a new hospital or civic center today without conjuring up for myself the murderous thoughts that must be going through her head under the widebrimmed hat. Wives, just like me, just like any woman, wanted to get their hair done, sleep in late, and if they were lucky, visit a picture gallery or go to the theater. They simply didn't want to review the entire Brownie pack at 9:30 A.M. So I quickly organized a whole new system for visiting wives, cut down their schedule to the bare minimum that I would have wanted myself and tried to introduce at least some informal time.

On their arrival in Ottawa I offered them a choice—either a relaxed tea with myself and the children in the gardens of 24 Sussex when the weather was good, or in the freedom room when it was bad, or a formal tea party. The formal occasion would be complete with hats, and one of my by now impressive selection of teasets, and we would be waited on by a maid. I had to be careful. The older wives, inured to the point of dependency by decades of small gilt chairs and conversation about the weather, needed the formality. What's more, they felt insulted if I neglected it. If they expected to find every diplomatic lady in Ottawa lined up in a sycophantic row, they were understandably thrown if presented with the alternative of me in my blue jeans with the latest dribbling baby. It was all a question of matching hospitality to expectations.

Those tea parties provided some of my best official moments. Freed from the constraints of their husbands and the other ministers, some of the wives revealed comic and unexpected sides to their natures. In Moscow I had formed no very strong impression of Mrs. Gromyko, other than of a large and obviously intelligent woman. A very different person came to tea in Ottawa. To my surprise she had opted for a simple afternoon with the children and I was somewhat nervous when her official car drew up at 24 Sussex. Would Justin dribble all over her? Had the cook remembered the cake? She couldn't have been easier, chattering away and plying me with advice and hints about how to bring up the children. As she left, to my astonishment she said to me: "Do you realize that you live in *paradise*? No country in the world has the luck and the opportunities that you have here."

As surprising, though in quite a different way, was my morning with Mrs. Nixon. My impression of her up until then had been of a woman who tried hard to compensate for her husband's extreme lack of sociability—tried, and usually succeeded. She had a hard veneer, but she was agreeable enough. In 1972, when Justin was just three months old, the Nixons came to Ottawa. Among the other various entertainments, I received a note from the ambassadress asking whether Pat Nixon could come to 24 Sussex to call on me and Justin at eleven o'clock. "Delighted," I replied, rather flattered. The question was swiftly followed by a second note: "Which room can the press photographers use?" We sent back our usual answer: "I'm very sorry—none." Pierre and I had a rule about having no press in our home.

Nothing seemed to daunt them. Another note: "Please, just this once. To cover an historic moment." Laughing somewhat at the "historic" nature of the occasion I said that if she really wanted it so badly Mrs. Nixon could bring along one photographer.

As the United States limousine drew up to the door Justin chose the moment to pee down my sweater. It hardly mattered. I don't believe Pat Nixon cast so much as a glance in my direction. She strode in, refused all offers of tea and coffee, took Justin from my arms, plastered a gracious smile across her face, turned toward her photographer: snap, snap.

"How are Tricia and Julie?" I asked her, in an attempt to make conversation.

"Very well thank you." She defeated my attempt. And she was gone.

I made companions of these women, companions in a common plight, but few became my friends. Of course there were exceptions. Mrs. Gvyshiani was one of these, a very pretty and elegant woman, and her return visit to Canada was one of the most enjoyable during my years with Pierre. She and Prime Minister Kosygin came at a perfect time of year, October, when the weather was calm and warm, and the leaves had started to turn: there is nothing more spectacular than the fall around Ottawa, one enormous blur of scarlets, oranges and strident yellows, crowning the parks and the landscape like the brilliant plumage of a tropical bird.

An official visit to a civic center had been planned for Mrs. Gvyshiani's first afternoon, but at lunch that day, looking out of the window together at the very blue sky, we changed our minds, cancelled the visit, and took off for Harrington Lake, leaving havoc in our wake. Up at Harrington nothing was ready for us. Brushing aside maids, assistants, major domos and secretaries, we ensconced ourselves in the kitchen where Mrs. Gvyshiani taught me how to make tea her special way, pouring a little hot water on the leaves first to make an essence, and only then adding the rest of the water. No tea has ever tasted so good.

By now the boats were ready and we took our places in the most comfortable of our fleet of small and extremely uncomfortable summer rowboats with outboard engines. We chugged off merrily across the very black, still water having a thoroughly good time. But we were not reckoning with the forces of order behind us. It wasn't long before a second boat had put out, this one crammed to the brim with K.G.B. men, presumably to ward off the bands of terrorists that menace those wild shores. So there we were, Mrs. Gvyshiani and I in one boat, giggling wildly, while behind us, in considerable danger of sinking, chugged a boatload of agents peering wildly from the prows to glimpse a rifle among the autumn leaves. It was a comic outing.

As I went along, watching and listening and learning, so I came to admire the women who put up with this life, and particularly those who handled it with style and dignity; women like Queen Alia of Jordan who later became a real friend. No one, however, impressed me more than our Queen, with her warm friendliness and utter dedication. I have reason to be grateful to her. On one of our first encounters I was wearing a brand new *haute couture* suit I had bought in Rome, with very high heeled shoes. I was extremely nervous. As I sank to the ground in a deep curtsy it became crystal clear to both of us that I was not going to make it up again. Without altering her expression by as much as a flicker, the Queen strengthened her grasp, tensed all the muscles of her right arm, and drew me up to my feet with a grip of iron, smiling impassively the while.

ON THE
CAMPAIGN TRAIL

NOT LONG AFTER we were married I was approached by the ladies of the Liberal Association: would I become their honorary president? All previous prime ministers' wives had accepted; it never crossed their minds that I wouldn't follow suit. Would I care to be on various Liberal committees? Play a part in the parliamentary wives' meetings? To everyone's amazement, I refused. I agreed to help out on special occasions, but said that at this stage I didn't wish to get involved in any work I could not give myself up to completely. If I took a job on, I wanted it to be not a token, but a proper one.

The political ladies took my excuse in good heart. They put it all down to youth and timidity. What they didn't realize was that I had a very different reason for refusing, and they would have been shocked had they learned what it was. I didn't get involved with their activities, because I didn't *feel* involved. I never had been a card-carrying Liberal. I couldn't seem to summon up any party fervor—indeed, I sometimes felt that there were as many "nincompoops" in the Liberal ranks as there appeared to be in the Conservative and National Democratic parties. A heresy, I know. And with that sort of attitude it would have been worse than hypocritical to become a fake Liberal lady.

Without fully appreciating these subtleties, Pierre backed me nonetheless in my resolve to keep my distance. After all, it fitted in perfectly with his policy of isolating me from his political work. He really seemed to prefer me this way. The very fact that I didn't beg him to discuss the contents of his briefcase with me each evening meant that he had a genuine private life to come home to, while other cabinet colleagues rehashed the day's events nightly with their wives. In fact he's the only man I've ever met who is able to split himself so perfectly in two: work is work, family is family.

The only times he used my fresh eye politically was when he had to make some major decision, like a cabinet reshuffle, and then he would talk it over with me late into the night, rehearsing the arguments aloud, while I tried to ask the sort of questions any unbiased layman might ask. I was learning about politics all right. They weren't party politics perhaps, but as an observer, reading, listening, talking to the politicians who surrounded us, I was gaining an incredible amount of unpartisan knowledge every day and filing it away in my mind. In time Pierre found this increasingly useful.

I didn't entirely escape the wives' jamborees, however. Political life in Canada would collapse altogether were it not for legions of dedicated political women making coffee and sandwiches for rallies—and I took my place alongside the others when there was no avoiding it. About a year after we were married Pierre decided to hold one big caucus party in the confederation room of parliament; it was to be the last major meeting before the 1972 election. I was invited to be on the flower and decoration committee and to my surprise I had fun, caught up in a good spirit of political camaraderie.

When the Liberals got back in again at the election I allowed myself to be drawn closer into the fold—but always in a social, never a bureaucratic, capacity, I gave caucus parties up at the Lake, barbecue lunches by the waterside, to which candidates and members brought their families. One night we even held a candlelit barndance up there; the flares from the marquee reflected in the still black water of the lake. I soon observed, and began to revel in, the great difference in style between the parties, particularly between our party and the Conservatives. It brought out both the best (a longing to excel) and the worst (a taste for malicious teasing) in me. I passionately wanted the Liberals to dress better, look better, do things with greater taste and panache; at the same time I dearly wished to poke fun at our rivals.

Mrs. Mary Stanfield, the wife of a former Leader of the Opposition was, I soon discovered, the traditional Conservative lady, of quite another political generation to me. The Stanfields were succeeded by Joe Clark and his lawyer wife Maureen McTeer (she refused to call herself Clark, something that soon led to the Wick's cartoon "There must be something wrong with the guy if even his wife won't take his name!"). In that sort of game it was impossible not to be aware of other politicians and their wives, particularly as I read the newspapers avidly and had a couple of friends in Pierre's office.

Comparing Joe Clark and Pierre Trudeau soon became a popular party game in Ottawa. Spot the Difference. Joe was the party man, the dark horse of the Conservatives who had won the leadership as a result of a freak split vote, to his own great surprise. From the start, he modelled himself on John Diefenbaker, the former prime minister, right down to the tremulous shaking of his head. Pierre, everyone agreed, was no party man. But unlike Joe he was a statesman, a philosopher-king, with political appeal Joe could never hope to match.

From 24 Sussex I watched Maureen McTeer's arrival on the political scene. I felt sorry for her in those first few weeks.

She had been even less prepared than Joe for victory. Immediately after the election she held a naive and unfortunate press conference that she must have regretted bitterly. She told the assembled reporters that she and Joe don't like to dance, don't like to do sports and furthermore, don't like to spend time with stupid people. (Not to be condescending, I must confess myself to being prejudiced against *boring* people).

As Leader of the Opposition Joe Clark inherited Stornaway, a house standing in residential Rockcliffe Park; unlike the prime minister's residence it comes unfurnished and the Clarks had a considerable battle filling the imposing reception rooms. When, later, I was redecorating, I sent Maureen over the blue Wedgwood set I had turned out to make way for the red Italian china.

Though Maureen and I had nothing to do with one another, and indeed almost never met, we kept a close eye on each other's behavior via mutual friends and the newspapers. The night we gave our party up at Harrington Lake the Clarks held their Conservative caucus party at Stornaway in the back yard. Maureen prides herself on being Canadian. To celebrate the evening she had all the food and drink neatly labelled "Cana-

163

dian cheese, Canadian caviar, Canadian wine," with little red and white maple leaf flags. The press went to town on that as well, particularly as Canada is not known for the taste of its wines or caviar.

Yet it didn't always go my way. Maureen McTeer is emancipated in a way I never shall be. I may laugh at her wash-and-wear shoes and her polyester drip-dry clothes, but the very fact that she is so politically attuned keeps her sane. And I sometimes used to wonder whether her possessive defensiveness of Joe, so possessive she sometimes seemed like a frantic mother hen, wasn't one of the few solutions to a successful political marriage. How sensible was I in being so stubbornly different?

While Maureen was chairing the Conservative women and singing loud praises of Joe, I sat back at home and nursed babies. When Pierre asked me to, I went down to the House to listen to his speeches, sometimes taking a small child with me. He didn't often ask. He usually preferred me to stay at home. Rarely did I accompany him on the regional trips he made every couple of weeks. When he was off somewhere remote and new I used to go too; if it was to a large city I stayed put. I hated bustle, jostling crowds, smoke-filled meeting halls, all the hurly burly of party politics that others are engrossed by.

Though I spoke in public myself as little as possible, pleading everything from pregnancy to a sore throat, there was no escaping it altogether. I was agonizingly nervous the first couple of times, my knees trembling so violently that I couldn't see how I would avoid keeling over on my way to the stage. Sometimes I didn't even get any warning of what was about to hit me. I would be daydreaming in the front row, wishing I were at home reading a book, or hiking in the mountains with Pierre, when a tag end of a sentence would impinge like a hammer on my thoughts: ". . . and now I will call on Mrs. Trudeau." There was nothing for it then but to ad lib, which invariably got me into trouble with the sorts of things I came out with.

One day in Vancouver, at a meeting in the area where my parents live, I suddenly found that I had a microphone in my hands. There was silence all around; just row upon row of expectant eyes. The room swam before me. Fearing that unless something could be forced from my lips I would take my easy way out and faint, I said the first thing that I could think of: "Pierre has taught me everything I know about loving." It is quite true, but I didn't mean it quite the way it came out. There was an enormous guffaw from the audience and a good deal of smirking. I turned crimson and got deeper into the mess. "No, no," I said hastily. "I mean about being a loving person." Ha, ha, ha, they all roared.

But I got better. The day even came when I gave a speech of Pierre's for him. He was called away suddenly to a summit meeting in Germany on the day he was to receive an honorary degree from Ottawa University. I read out his words and just hearing them come out gave me a heady rush of confidence.

I never got around to the heights of Ms. McTeer's feminist indignation, but paradoxically it was in the name of feminism that I had my one memorable experience of political speaking. It was at the Commonwealth Conference in Jamaica and Beverley Manley, the wife of the Jamaican prime minister, an ardent feminist herself, had decided to organize a woman's seminar to run concurrently with the conference, and had asked all the wives to prepare papers on the condition of women in their own countries. It was unexpectedly successful.

Some of the wives lost their nerve and simply read out briefs that had been prepared by men executives in their husbands' offices. To listen to the Nigerian delegate Victoria Gowan, you would have thought the women of Nigeria the luckiest in the world. Others were very brave. Mrs. Forbes Burnham tore the Guyanese to shreds, painting a picture of everything from penis envy to sloth. Mrs. Whitlam gave a stirring address on the plight of Australian women. The wife of the prime minister of Samoa put us all to shame by her account of starvation and poverty. Then it was my turn. I had collected quotes from everyone from Napoleon to Dr. Spock illustrating the sexist attitudes of world leaders across the ages, ending with some of Pierre's more unfortunate remarks. I was over-joyed with the laughter and applause it received.

In those first few years Pierre and I handled that awkward balance of political and home life reasonably happily. I felt lonely, yes, but not left out. That was perhaps due to Pierre's tact and the way that whenever someone interesting was in town, like Marshall McLuhan or Richard Burton, he made a point of having me at the lunches he gave for them. When something really bothered him then he did discuss it with me: he knew that, because I kept my distance from the other political wives, I was perfectly safe. If it was just some old wheat policy speech he kept it to himself. I was grateful: nothing could have bored me more, though my attitude would have scandalized the other political wives. And there was a comic side to it all. When Pierre and I first married he told me solemnly one night: "One of the best things about Mother was that she never disturbed me." I liked watching television; Pierre wanted to work—yet he insisted I be in the same room as he was. How to solve the dilemma? A visitor peering through the window of the sitting room would have seen Pierre poring intently over the contents of one of his seven brown boxes and me curled up in front of the television with an enormous set of earphones, like a disc jockey watching a silent movie.

In the spring of 1974 Pierre called an election. It was only eighteen months since the last one, but he had had such a very close shave that time, with barely a working majority, that he dared not wait any longer. It was now or never. A bid for a real Liberal victory.

Yet it wasn't going to be easy. The dwindling majority, said the political pundits he consulted, came not because of Liberal policies but because of Pierre himself. His manner with the public, they told him, was too dry, too professorial, his voice too hard and cold. They expected rousing rhetoric; what they got was a boring, highly intellectual lecture. People simply thought him arrogant and aloof, a brilliant but cold man, abrupt and remote. Trudeau worship was over.

When in May he had decided to take to the hustings again, Pierre hadn't wanted me to campaign. He insisted that politics was *his* work and the children and the houses *my* work, and to mix them now would only confuse our lives. Yet from my close observation of the last election tour, and from my endless scouring of the newspapers for opinions of Pierre, I sensed that this time his reputation for coldness and arrogance might swing the voters so far against him that the Conservatives would get in.

I am probably the only person alive who really knows how very unjustified this reputation is: Pierre is one of the gentlest of men, a loving father and a very loyal friend. But he is also painfully shy, a genuinely private person, quite incapable of expressing his feelings at all convincingly. I had a hunch that if I fought the election by his side, demonstrating on every platform and in every convention hall of the country just how happy we were together and what a devoted family man he was, then Pierre would have a better chance to convince people that he was the man to lead them.

My immediate problem was that I couldn't get Sacha, then just four months old, to accept a bottle, however much I tried. I was also secretly troubled by the thought that having fed Justin for six months I should do the same for Sacha. So if I went, the baby would have to come too.

Pierre took some persuading. I pleaded, I bullied, I begged. In the end, reluctantly, fearing that Sacha would fall ill, and I would grow bored, Pierre gave in. And once he agreed, he appeared delighted to have me along—we had one of the best times of our marriage. We decided to leave Diane in Ottawa with Justin, and asked Mary Alice Conlon, the ex-nun who had come to us as a maid a couple of years earlier, and who was fast turning into the lynchpin of my domestic life, to come with us and help me with the baby.

The real daily, not to say hourly, dilemma was to be how to feed him surreptitiously so that no one would be shocked. At the start of the campaign I was exceedingly modest, retiring behind curtains, into restrooms, empty offices or halls where I could settle down with some degree of privacy. Later I threw all modesty to the winds, and became adept at giving him snacks in places and at times that would have appalled any advocate of oldfashioned habits. At times I became so engrossed in the campaign strategy being discussed at the table alongside me that I forgot to take him off the nipple for hours on end. I got so that I could talk, stroll about, answer the telephone, with the baby tucked up discreetly at my breast and no one could have noticed a thing.

We decided—for by now I too was part of the decision-making team, a team that really worked well together—to handle the 1974 campaign quite differently from previous ones.

We weren't going to court the press, and we weren't going to canvas in the traditional big cities any more than we strictly had to. Instead we resolved to make for the wilds, for the villages, for the small towns, attend local rallies and fêtes, picnics and meetings and get to know as many people, in a totally informal way, as possible.

Pierre and I started our campaign on a train, a whistle-stop trip of the north, starting in New Brunswick, on to Nova Scotia, Cape Breton and the Gaspé Peninsula. We had our own engine and four special cars to carry our party, the campaign men, and the reporters. Pierre and I and the baby were given the last coach, which had a porch at the back, like an old-fashioned western railway, and as we whistled our way into remote country villages in the pouring rain we stood out at the back waving. Pierre and I each had an adjoining suite at our disposal: Sacha and Mary Alice were next door. We had our own cook and steward, and as we crossed boundaries into a new district we would be joined by the local candidate and his manager for lunch, and a talk with Pierre before arriving in the home town. Our living room was always full of people smoking, drinking, talking, in an atmosphere of ever-growing excitement. A songwriter had written a special campaign song for Pierre in Quebec French, and as we steamed along into a town it would blare out ahead of us, a catchy, infectious, winning song that everyone soon had on their lips.

The weather was appalling on our train trip. We chugged along the craggy, rugged coastline watching the sleet against our windows as we looked out over the little villages with their whitewashed clapboard houses, and the occasional turquoise or pink house set among them, and then on out into wild and hilly country of pine trees, lakes and rivers. That chugging train set the pace: we were moving, we were winning, we were happy.

As we puffed and blew to a halt in a fishing village the tracks would be lined with people, drenched by the heavy rain, but full of welcome, waving to our campaign song. I used to bring Sacha out on to the platform and there would be cheers of, "Hurray for the baby." Sometimes the sleet and hail would be coming down so fast we could hardly see the tracks. In Cape Breton, New Brunswick and Nova Scotia I soon discovered that one family seemed to dominate the whole village. So as I shook hands I used to ask: "Now are you the Macdonalds? The Campbells? The MacNeils?" It was always one of these three. One village I found was entirely MacNeil: "Hi," I would call out, "You must be a MacNeil too?" "Ay indeed." And there would be hoots of laughter all round.

We got back to Ottawa with a few days to see Justin and gather our strength for the real onslaught of the campaign that was to come—sixty days of traveling, sometimes two to three cities in a day, home once a week for a glimpse of Justin, a bath, a change of clothes and off again.

I took time to assemble the most practical traveling wardrobe that I could think of—with Pierre's advice on how formal or informal I would need to be. Money, I reasoned, was not in question; what I needed was a small collection of extremely smart clothes that would coordinate with one another. With this in mind I set off for Toronto's better shops and came back with a beautiful navy blue pants suit, three different silk shirts, a blazer, a second pair of pants and a shirt to match, two white wool skirts and an assortment of T-shirts. Nothing formal, smart, not dressed up.

Since Sacha was to accompany us I fitted him out with a bouncing chair for the plane, a little backpack so that we could walk him around the cities, and a baby carriage that came to pieces, so that we took the top for a bed and had the wheels to push him with. Most nights we were to spend in a hotel or a motel, and while Pierre canvassed, the plan was that Mary Alice and I would convert the hotel suite into a nursery. Then I would go and join Pierre at his rally, leaving her to look after Sacha and take him for walks in his pram. However lightly we determined to travel, we never quite escaped the sheer absurdity of our arrivals—Pierre's campaign aides scuttling off the plane with embarrassed smirks on their faces, clutching stuffed bears and carriage wheels, and the prime minister's car filled to overflowing with pots, diapers and back packs.

The diapers were the worst of it. Since paper diapers seemed to give all my babies rashes we always had a diaper service at 24 Sussex. Every Thursday the van would drive up with 150 fresh diapers and take away an immense sackful of dirty ones—

the prime minister's residence must have the longest standing diaper service in Canada: six and a half years of solid deliveries. Flying, however, posed a problem. How was I to keep Sacha free of rashes? So we took along the diaper service and the huge green sack (only adding to the ludicrousness of our arrival). I couldn't bear to see this baby with goldplated diaper pins (all the boys were given gold pins as christening presents) looking on the outside like a baby out of a posh baby magazine and inside like a deprived slum child.

The election plane had a special private suite for us up at the front; no bad thing as the rest of it reeked with tobacco and alcohol, since it became a flying pool hall for the newsmen accompanying us. Pierre held his meetings and conferences at the front of the suite, while I snatched quick rests on the beds at the back or fed Sacha, protected from the boisterous camaraderie and dense cigar smoke only by a flimsy curtain. Sacha slept in his crib, though toward the end he was growing out of it fast, crammed in, his head and toes wedged against the ends, like the proverbial sardine. He was a good, happy baby and he reveled in the constant attention. It seems to have left its mark on him. Ever since then he's been the child who has traveled most with Pierre on his own: at two and three Pierre took him to meetings for hours on end and he would never complain, returning home to tell me with great pride: "Daddy says I have been *good*." Wait for applause. "So I can go *next* time with Daddy."

It was a grueling life: up at dawn, in the air seven or eight hours a day, then new arrivals, new crowds, new speeches. It wasn't surprising we got on one another's nerves. Ivan Head, an old adversary of mine and Pierre's special assistant in international relations, was along as Pierre's speech writer and did his best to ease me out, creating an indefinable but unmistakable aura that I was totally redundant to the trip. He was always smiling, always whispering something in Pierre's ear, and I felt moments of pure childish jealousy. To fight back, I worked.

When we arrived at some big rally Pierre would make his way toward the middle, mobbed by the crowd, shaking hands and smiling. Here he was at his best: flirtatious with women, jokey with the children, excited by the crowds—he took advan-

tage of every gimmick that came his way: if he saw an abandoned policeman's motorcycle, he leaped on to it and roared
off. If a swimming pool, he dived in, delighting all with his
spectacular dives. It was laughter everywhere.

Meanwhile Bob Murdoch, his executive assistant, a policeman and I would amble our way around the edge of the crowd,
chatting. I learned how to talk to people simply and draw them
out; I tried to have real conversations and got pretty good at
knowing what sort of advice to give and what answers were
politic to make. The only thing that bugged me was police
protection. The security men would lay their great arms on me
and jostle me along far worse than any crowd. After one episode
which had ended in me disgracing myself by shouting, "Take
your fucking arm off me," to the policeman with us, the order
went out: "Do not touch Mrs. Trudeau." That was the first
thing that Bob did everywhere we went: warn the police not to
lay a hand on me.

The other thing that enraged me was the terribly sexist
nature of Canadian provincial politics. In every town we went
to I found I was the only woman on the platform. When I remonstrated, I was told that there wasn't room for any one else on the
stage. "O.K.," I took to replying, "well, there's a lot of room
down there for me." And I would scramble off and join all the
other wives in the front row. Nor was I prepared to play at
protocol over the flowers: when they were nosegays of wild
flowers I loved them, and wore them all day; when they were
dry, tatty bunches of boring red carnations, I shipped them off
to the local hospital.

The Liberals were fielding 265 candidates throughout
Canada. It was obvious we couldn't support them all, so Pierre
and Ivan Head worked out the most sensitive seats and we
tackled those. I even made one short trip on my own, with
Bob Murdoch to British Columbia, where I made my own
speeches, and canvassed the streets. By then I too had become a
Liberal political animal: I knew just what to say and when and
how and I liked the way I was good at drawing crowds. "Why
can't it all be like this?" I remember thinking sadly after one
particularly good day.

As the campaign progressed, it became increasingly clear
that Pierre had to adopt a new, relaxed, intimate style and

I worked away at him. He needed to be down to earth, emotional, committed—not rational. It was quite a battle. Ivan Head had views of his own about Pierre's style, and even stronger views about my role, or, perhaps lack of a role, in the campaign. And though I had my friends in the informal camp, Ivan Head was powerful and my cries about how terrible Pierre's speeches had become, full of heavy rhetoric and ponderous, interminable paragraphs meaning nothing, fell on deaf ears.

Then I got a lucky break. Pierre was to give a wheat policy speech at Humboldt, up in Saskatchewan, and a small group of us flew up there early one morning by private plane. Now I knew all about Pierre's policy speeches: they were all alike, written by the minister concerned, handed to Pierre the night before, and delivered by him half asleep to a yawning, unsuspecting crowd, while a photostat went off to the press.

It was a magnificent late spring day, with that pale blue early sky, and warm enough to give a picnic-like feeling to the occasion. A great crowd had turned out to see us. After greetings and cheers Pierre stood up and embarked on one of the longest, most tedious of speeches, written by the very minister in charge of the Wheat Board who was sitting complacently on the podium with his wife. I looked out across the sea of faces with pity and fury: "These people are bored rigid. They haven't come here to listen to this," I said to myself. Worse was to come. The last five minutes of the speech were a highly embarrassing eulogy of Pierre, and even he looked ill at ease as he delivered the fulsome words. He sat down, to muted applause, and I was called to the microphone.

I was too cross to be tactful. In any case I was made more courageous by the great roar of welcome that went up from the crowd. "I must apologize," I started, feigning contrition, unable to prevent the malice rising in me, "but neither the good minister here, nor his lovely wife have been kind enough to write an elegant speech for me to make. So you will have to make do with plain, honest words." And I went on to talk about the new programs for women and children which the Liberals were embarking on, reminding them of things we had done and trying to inject a note of sincerity into the proceedings. Behind me, I felt the podium stiffen with rage. The people, however, loved it, and laughed and cheered.

172

I returned to my place and looks so hostile that I could almost feel them. All the way back to Ottawa I was in disgrace; no one spoke to me, no one came near me. Typically Pierre just laughed. He thought it was wonderful. And from that day on he *did* change his tactics. He asked his ministers to prepare bald policy statements that could be given out to newspapers, and he simply used the words as the basis for his own speech, a real, heartfelt, interesting, imaginative speech that people could follow and even enjoy. He stopped being a professor, and started shouting out the words with real emotion. The effect was dramatic. And, like magic, so was the change in the weather.

There had been something funny about the 1974 campaign from the start, and the press was the first to notice it. A lot of reporters were traveling with both parties, the Liberals and the Conservatives. They would be with us for a week, and then with the Leader of the Opposition for a week, and then back to us again. More and more, everywhere the Conservative leader went it rained; everywhere we went the sun shone.

When I reached Vancouver I took a couple of days off. Pierre was campaigning in the rural areas, and I stayed with close family friends. Gingy Meyers was older than I, and a very good family friend, and she took one look at me when I showed up. "Margaret," she said, firmly, "leave Sacha with me. You can't go on like this. You look absolutely exhausted. I'll take good care of him."

I knew she was right. I *was* exhausted and the strain of constantly moving was beginning to tell on him. But it was hard. Gingy lived in a house right across the street from my childhood home, and I was filled with nostalgia. I'll never forget sitting by her pool, listening to John Denver singing "I'm leaving, on a jet plane" on the hi-fi and feeding the baby for the last time. Sacha's head was wet with my tears.

I joined Pierre in Edmonton, trying to choke back my tears on the plane. They were tears of exhaustion as much as anything, and I was ashamed to think of Pierre seeing them. When I met him he was astonished: "Where's Sacha?"

"I've left him with Gingy."

He was kind, gentle; he knew how much I minded. As for Sacha, apart from the fact that his meals were reduced from the fourteen a day he got from me to a more conventional four or five, he couldn't have given a damn. The first food Gingy gave him was a frozen fresh orange popsicle and he lapped it up. I did keep my milk up throughout the rest of the campaign but when I went back to pick him up and tried to feed him he spat out the nipple with distaste. He was *into food*.

As May became June, then June July, so our exhaustion grew stronger and our enthusiasm more forced. After forty rallies every one blurred into the next and seemed the same; the speeches were the same; even the people were the same. We were kept going only by a growing sense of victory, a swelling tide of success. Everywhere we went the crowds turned out in their hundreds and thousands. Never had Pierre received such ovations; it was Trudeaumania all over again and I was happy for him. Yet the press, for all the good weather and the enthusiasm, kept predicting that we would lose. The last day that there could be an editorial on the election, every major newspaper in the country turned against Pierre. Do *not* vote for Trudeau, was the message.

The political touchstone in the country is Toronto, an ethnically mixed, fickle, and changeable city. If Toronto didn't want Pierre, then neither would Canada. We left it till last.

It was a marvelous, blue, unclouded day. One hundred and fifty thousand people had brought their picnics to Toronto Island to eat on the grass and hear what Pierre had to say. When he stood up there was a hush. He talked for about twenty minutes: clearly, calmly, radiating confidence. When he sat down you could have heard the ovation twenty miles away. Then I got up to speak. I talked about motherhood, my children and the family, and before long all the moms in the crowd had tears trickling down their cheeks.

When I finished, others spoke, and the atmosphere grew better and better. It was all very moving, not just for Pierre and me but for the whole crowd, who sensed how important the occasion was, and rose to it. From that moment I had no doubts that we would win, though everyone kept repeating that we wouldn't.

When we got home that night tension was growing. It was only then that I realized that I had never in the last two-month dash paused to consider what we would do if we lost. I had become so involved in the political life that I had even dreamed of running in the next election for my father's old parliamentary district in north Vancouver. Was I going to have to pack up my two babies and the entire house next morning and move out? On the one hand I wanted out, badly; but then why had I worked so hard to stay? Pierre, I knew, had no doubts; he still has no doubts today. But I was really torn. And when, at midnight, the news of our success came, my tears might have been those of pain or pleasure.

Next morning was a brilliant sunny day and I sat having my breakfast on the porch of the freedom room watching the white sailing boats in the sparkling bay. I waited for a phone call of thanks, of praise, of something, from someone. I waited; and I waited. It was absurd of me—everyone was exhausted, why should they have thought of me? But something in me broke that day. I felt that I had been used.

On the campaign trail—so many contacts with so many good Canadians.

My spontaneous toast to Mme. Echeverria obviously charmed our husbands, but it was another step out of line for me.

Micha, "the most important member of the Canadian delegation" on our visit to Cuba in 1976, in the arms of a man whose affection for children was obvious and delightful.

OPPOSITE: *I arrived in Cuba splattered with blood but Castro didn't seem to notice.*

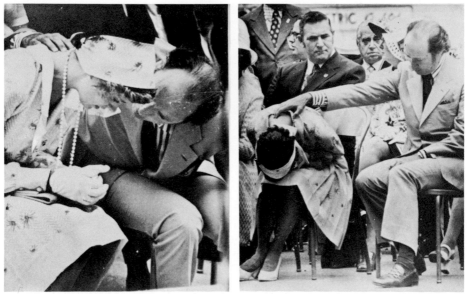

Maggie faints again—thank heaven someone who cared helped me through. On this occasion we were in Charlottetown and the Queen was speaking.

We are showered with rose petals on our arrival in Mexico in January 1976.

In Japan, 1976, with Prime Minister Miki and his wife.

Mickey Mouse, on my Italian dress, sits next to Mrs. Mondale and has the cheek to let his silk slip and reveal too much thigh.

The famous mini dress (hardly) that shot me to infamy (again) at the White House.

A former flower-child receives an instant lesson in auras: Pope Paul VI emanated warmth and spirituality.

Masada, Israel at high noon, a hot, bad-tempered lady—it was not a happy vacation.

Healthy boys and their happy father—how could I not trust their care to such a good man.

OPPOSITE: *With my two boys, Micha and Justin, on a visit to my parents in Vancouver.*

A photography student on her way to class is snapped with her husband.

Margaret Mead and I attend a demonstration calling for clean water in the world.

With Mommy away, nannies Monica and Leslie guard over my three sons at a Parliamentary Christmas party.

Turning the focus the other way, I catch a paparrazi at work.

The ultimate performer at his lewdest, crudest best: one of the photographs I took of Mick Jagger in Toronto.

My proudest achievement as a photographer: Yasmin Aga Khan hanging out on the street where she lives.

Photographing Sophia Loren: her grandeur is matched by her heart.

I don't know Jackie Onassis but I admire her enormously.

New York high life in April 1978 finds me with Andy Warhol who thinks everything is wonderful.

A new family for my first film, Kings and Desperate Men: *Patrick McGoohan and Jamie Brown.*

A girl like me should have known what trouble nice boys like Ronnie and Mick could get me into.

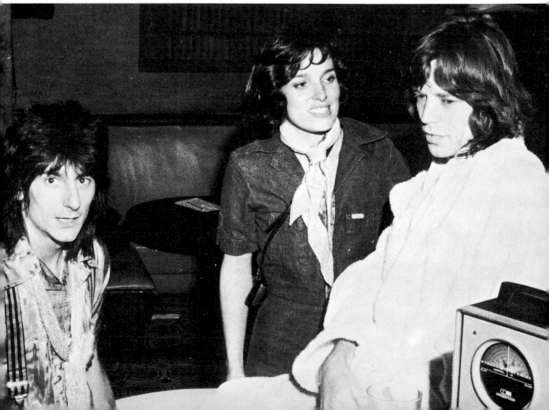

Searching for my Guardian Angel in Cassis—the location of my second film.

IF YOU CAN'T PLEASE EVERYBODY, PLEASE YOURSELF

MY REBELLION STARTED in 1974. From then, until the day I walked out of 24 Sussex three years later, it built up momentum in fits and starts. It took many different forms: a sad ending of my love for Pierre; a return to the inner turmoils and confusions of the weeks after Morocco; a sense of mounting claustrophobia that had, like some enormous bubble, to burst soon.

The first visible explosions were all directed at the official life, by sad irony the very life of protocol and formality that I had finally and so painfully mastered. By 1974 I had become good at it; very good at it. But it was too late and I certainly hadn't managed to make it fun.

At home, with our children or alone together, Pierre and I struggled and often managed to re-create the happy intimacy of our earlier days. He worked. I looked after my children and spent what time I could with friends. Confusion came when official life intruded: that as such was my only *work*, a chore that even Pierre despised and considered mouldy icing on top of a cake. But whereas he didn't have time to be obsessed by whether or not the Governor of the Northern Territories should have sole for dinner, or Mrs. Nixon sit next to a general, I did. More than enough. The details whirled around and around in my head in an ever-growing nightmare.

Absurdly, Pierre had been and still was my staunchest friend in my efforts to reduce the protocol, and when really grotesquely formal occasions were forced upon us. We joked about them together, laughing, often hilariously, over narrowly averted disasters or comic incidents. More and more often, though, the laughter turned sour: Pierre began to find my rebellion heavy-handed and tedious (and so did the Canadian public). My outbursts didn't strike him as quite so funny, nor my independence quite so endearing. I in turn found petty ways of getting my own back on him, inching my way back toward the very style of life he had so earnestly begged me to give up. It wasn't all malice on my part; it was desperation too. A split appeared in the ground between us and it widened with each episode—episodes that every newspaper reporter who wrote about us was by now on the alert for. What *will* Mrs. Trudeau come out with next? Everyone, it seemed to me, was watching me, longing to find a good juicy story for the front page.

At home, where I was under less observation, I could usually conceal my outbursts. It was on the official trips abroad that the strain began to show; then, surrounded often by as many as a hundred predatory reporters, I was a sitting duck.

Michel, the last baby, came in October 1975, and in the January of 1976 Pierre was going to Latin America, a big three-week, three-country trip to Mexico, Cuba and Venezuela. A very important trip in terms of Canadian–Latin-American relations, particularly as it was the fruit of Pierre's attempts to expand Canada's ties with the Third World. It was made all the more important by the fact that the United States was still entirely cut off diplomatically from Cuba.

I had assumed that I would have to skip the trip with Pierre because I was still nursing Micha, and from what I had heard Mexico was no place for a baby. But once again my doctor reassured me that as long as I stuck to breastfeeding he could come to no harm. Once Pierre heard this he relented and went so far as to let me take a nanny: I chose Diane, the most hippy member of our staff, who I felt was just the kind of friend I needed in Latin America.

We flew first to Mexico. It was like coming home—magic and drugs, all my old stomping grounds. We stayed in a luxurious hotel in the center of Mexico City where the butter was brought to our table moulded in the shape of a bunch of roses. Mexico seemed to me like the center of the sun. The places we went to, the things that we did, the warmth and hospitality we encountered everywhere made me feel excited in a way I hadn't felt for ages. Micha stayed in our suite with Diane, and I popped back and forth to feed him, spending the rest of the time with Señora Echeveria, the first prime minister's wife I had ever met who was not only charming and motherly but an extremely hard worker, with a fleet of mobile health units she directed herself.

I felt so good in fact that my normal caution began melting in the sun. One day Pierre and I were taken on an official trip to Palenque, the Mayan ruins in the jungle not far from Mexico City. All the way from the airport to the ruins the roads were lined with posters reading: *"Bienvenido Pierre Trudeau."* When we got there I found two old friends waiting: they had seen news of the official visit, broken through the tight security cordon and lain in wait for me. I was overjoyed.

And when one of them whispered in my ear: "We've got something for you," I didn't protest. I left my bag casually on the ground near the car while I went to look at the ruins. When I got back our policeman hurried up to me. "I think you should know, Mrs. Trudeau, that that girl has slipped something into your bag."

"Thank you so much. Those must be the cookies she told me about." And, opening my bag, I drew out the biscuits I had packed from my breakfast table. What he didn't realize was that tucked underneath was a little plastic sack of peyote mushrooms. That night at Cancun I allowed myself a secret taste. It made me look forward to more.

From Mexico we flew on to Cuba. I had intended to land in full regalia: a beautiful silk dress I had bought in Rome, with matching shoes, hat and handbag. Just before the plane started its descent over Havana I went to consult Pierre, working in our suite at the front of the plane, about whether I should wear any jewelry. He considered the matter carefully. "How about that diamond pin?" I went back to my case, took the pin from its box and just as I was fastening it to my dress the plane lurched, embedding the tip into my finger. Blood spurted down the front of my dress. Since by now the plane was taxiing down the runway I had no time to change. Another gaffe: here comes Mrs. Trudeau, on the first Canadian official visit to Cuba, with blood all over her clothes.

It was very hot when the plane doors were pushed back, a

great blanket of steamy heat that hit us in the face. Castro was standing waiting on the runway. I was immediately mesmerized by what I saw: a tall man, with incredibly beautiful eyes, and a wild, almost fanatical, look which made him physically very attractive. In a heavily accented voice, deep and gruff, he purred out a stream of romantic and flowery English. Always he appeared impeccably dressed in green army fatigues, but of the best cut imaginable and shoes polished until they glowed. Never was he at a loss for a compliment: "When I saw you come down the steps of the plane," he said to me on my first evening, "I told myself, oh, the prime minister of Canada has a very pretty wife. Now I discover that not only are you pretty, you are too intelligent for your own good." I fell for it all.

He endeared himself to me from the start by his attitude toward Micha. At the airport, in his speech of welcome, he declared: "I am very glad to have the distinguished prime minister of Canada and his lovely wife and his intelligent entourage, but I want you to know that as far as I am concerned, as far as the people of Cuba are concerned, the most important visitor today is Miche." (He always called him Miche.) From that moment on Castro had Micha in his arms the whole time: I have pictures of Micha slobbering over the immaculate army fatigues. He even went so far as to have special badges made for him to wear: "Miche Trudeau, V.I.P. Official visitor of the Canadian delegation." Whenever he came to collect us to go off anywhere he'd say: "Where's Miche?" And if I replied "He's upstairs with Diane," he'd run up the stairs shouting, "Diane, Miche, get ready, we're going. You're late."

Pierre and I were staying in a charming guest house in Havana, built in natural wood and stone, kept cool by channels of water, across which we stepped on huge, flat stones. Every window opened onto tropical gardens. This visit to Cuba marked a change in me, almost a reversal to my student days. During my years with Pierre I had coached myself away from politics, so that when people abroad asked me what party I supported, I used to reply, half joking, "I'm a monarchist," which let me off the hook. Now, looking around Cuba, hearing about Che Guevara and remembering all the stories in the Canadian press about how the F.L.Q. terrorists who were flown there in exchange for Cross's release were now extremely unhappy, I felt a resurgence of political consciousness. How wrong they were. This is the answer to Utopia, I said to myself, looking out over the flowers, the tropical paradise all around me. If this is revolution, it is truly marvelous.

Once I had convinced myself that Cuba could do no wrong, everywhere I went I found my enthusiasm confirmed. Everyone was happy; there were spectacular entertainments, water displays, gymnastics, dancing. Even women seemed properly valued: Castro appeared as anxious for me as for Pierre to see the sugar factories.

I was taken off to see Castro's program of day care centers, which are unlike any of the hundreds I have visited all over the world. The Cubans are still basically Catholic and family unity very important, but the economic fact is that both mother and father work. It seemed to me that every Cuban I spoke to had four jobs at least. Each morning on their way to work parents take their children to the local day care center where they receive skilled care, an excellent diet and a superb education. Doctors visited the centers constantly, and every child has an up-to-date dental and medical chart. But what impressed me far more was the fact that the children are even dressed by the centers: I was taken to see laundries piled high with every conceivable size of jeans and T-shirts. This means that the mother can spend what time off she has actually playing with her children and talking to them, rather than frantically doing their laundry and trying to keep them clean, healthy and properly fed.

I saw happy children everywhere I went. One day I even took Micha on a visit to a day center: he was whisked out of my arms and carted off to join his own age group while Diane and I talked to the rows of matronly ladies in charge and inspected crib upon crib of spotless babies. Suddenly I heard an all too familiar yell reverberating through the open partitions of the center—being a tropical island, all the buildings are open and the sound carries. I would have known that hollering anywhere. I hurried in search of him and found that the cause of the trouble was a bottle a kind nurse had tried to offer him. His yells of outrage ceased only when I unbuttoned my jacket and offered him a snack, amid much laughter from the assembled women.

197

Castro is one of the few world leaders I felt I got to know well. From the start I was charmed by the ease and spontaneity with which he handled our visit, his obvious friendliness toward us and the sense of a good time he seemed to radiate. Whenever I could I talked to him about Cuba and his own background. We had one curious conversation—curious only in retrospect because at the time it seemed perfectly natural.

The war in Angola had been going on for some months and Pierre and Castro were discussing—extremely cagily—the presence of the Cubans in Africa. Castro told Pierre that a small contingent of Cuban advisers had just been sent in. One day while we were walking through Havana it suddenly struck me that I never saw any black men; black women, yes, but no men, apart from an occasional elderly one. "Where are all the black men?" I asked Castro during our next conversation. "Have you sent them off somewhere?" (It was a genuinely naive question.) He hesitated. "I have worked seventeen years to give my people peace and equality and education. It would be sad to see them die on foreign soil." "Oh," I said, meddling where I shouldn't, but still half teasing, not realizing quite what I was saying. "So you're having to pay the price for all that aid. Maybe they want a charismatic leader in Africa too?" It was only two weeks later that we discovered the full extent of the Cuban presence in Angola, and that Castro had been far less than honest with Pierre.

The days passed by all too quickly; never had an official visit seemed so enjoyable—nor so completely devoid of stuffiness. One day Pierre and Castro announced they were going off for an evening's private talks at an undisclosed destination. I was to stay in Havana with Micha and see a Canadian dance troupe give a performance. Ivan Head, who was once again with us, and fast becoming the Tom MacDonald of my official life, informed me that I couldn't accompany them, because there would be nowhere for me to stay, and my presence would only embarrass our Cuban hosts. That day, at lunch, I was sitting next to Castro. "Why aren't you coming with us?" he asked.

"I'm not allowed to," I replied sourly.

"Why ever not?"

"Because they tell me it would be an imposition with Micha and that you're working."

He looked at me scornfully. "I thought you were a photographer. You should be working." Then he went on. "I am not inviting any press up there tonight. You shall be our photographer and, of course, you must bring Miche because there's no one else who can fulfill his needs."

Wonderful. I hurried back to the Canadian delegation and searched out Ivan Head, that pompous and somewhat self-important man, who saw himself as Canada's Henry Kissinger and didn't want anyone to forget it.

"Castro has invited me," I told him smugly. He was furious. Fifteen love to me. He was all set to protest when Pierre overheard us and laughed.

"Oh let her come," he said. "We'll really make her work."

We got up to the "undisclosed destination," which I later discovered was a military installation looking out toward America, in the late afternoon. We were to stay in the only house, a single bungalow with two bedrooms, but far from being primitive it was enormously comfortable, with a complete layette for Micha, exquisite baby clothes, a changing table, a crib with a mosquito net that had been lace edged all around the bottom, blankets, wrapping sheets, every conceivable luxury. We could have taken him up there naked and he would have spent the most comfortable night of his life.

In the late afternoon Pierre and Fidel went out to catch the dinner. Pierre is such a pacifist that he won't kill anything, not even insects. But that day he had no choice: Castro simply handed him a spear gun and the two swam off in search of fish. There was no other food. Castro is a marvelous diver, with no qualms about killing anything, and before long they were back with a splendid haul. Castro appeared clutching a wriggling old lobster by the back, which he threw down onto the dock, and went off to fetch a lime. Under my stupefied gaze he then ripped a leg off, saying: "How do you like your lobster, with or without lime?" and handed me a claw. I was dubious, not only because the leg felt alive, but because I had been warned never to eat any shellfish raw, other than oysters. But it was delicious.

Apart from our comfortably furnished quarters, the radar station was pretty spartan. There was no kitchen. Dinner was prepared over a barbecue, course after course of grilled fish, each one more delicious than the last. While they were being grilled, sizzling away and giving off a delicious smell, we were handed bowls of fish soup. As I was delving about with my spoon I caught sight of a clam. "Aha," I said to Castro. "You caught these too?"

He laughed. "You found us out. But those are the *only* things you'll eat tonight that we didn't catch. I simply didn't dare rely entirely on our skills as fishermen."

It was a memorable evening. Lights had been strung up in garlands around the table, one long trestle table with benches, at which we all sat down to eat together, everyone from our nanny to the drivers. Castro and Pierre spoke mainly in Spanish, and when they got to topics Castro thought would interest me particularly he would turn to me and explain them all over again in English. It was a crazy, informal evening: even the policeman and the nanny were canvassed for their views.

Late that night, after I had fed Micha, Diane and I wandered down to the seashore again. Pierre was working at a speech he was to give next day. Suddenly we noticed that a family of deer were eating the scraps under the trestle table; they seemed so tame that one of them came close enough to take something from my hand. Then, out of the darkness, we heard the footsteps and muffled tones of two men coming in our direction. It was Castro and a senior aide, and they were as astonished as I had been to see the deer. It was as well that Castro and I were not alone, for he paid me the most outrageous compliment I have ever received.

"You know," he said to me in his silken English, "my eyes are not very strong, so every day to make them stronger I force myself to look at the sun. I find it very hard. But do you know what I find harder? That is to look into the blue of your eyes."

Castro is a ridiculously romantic man and obviously worships women. The tidbits I discovered about his life only added to his fascination: how he never sleeps in the same bed two nights running for fear of assassination; how he has never seen his seventeen-year-old son (his wife left him after the revolution).

The Cuban visit showed up more sharply than ever before the contradictions between what I felt happy doing and what I was actually expected to do. The two I was beginning to see, were just not compatible. Next morning I muffed it again. We were to visit a chemical plant and Castro suggested that I stay on in my jeans and keep photographing. I was delighted. I knew I would get jostled around with the other photographers so I fished out an old T-shirt from my suitcase and off we went. It had "Margaret" stamped across the back; unfortunately it also had a little Liberal logo on the front alongside the Canadian flag. And this made people angry; very, very angry. To wear a scruffy old T-shirt on an official visit was bad enough; but to wear a Liberal T-shirt when I was meant to be representing not the party but the country was sacrilege. Murmurings were heard in Ottawa. Nor did the press much like me around. They wanted me up there on the receiving end of the photographs, not down there with them.

There was one funny incident before we left. Castro held a formal reception for us, and his sister-in-law, Wilma Espin, wife of his brother Raoul, a goodlooking woman in a white dress and gold shoes with elaborately curled hair and immaculate make-up, was acting as hostess. After a while, when no one had introduced us, I went up to her.

"I don't believe I've met you before."

She looked puzzled. "But I've been with you every day."

Then I remembered a dowdy, serious companion, in navy blue sweater, flat shoes and skirt dragged tight over her bottom, who had been dogging my footsteps for days and whom I had taken for a policewoman. I felt very ashamed. I realized that I had completely misjudged not only her but many of the Cuban women, and how it is perfectly possible to consider oneself an almost sexless worker by day and an absolutely feminine woman by night.

Even on this, our last formal evening, protocol and formality soon vanished: it wasn't long before the whole table were clapping their hands and tapping their feet to the music. Loud music, good food, bright colors; these are the memories of Cuba I am left with. When the moment came for us to leave, weighed down with gifts of three matching cowhide chairs for the little boys, I was tearful. Pierre teased me. "I'm glad you're still with me. I thought you would ask for asylum."

Our next stop was Venezuela. As part of my briefing mania I had already been in touch several times with Mrs. Schwartzmann, our ambassador's wife, an extremely conscientious woman who had sent me details of Mme. Perez' work with day care programs, and informative notes about the sort of people I was likely to meet. I was all set to like her. On arrival I discovered she was a Cuban émigrée—and there is no one in the world who hates Cuba more. (I was to learn this at Key Biscayne a couple of months later. I was on holiday in a high-priced, fat-cat camp when I was mobbed by outraged Castro-haters after I'd offered a local reporter a Cuban cigar.) My enthusiasm about what I had seen fell on not just deaf, but decidedly chilly, ears. I also soon saw just why the briefing notes had been so informative: people, social people, were her life. Their rank and pedigree were the spice of life to her, not some dreary chore to master. We weren't destined to get on; I was not in the mood for silly pretensions. Nor was I in the mood for all the tedious lunches and cocktail parties she had laid on for me. I took refuge in the guest house we were staying in—a charming, luxurious little house run by a friendly girl about my age—and brooded on the contrast between this social hell and my good times in Cuba.

Mme. Perez changed all this. I had asked to see her day care program in operation and been told that it was out of the question, that Mme. Perez ran it from an office in the city and never went near the poor areas herself. I felt bolshy. "O.K.," I said to Mrs. Schwartzmann, "why don't Mme. Perez and all the ladies around her go and get their hair done and I'll take a taxi down to the slums and have a look for myself." Consternation. Very sourly Mrs. Schwartzmann said she would see what she could do.

I hadn't, until now, really spoken to Mme Perez, beyond the initial civilities. When I met her to discuss her work I was immediately charmed. Here, I found, was a delightful, warm figure with a great sense of humor and sparkling eyes, who, far from never visiting her centers, went there five days a week, and kept the whole thing going by cajoling rich Venezuelans to part with their diamond earrings and ruby necklaces. She was only too happy to show me how it worked.

We set off in a private coach, Mme. Perez in a simple white dress, sturdy shoes and a plain gold cross around her neck, me in a safari suit and slung around with cameras. We took Micha with us. When the bus drew to a halt, I happened to look behind at the other ladies—Mme. Perez' entourage and various diplomatic wives. An identical expression of dismay and distaste was on all their faces while their clothes were the most inappropriate I have ever set eyes on: high-heeled crocodile shoes, silk Pucci dresses, heavy gold jewelry, suede handbags. They were terrified: what had they let themselves in for? They could scarcely get off the bus, let alone walk along the rough, unmade roads.

Mme. Perez had arranged her program with ingenious simplicity. She had asked a number of middle-aged women in the ghetto, whose own children had grown up and left home to act as "caremothers" for six local children—orphans, or children who were simply left to roam the streets. She had arranged for the women to be given an allowance for food, and supplemented it with meals sent down by mobile vans. Then she had recruited volunteer teachers to come down and supervise some kind of lessons, and volunteer mobile health units to check on the children's physical condition. It was inspired: it took the children off the street, gave the women a job, and involved Caracas' university graduates in serious social work.

Mme. Perez herself blossomed among the ghetto children. All the families we called on seemed to know her very well, and the children crawled up on to her lap with cries of pleasure. The sight touched me profoundly, actually finding one of these social figures—and who more protocol-ridden, one would have thought, than Mme. Perez?—engaged in an extremely demanding job of her own, with no self-publicity and no fuss. So profoundly, in fact, that I decided to make some special gesture toward her. I had a sudden urge to write her a song, and sing it to her myself. We were due to have a final dinner, just the four of us, the Perezes, Pierre and me, and my plan was to sing it afterward. Pierre was all for it.

Then our program got switched around. I find the memory of the scene almost too embarrassing to describe. Instead of our informal little dinner, the evening turned into a massive reception, possibly the most formal and pretentious dinner I ever went to in all my years as Pierre's wife. The whole of smart Caracas was there, in full evening dress, with tiaras and medals. I had half decided to abandon my plan but Pierre (to tease me? in malice?) persuaded me to go ahead with it. So

when the plates were cleared away I rose unsteadily to my feet
and delivered my little aria:

> *Señora Perez, I would like to thank you.*
> *I would like to sing to you.*
> *To sing a song of love.*
> *For I have watched you*
> *With my eyes wide open,*
> *I have watched you with learning eyes. . . .*

I hardly need to describe the effect. Half the guests were so
embarrassed they kept their eyes riveted to their plates. A few
of the Venezuelan women seemed touched and smiled their
support. The Canadian delegation, to a man, was horrified.
This, in the eyes of people like Ivan Head, was the last straw.
Mrs. Trudeau has gone *too far*. I could see a smirk from ear
to ear.

I wasn't exactly delighted with my performance but the deed
was done. (In my own defense I have to admit that had it not
been for the liberal dose of belladona a Caracas doctor had
prescribed for stomach cramps I undoubtedly would never have
dared make such a fool of myself.) I didn't regret the thought
that was behind it, though. I got my reward the next night in
the form of a delightful and intimate supper with the Perezes
and their children at their private villa, a sumptuous presiden-
tial house with a pool, tennis courts, fountains and terraces
covered in bougainvillea. There we sat out in the magnificent
gardens, played bowls, and laughed: Mme. Perez returned my
compliment by inviting one of Venezuela's best-known bari-
tones to come and serenade me.

The episode was to have its repercussions. The first morning
we were back in Ottawa, having reached home late the night
before, I set my clock radio to wake me at nine. It was an Arctic
cold morning. I was lying snugly under the quilt half asleep
when suddenly I heard an outraged voice saying: "I think she
is an absolute disgrace to this country. She is a disgrace to
every Canadian woman. She has no right at all to sing ridiculous songs in official company."

This was followed by a second, more reasonable voice, a man
this time: "Well, no, I don't quite agree with you. She's *trying* to

be honest at least." In an instant I was as frozen inside the bed as the air was outside; I wanted to crawl to the bottom of that bed and never come out. My instinct was to switch off the sound, but then I forced myself to listen.

A caller came on: "Hey Margaret, if you're out there listening, just you keep doing it. You are a gift to us."

This friend was a friend indeed, but there were all too few like him. The next six callers had nothing but venom and spite.

At this point the interviewer chipped in. "I doubt you are listening, Margaret Trudeau, but if by any chance you *are*, why don't you give us a call. Here is the number. The lines are now free. Call in."

I shot up in bed, seized the phone and dialed. "I meant no insult to anyone," I said stoutly in my own defense, stirred out of my terror by what I felt was monstrous misunderstanding. "I admire Mme. Perez. I don't only think she's an excellent prime minister's wife, but she's working very hard for her own people in her own right. I wanted to sing a song in admiration."

The critics were momentarily silenced. But that phone call started a whole new area of criticism. Should the wife of the prime minister of Canada phone in to talk shows?

The following week I was offered a phone-in show of my own on the local Ottawa early morning show. Luckily, Pierre was away, so he wasn't in a position to forbid it. I decided to accept the invitation simply because I had reached breaking point. I was sick to death of all the sneers and criticism that I was never allowed to answer. My sharp tongue, it seemed, got me into trouble whatever I did. I was tired of hearing people say: "How can such a lovely girl say such terrible things?" Now I was really going to give it to them.

The presenter, Michael O'Connell, opened the show by asking: "Now Margaret, is there any song that you would like us to play to start the program?"

"Yes," I replied immediately. "A song called 'Garden Party' by Rick Nelson." (It was about how he went to a garden party and everyone was either rude or unpleasant to him. In the song he sings: "If you can't please everybody, you might as well please yourself.") Then the phone calls started. Many, I was relieved to find, were friendly, and they grew friendlier as the show went on, and as I put across some of my own feelings and difficulties without having them misrepresented by the press. A few were censorious, like sharp-tongued nannies. A couple were outright hostile. I tried to be as reasonable and calm as I could.

My rage was really with the press, not with the public. I felt that there had been a growing campaign among the more malicious newsmen to put me in as bad a light as could be found and distort everything I did or said. The battle had reached its peak on our return flight from Venezuela. That day, prompted by a feeling that we had, after all, spent a frenzied three weeks of hard work all together, and yet scarcely met, I decided to leave our suite in the front of the plane and go back and talk to them. It was the first time I had done so, and I was taken aback by the boozing and jollity I found. Nonetheless, I made my way somewhat awkwardly to where my photographer friend, Rod McIvor, was sitting and sat chatting with him about the song in Caracas. "Will you sing it to us?" asked one of the reporters in a friendly manner. I hesitated. Then I thought it would seem standoffish to refuse so in a wavering voice I obliged. Meanwhile another man had handed me a bottle of good Cuban rum, and though I don't drink, I took a swig to play my part. That was my error. The papers next day were full of stories about my carousing with newsmen and swigging back booze straight from the bottle, and transcripts (they had, it turned out, switched a tape on) of my song circulated around Ottawa for weeks. I felt shattered, totally betrayed. And that was enough. I didn't go with Pierre on his next official visit to Britain and Germany. I simply refused to go. I felt too scared.

I wasn't let off the hook for long—1976 was official year *par excellence*. No sooner was one case unpacked, it seemed to me, than I was back up in the attic dragging it down again for the next round of parties, receptions, airports and pleasantries.

It was Olympics year. Pierre and I received the whole world in Montreal. I was looking forward to it enormously; for once formality was to be mixed with fun, and dozens of people were coming through Canada whom I had wanted to meet for years. Before moving up to a suite at the Queen Elizabeth Hotel in Montreal for two weeks, we had a series of informal lunch parties at Ottawa.

The sailing events were being held in Kingston, and when the Queen arrived on *Britannia* she invited us for dinner to watch the final heats. It was a horrible evening, blustery, raining hard, the sea as gray as the sky. Pierre and I were accompanied by the lieutenant governors and premiers of all the provinces and their wives. We were picked up from shore by the Queen's barge. As we climbed on board the *Britannia* in the pitching seas I was standing chatting to Mme. Léger. She had the Order of Canada pinned to her black chiffon evening dress. As she reached up to clasp the steps her brooch became loose and slipped off her bosom and down into the water. There was an outcry. The security frogmen patroling the boat were immediately alerted and spent a fruitless evening diving for it in the gray, opaque water, while poor Mme. Léger never ceased bewailing her loss.

I was deeply disappointed by what I found on board. I had expected luxury and style; instead I found overstuffed, faded chintz sofas, bland, wishy-washy colors and a total lack of elegance. It was like finding the Queen herself in an old cotton print dress. The main salon looked more like the drawing room of an English country house than a luxury liner. The sheer lack of pretension verged on the shabby. None of this extended to the staff, however, who were immaculately turned out in starched white and waited on us with naval promptitude, nor to the china and linen. Nor to the food, which was superb. As the Queen swept down the massive staircase in the main salon— which made the boat more like a house than ever—she imposed her own grandeur. It was my first taste of that curious blend of the shabby and the very grand.

A few nights later, installed at the Queen Elizabeth Hotel, I found myself unexpectedly receiving Prince Charles for dinner. Hearing how well his sister was doing in the Olympics' horse events, he had decided to make a flying trip to Canada to join his family. This was the evening of our big reception for the Queen—dinner for three hundred in the Beaver Club. The seating had all been arranged. When I heard of his arrival I sent for the plan. Prince Charles, I found, had been squeezed in next to Maureen McTeer. Out came my pencil. I switched him and put him next to me, in place of Prince Andrew.

This wasn't my first real encounter with the Prince. That had come years before when I was pregnant with Justin. As he led me out to dance in my décolleté Valentino dress I had caught him peering down the front. He blushed.

"My father always told me to look into my partner's eyes when she is wearing a low-cut dress," he said laughing.

"Feast ye while ye may," I replied. "If I wasn't three months' pregnant, there would be nothing to see."

That night at the hotel we had a marvelous time, so wonderful and full of jokes that a photographer caught us giggling together behind a shared menu and splashed the picture across the papers. Prince Philip reprimanded his son for monopolizing my attention. Prince Andrew kept the table in tears of laughter and even Sir Martin Charteris, the Queen's secretary, a charming, affable man whom I had become very fond of during the Queen's frequent visits to Canada, felt relaxed enough to take snuff. He offered me a pinch; laughing, I took one and breathed deeply. At that moment the table rose and, in a procession led by the Queen and Pierre, we paired off two by two to walk through the crowd. I simply had to sneeze. As we swept into the crowd a huge gob of brown snot landed on my exposed bosom and a photograph I still cherish shows Prince Andrew, Prince Philip and Prince Charles all staring down with a mixture of astonishment and disgust.

That was the only evening I ever saw the Queen really let go and literally kick her shoes off. After the reception she asked Pierre and me to go back with the Royal Family to the *Britannia*, where she ordered sausages and scrambled eggs, while we sat around in tears of laughter over Prince Andrew's jokes and impersonations of people he had met. He and Pierre got on marvelously. Both share a particular taste for practical jokes, Pierre's taking the form of pointing out trees in the forest when we used to take the children for walks, and saying "How much do you want to bet me I can knock down that tree?" The children gaped, when, sure enough, with one mighty kick the tree came thundering down. Pierre had developed a keen eye for rotting trunks.

In late August King Hussein and Queen Alia of Jordan invited us to spend a holiday with them. It was a tricky situation, because of the politics involved, but since I wanted to go so badly, and Pierre felt it would do me good, we solved the diplomatic hurdle by saying we would spend one week in Jordan, and a second week in Israel, thereby offending no one. Actually we were delighted. Both Pierre and I had dreamed of a biblical pilgrimage to the Holy Land.

Our week in Jordan was delightful, and Alia, whom I had first met and got to like in 1974, became a closer friend than ever. But from the moment we hugged goodbye at the Hussein bridge on the Jordan side and walked across into Israel everything changed. A smartly dressed business delegation was waiting to greet us; ambassadors were lined up and bowing; from that second on, protocol reigned. We were never alone. We were pressured and propagandized and lectured and harassed. I was so furious that my manners got worse and worse. Pierre went as far as to call me a "detestable" traveling companion.

I should, of course, have given in, accepted what was happening and gone along with it. But this was supposed to be a holiday, not an official visit, and God knows we deserved one. We *needed* to be alone. Driving back from Tel Aviv to Jerusalem one night after dinner, the Canadian ambassador climbed into the back seat with us. I kicked him straight back out. "Go get a lift in the other car," I said rudely. Pierre was furious. "I don't care how rude I am," I said, by now in tears. "We have had a romantic dinner, and even then we barely escaped having it with twenty-five other people. I want to drive down and cuddle in your arms. I don't want to sit here while this ambassador goes on chit-chatting the whole way about arms and defense."

Another day we went up to Masada. It was midday, and the sun was beating down uncomfortably on our heads, made worse by the pressing, jostling crowds and the fact that the turban I was wearing cut into my forehead. I wondered whether I was about to faint. Then a reporter appeared at my elbow, and began to ask me questions. I very nearly told him to fuck off.

"Just leave me alone," I wailed. "Pretend I'm not here."

He tried to explain. "But you are here. The Israelis are so pleased to have the prime minister of Canada visit them at this time. It's important to us. You aren't just any old tourists."

"Yes, we are, we're on holiday," I said stubbornly.

He shook his head.

The point of it all was that I was perfectly willing to behave as well as I could on an official occasion, but not on vacation.

This, I felt, was a shabby and disgraceful trick. This time even Pierre lost patience with me. Not only are his manners naturally better than mine but he also wanted very much to hear what the Israelis were thinking at that moment. He was incensed too at my atrocious behavior, and felt it reflected badly on me, on him, and on Canada generally.

From Tel Aviv we flew to Rome. This was to be a semi-official visit so by now I was ready to start acting again. It started very promisingly, with a dinner party given for us by our ambassador at which one of my great heroines, Sophia Loren, was present. She was funny, and easy and engaging, and both Pierre and I got to love her dearly.

Part of our reason for visiting Italy was to see the Pope who had granted us a private audience at his summer residence at Castel Gandolfo. Before leaving Ottawa I had inquired whether I needed to wear anything special, and had been told that a plain dress with long sleeves would be correct. Did it have to be black, because I didn't actually own a long-sleeved black dress? No, no. Did I need to wear a hat? Absolutely not. So I had decided on an off-white coat and skirt with a long-sleeved silk shirt, a beautiful *haute couture* outfit I was longing to show off. The first thing I found on landing in Rome was a note from the Papal Legate enclosing a document headed "Presentation to the Pope" with the rules all typed out. In them I was instructed to wear a formal black dress and a hat or some kind of cover for my head. What could I do? It was too late to buy anything. The ambassador's wife lent me a black lace mantilla for my head, and I resigned myself to the inevitable "Mrs. Trudeau defies protocol" again.

At this stage Pierre and I had both realized that something had gone seriously wrong with our marriage. We had had too many arguments, too much bitterness not to feel that this visit to Rome might be our last chance. Or a second honeymoon. This made our audience with the Pope all the more important, particularly as I felt that my faith was slipping fast. Since we were being given a private audience with the Pope, Pierre said that I should be ready to talk openly because if there was anyone in the world who could help it was surely him. So I wrote out a little list of questions and put it in my bag.

We set off in the morning to Castel Gandolfo, the superb

summer palace of the popes, overlooking the lake of Albano, south of Rome. We were led out on to the terrace to wait for our audience. This was true solemnity, protocol carried to its ultimate degree. Every step had to be right; every movement. We were escorted from room to room, ever closer to the inner sanctuary as the moment of our audience grew nearer. The Swiss guard stood rigidly to attention. There was a profound atmosphere of dignity, elegance and awe. Then the summons came; I was trembling. The Pope, I felt, was surrounded by an atmosphere of intense spirituality; the sort of spirituality that even I, who question everything, would not question. Pierre and I were seated opposite him, across a desk. He and Pierre began by discussing the problems of the world, international politics, and how to bring about a peaceful solution in the Middle East. Pope Paul was impressively well informed and full of unexpected insights. He brought their conversation to a close by asking Pierre if he had any special problems with his faith that he would like to discuss, any problems that needed solving? "No, thank you, Holiness," said Pierre.

Pope Paul turned to me. "Mrs. Trudeau, I understand that you have beautiful sons, and that you are a very good mother to your three lovely boys." I sort of bowed my head and smiled. "Ah," he went on reflectively, "aren't the children of the world our hope for the future?" He turned back to me. "I understand too that you are a very good wife to your husband and have always supported him throughout the difficult job of being prime minister. God bless you." He made the sign of the cross over us. The audience was over.

A second later we were out of the room and walking down the stairs. Pierre burst out laughing. "Bad luck, you didn't get to ask your questions." I was piqued.

"Well, I could hardly raise them without him asking me. You got asked whether you had any problems. You old hypocrite. Why didn't you tell him?"

Pierre said smugly. "I've nothing to say that I would be willing to say in front of you." I was forced to laugh too. Inside, though, I felt bitter; I'd come all this way just to be told to go on being a good wife and mother.

In the fall there was still one more major official visit to pay, this time to Japan, the apogee of protocol. We were put up in the Akasaka, a splendid palace modeled on Versailles, where our bedroom was all peach silk with carved wooden ceilings, rich tapestries and magnificent paintings, with sheets of the finest muslin I had ever seen. Before we went to sleep each night we were visited by two tiny masseuses with hands and muscles of iron who pounded us so hard that I finally begged to be let off, complaining that I had no wish to be beaten up after such intolerably hard days.

For they *were* hard. The protocol and the stuffiness exceeded anything even I had come across. Every outing we made was planned down to the last second: 10:28 step into the car; 10:32 step out of the car; 10:37 greet curator and so on. Everywhere politeness. I was always late, rushed, hassled. Even the grandeur had lost its charm, though I was startled out of my complaints when I found that the melons that 120 people ate at the Emperor's lunch party cost forty dollars each.

One of the things that I always enjoyed on the official trips was the press conference Pierre inevitably held on his last morning. It was a custom between us that I should attend it with him. In Japan, the morning he was to give it, I found a separate day's timetable typed out for me; "Mrs. Trudeau: free day. Perhaps a walk in the garden?" I stormed up to Ivan Head. He explained patiently but not without a touch of malice that there were to be no women at the press conference and that my presence would therefore be rather tactless. I made a scene. Finally, with a resigned sigh, Pierre agreed. When the time came to leave for it, we proceeded down the fifty stairs of our palace, lined by dignitaries and officials bowing, and reached the cars. I was steered away from Pierre's car. I balked loudly. Pierre sighed: "O.K., let her come with me." By now I knew I was behaving badly, but I seemed to be possessed. I climbed into Pierre's car; the doors were closed. Unfortunately Pierre chose to be very patronizing. It was too much. I leaped to my feet, clasping the door handle. It didn't open: we were locked in. I started screaming. The horrified Japanese guard hastily unlocked the door and under the amazed and startled gaze of the officials standing in serried ranks up the stairs bowing, I rushed up, three steps at a time shouting, "Fuck you" at the top of my voice. It wasn't easy to live that one down.

As Pierre grew more worried about my outbursts so he kept repeating: "You must do exactly what you want to do. You can do anything you want." The trouble was that I needed direction, not freedom. My outbursts were cries for attention.

ℱALSE
PROTECTION

No AMOUNT OF CAREFUL schooling, no amount of anxious warnings by Pierre, could ever really have prepared me for the role of prime minister's wife. Being only twenty-two was in many ways a help—with the protocol, the clothes, the publicity—but in other ways it was a disaster. In any case I hadn't wanted to listen to advice, and when the régime was upon me it was far too late to do anything about it.

Had it not been for Pierre's policy of keeping me taboo from the rest of the world, I might have learned far quicker what I was up against. As it was the isolation left me curiously vulnerable; ignorant and so undefended.

From the day I became Mrs. Pierre Elliott Trudeau, a glass panel was gently lowered into place around me, like a patient in a mental hospital who is no longer considered able to make decisions and who cannot be exposed to a harsh light. The result was that for five years I lived in cotton wool, struggling to grow up, to shape my own life, uncertain about whom exactly I was fighting against, but increasingly convinced that this artificial life was slowly crushing me to death. With so much civility around, whom to attack? With so much comfort, how dare I complain?

On March 3, 1971, I was an ordinary, averagely intelligent and well-educated Canadian girl, who smoked a bit of grass and had for years lived an uneventful if perfectly responsible life. Overnight I was turned into a child, a quirky, spoiled, rebellious child, who must be humored, yet kept in place. Where once I had opened my own front door, got into a car and driven to see friends, now I had the door opened for me by a changing parade of butlers and maids, was not allowed to drive, and could see approved friends only by appointment, and then closely guarded. Where once I had picked up my mail from the hall table, called my friends, and wandered into the kitchen to have a snack, now all my letters were opened and screened, my friends contacted by my secretary, and I was rarely brave enough to invade the kitchen with its chef and assistant cook to dig around for something to nibble on.

Nowhere did the restrictions on my life bite harder than over security. It was a word I came to hate. For five years, whenever I left 24 Sussex I took two policemen with me. They stood behind me in shops, they dogged me along the street, they sat at the next table when I was lunching with friends, they hung about at the door when I was in a boutique buying clothes. They even cycled along behind me when I was out on my bicycle.

The worst of it was that they changed all the time. Whenever I decided to leave the house I had to call up the security office, wait fifteen minutes for my escort to show up, climb into the Pontiac or Chevrolet at the front door, only to find myself confronted by two total strangers. "Where to, ma'am?" sometimes courteous, sometimes cheery, always a little disdainful. And once I had told them my wishes I had to sit there listening as it went out over their car radio. "Mrs. Trudeau is going to such and such a shop. Then she's going downtown to pay a call on so and so. On the way back we shall be stopping for fifteen minutes to pick up such and such." It certainly takes the spontaneity out of a morning's outing.

After a while I defended myself by not giving them advance information of my movements. Because I found that if I was foolish enough to tell them in the morning that in the afternoon I would be going to a certain shop, by the time I got there it would have been visited and checked out by a police patrol. So as I walked in the door, struggling for what anonymity I could get, everyone was alerted and waiting for my arrival, and little groups of people had collected by the street door.

Then I really started playing games. I wouldn't tell my two guardian angels where I was going, even once I was in the car. I'd be the flighty woman, always changing her mind, one minute saying "Let's go to the Market" and the next, "Oh no, I think we'll try the Place de Ville instead."

But I couldn't win. The police tried to make it clear that they were *guarding* me, but I always felt that I was simply under surveillance, a prisoner. Indeed I was, there was no getting away from it. There was always someone watching me, always someone on guard.

I soon found that I wasn't the only prime minister's wife to hate the security. Stories about different police forces and brushes with security men became a favorite topic of conversation at the wives' lunches and tea parties. I began storing up tales that made my own life sound like a picnic.

When Nancy Kissinger visited Ottawa she kept the lunch party I gave for her in tears of laughter over stories about what it was like sharing her small Georgetown house in Washington with a patrol of secret servicemen. She told us how she couldn't open her bedroom window without getting a key from one of the security men downstairs to disconnect the entire alarm system. Her guards patroled not only outside the house, in the street, but inside as well.

"You have to imagine," she explained, "a very small town house, with small neat rooms and lots of priceless and fragile furniture, and dozens of enormous, clumsy policemen with great beefy arms and huge feet stomping about. "

Nancy even had to put up with a man outside her bedroom door, so that if she felt like roaring with laughter or crying or putting her hair in curlers and going to fetch a book, she always bumped into someone skulking about the passages and felt their critical presence all around her like vigilant ghosts. She said that once it made her so angry that she got dressed, stormed out of the front door, slammed it, refused her policeman's offer to climb into their car, and marched off down the street. Even here she was defeated; the policemen jumped into their car and followed her at twenty paces in low gear, grinding along the narrow Georgetown roads.

All the women had their own stories to tell and most of them shared my fantasy about running away, escaping, breaking free. Only Mary Wilson, the wife of Britain's prime minister, said crossly that *she* didn't have a policeman at all, and that she wished she had because she would have found his help invaluable with the shopping. She can't have realized how lucky she was. And if I felt persecuted—what about the restrictions royalty had to put up with? Their's was a life sentence of constant police surveillance.

Inside Canada the Royal Mounted Police provided the security team to guard Pierre and myself: twenty-eight men on a system of shifts, but the number increased as the babies came. Then a special squad of nine, purely for their safety, was formed. There had to be someone on call always for each child, though later when Justin and Sacha went to the same school they shared a bodyguard.

We had a second team of security men, full time, stationed up at Harrington Lake, though we soon found that the men on duty up there tended to treat the assignment like a holiday, using our boat, snarling up the fishing tackle, swimming freely in the lake. Hard as we tried to, neither Pierre nor I could quite bear the way our possessions were somehow taken over, like public property, so Pierre asked that the men wear their uniforms—in Ottawa they are all plain clothes—because he felt it less likely that they would spend their days canoeing if they were in their distinctive khaki jackets and black pants.

When I had married Pierre he had a bodyguard, a charming man called Bert Géroux. He had once taken Bert snorkeling and only discovered, as the man clung frantically to the anchor of the boat, that he couldn't swim. Bert had forgotten, or been too ashamed, to mention it. Pierre's excellence in most sports caused the force something of a problem. We found, for instance, that we were always being assigned amateur skiers to accompany us to the mountains, so we spent wasted hours waiting for them to catch up with us. Pierre solved that by getting a specially trained skiing patrol.

Never was our security more ridiculous or ill-equipped than when Pierre and I went on one of our early romantic canoe trips down the French river. We were with two close friends, Eric and Pam Morse—Eric was a great traveler, a historian of Canada's waterways. I had pressed for us to be accompanied by two young constables from my patrol, both good canoeists and likable fellows, but unfortunately the prime minister of Canada cannot be guarded by mere constables. So we drew a stranger, high in rank and low in humor, and one of our own corporals.

217

The day we set out was misty and gray. We flew by helicopter up into the wilds, with our canoes, backpacks and sleeping gear ready for a four-day trip down one of the most spectacular rivers in Ontario. Six people; three canoes. We soon met with our first rapid; Eric and Pam took it first; Pierre and I followed. It was noisy and fast and frightening, but Pierre is a superb canoeist and we had no trouble. Then came the policemen. Of course, they thought they would take their own path and before a minute was up they had capsized in a bubbling pool with half our food and all their own equipment, and the rest of the day had to be spent drying them out. When we finally came to move on we found that their radio transmitter was out of order, so we made our way downstream with two soggy, mutinous policemen in far more danger than ourselves. The presence of these two policemen at our intimate fireside was far more irritating than the ubiquitous blackflies, and much increased when their badly put up tent collapsed in the middle of a downpour, like a scene out of *Deliverance*.

One more canoeing incident with the police freed us forever from taking them with us on our trips. One sunny early summer's day Pierre, Justin (then two and a half) and I went off for a lazy day's paddling and a picnic on a little river north of Harrington Lake. A police canoe accompanied us, and we organized a rendezvous with them for 4 P.M. Four came and went and there was no sign of the men. Finally we got a call over the radio: they were further ahead, waiting for us. Unsuspecting, we continued up the river and a couple of minutes later found ourselves caught up in fast, difficult rapids, the water churning around us. One moment we were even perched on a rock facing the wrong way. I kept my eyes shut, clung on to Justin and trusted in Pierre. Then we heard a deep, menacing roar ahead; in a split second Pierre got us to the side and heaved the canoe urgently out of the water. He walked ahead to look. There, just around the next bend, was a huge, rocky waterfall which we certainly couldn't have survived. When the astonished police caught up with us we discovered that they had been using the wrong maps—but by then it was eight o'clock, Justin was howling and exhausted and I swore that never again would we allow such idiots to endanger our lives. On our next trip down the Petawawa we went on our own—it was a truly good, simple trip without irritation or danger.

Security at home was one thing; but when we went abroad it was sometimes so intense as to be laughable. Tanya, my guardian angel in Moscow, followed me so closely that I couldn't even go to the washroom alone. That she was a guard as well as interpreter was made plain to me the day that I caught sight of a revolver in her handbag. Getting rid of her, even for a few minutes, led to some funny scenes. One day Mrs. Gromyko had laid on a delicious tea of chocolate cake and strawberry shortcake, and a group of Russian wives and I were gathered around a table talking in a stilted sort of way. For all my surreptitious pushing and shoving, Tanya was crouched close alongside me. Finally Mrs. Gromyko had had enough; politely, but extremely firmly, she marched Tanya off to the other end of the room and placed her with a plate of cakes in one corner. Then we settled down to a far more enjoyable and unguarded tea, with all the women questioning me closely about the west. Pat Nixon and I, so I later saw from a photograph, shared Tanya on our separate official visits to Russia.

The Americans, I discovered, give more protection than anyone. Staying once for a holiday with Pierre and Justin, then eighteen months old, on a deserted island in Hawaii, I found that our tropical hut, open on all sides and with walls made of screens, was guarded by four men, one stationed at each corner of the house. They could not only hear every sound we made; but they could see us as well. It put an end to the romantic holiday. I found, too, that the burly American police could be singularly slow-thinking. One day we ventured out to a wild, secluded beach, where we were alone except for a young hippy family with a little girl of Justin's age. The police soon made it plain that there was something very deviant about them; the wife actually bathed nude. The waves were enormous and the under-tow a killer and while I was by the water with Justin, the little girl, showing off to us, went too far into the waves and got swept off her feet. No one moved. So I plunged in after her, and scooped her up in my arms, but then I too was swept off my feet. I shouted for help. It was Pierre, not the six strong American policemen, who came to my aid.

At 24 Sussex, it was the police who laid down the rules of

morality for the staff: they put a security curfew on the house. Friends had to be cleared if they wanted to visit, and even then they couldn't come after certain hours. If one of the visitors looked at all hippy, then the police had him or her blocked. When I discovered what these vetoes were doing to the social life of the staff I objected, only to be told politely to mind my own business.

Diane had a boyfriend, a young boy who wore his hair in a pony tail and had a police record for trafficking in marijuana. When they discovered this, the police decided to get him banned. They waited a couple of weeks, then filed a report that one night they had been walking around the house when they had smelled an unmistakable trace of grass coming from the staff windows. It had to be Diane. By some lucky coincidence Diane kept a diary. It was discovered that the very night she was accused of having her boyfriend in, she had in fact been up at Harrington with the children. I made a great fuss, and that cooled their moralism for a while.

The irony was that the sweet smell was more likely to have come from my rooms. Not many years after we married, in a mood of desperation about the life I was falling into, I had defied Pierre and gone back to the occasional joint. It wasn't much, and I took great care never to be caught.

It wasn't long before I had my knuckles rapped. A nice young policeman rang our bell one day. I went down to see who it was. He handed me a little packet.

"I brought some incense for you," he said, smiling. "Sometimes when I patrol the house I can smell it coming from the windows so I know you must like it."

It was a warning, a friendly warning, but a warning all right. I took more care after that, on occasion even having to resort to shutting myself into cupboards for a quick smoke.

Like the stuffy protocol, I fought the formality of the police. I couldn't bear the way they would salute every time I came out, so I stopped that. The trouble was that there was nothing to replace it. So I used to mumble "Hi," as I went past, and they would just grin sheepishly. It wasn't very satisfactory. I also fought the way they were always there, even at the most intimate moments. Pierre, who got on fine with all of them, never notices a thing, but I used to be deeply conscious of their feet crunching through the snow beneath our bedroom windows, and the crackling voices from their transistors often woke me from a deep sleep in the middle of the night.

As the years went by my anger at the police system grew more intense. When Bert left, Pierre was assigned a marvelous guard called Barry, more friend than policeman, who came everywhere with us. He made the system tolerable—just.

But all too soon he left, to be replaced by a competent, unimaginative hulk of a man, who by the end of our Middle Eastern trip I hated so much I could have killed him. "If he stays with us, I'm off," I told Pierre in Rome.

Pierre was appalled. "But he has another three years to serve."

To which I said, "Well, it's him or me."

It was the first of many such incidents. One sunny summer's afternoon in Ottawa I decided to pay a casual visit on my closest friend, Nancy Pitfield, who lived just two blocks away down the street. A spirit of childish adventure overtook me: I wanted to go *right now*, not sit around waiting for twenty minutes until my police patrol could be summoned up to accompany me. Like a mischievous child I crept to the window, pulled back the curtain a couple of inches and peeped out to see where the policeman on guard was stationed. His bright red uniform and funny hat were clearly visible at the side door. I took off my sandals and tiptoed to the front door. Scarcely breathing, I opened it, crept out and stealthily made my way down the drive. Once out of the gates I started to run. It wasn't many seconds before I heard a "clong, clong, clong, puff, puff, puff" behind me. I stopped, shrugged my shoulders, turned around. There, heaving and puffing, was a beefy, redfaced policeman pounding as fast as he could down the street.

Another day I lost my temper. It was midwinter, and snow was falling very gently on Ottawa, turning the dreary streets into a silent, magical world. I decided to take Sacha and Justin to walk in the governor general's compound across the road, an enormous, empty park where I often took them. I bundled them into their parkas and set them in the pram. As I turned down the deserted path, the snowflakes falling, and my spirits rising at the beauty of the scene, I became aware of a policeman at my heels. I pushed harder, to get him further behind me; he hastened his pace. I pushed faster. Soon we were flying down the paths like people possessed. Finally red in the face, sweating, the silence shattered by the noise of my heartbeats and the steady pound of his feet, I whirled round: "Why don't you leave me alone?" The poor policeman flushed.

"Don't take it out on a poor guy who is only trying to do his job."

"Ah! If you can't take it out sometimes, somewhere, on someone, where does it all go, this rage? How do I get rid of it? I'm angry because no one ever leaves me alone. I'm always conscious that somebody's watching me."

The policeman looked pained. "You're not under surveillance. You're being protected."

"Oh no, I'm not. I'm under surveillance."

My feuds with the security became so frequent and so hostile that the day came when I decided to pay a visit on the assistant commissioner to discuss my security. Clearly things couldn't go on as they were. Edward Willes, a nice, sympathetic man, tried to be understanding. "We just want to help you. Can you make any suggestions?"

"Yes. First of all don't assign any more creeps to my detail."

"Creeps? What exactly, Mrs. Trudeau, is your definition of a creep?"

"A creep is someone who is very heavy, quite exceptionally heavy. He has his hand on his gun the whole time. He does not communicate. Either he chatters meaninglessly or he is stony cold. He refuses to reach out and pick up a bag for me even if he sees I have twenty-five bags to carry. That's not his job. He's a bully and he pushes me around psychologically all the time. Everything he says to me reeks of the very world I am trying to avoid: moralistic, censorious, riddled with formality. Can't you give me young men who have children of their own, who have ordinary wives, who aren't so superconscious of being big, tough policemen?"

By now I had got into my stride. It all came pouring out, the grievances and miseries of my first years. "Don't change the policemen all the time. Give me time to get used to them. I feel my privacy invaded each time I have to face up to a different fellow at the wheel of my car. I don't want so many people to know every single thing I do."

Assistant Commissioner Willes and I made a deal. He offered me Henry Kennedy, the best policeman he could think of—a nice, kindly man in his late twenties, who was making a good career for himself in the force but who had spent time with us before as a young corporal and loved children. Henry would look after me. In return I was to make no more trouble, no more unscheduled disappearances. I kept to my side of the bargain. Henry stayed with us two years—though he could have left as soon as he asked to. I came to depend on him more and more as a friend, to whom I could complain and bitch when things went wrong. In Henry's company I could drop the pretense; I didn't have to be formal and polite.

When Micha was born he got all dressed up in a white hospital robe and, while Pierre sat at one end of the corridor having intelligent conversations with the doctors, he marched me up and down to get the baby started. Henry's wife was having her first child in a couple of months and he was as obsessed by the coming baby as I was. He wasn't quite prepared for the screams and yells from the delivery room however, and when I emerged triumphant, proudly clutching a swaddled baby, I found him white and shaken. But it says much for our relationship that he was there in the first place.

During my discussion with the assistant commissioner he had also agreed to choose policemen for the children who don't feel that it is degrading for them to run after little boys who have escaped their nannies, and don't see guarding the prime minister's children as a job fit for a babysitter. Pierre and I felt that we wanted friends for the boys, men who understood that they needed guarding, but very discreetly, and that whatever happened to the children with their friends, the men must never interfere to defend them. The new team includes a couple of women police; they have become friends now, not resentful strangers. The boys marvel at their guns, for Pierre forbids them any toy weapons. We have told them the security men wear them to shoot snakes.

The day I discovered that all my oppressive security was nothing other than a myth, I was down in Jamaica with Pierre and his guard, Barry. It was sunset and Barry and I were drinking rum punches by the shore—there is nothing I liked better than a rum punch and Pierre wouldn't drink—and I said, absentmindedly: "Barry, is there anything that you think should be changed about our security?"

"Well," he said, "if it was up to me, I'd have it legislated, written into the law, so that there isn't always a tremendous element of doubt about it."

"What element of doubt?"

"We have no way of ensuring that you will be guarded the entire time."

The truth suddenly hit me. "You mean to say I don't *have* to have policemen all the time?"

He looked uncomfortable. "Er, of course you really should have them all the time, because you're always in danger from nuts. But it's not actually compulsory."

Within two weeks I had taken my driving test again and got a new licence. Pierre bought me a car, and the day I picked it up I waved goodbye forever to Henry. The feeling of freedom, simply to be able to drive my own car down the street, alone, was unbelievable. It was better than freedom: it was anonymity. Big burly men, with short hair and guns slung bulkily around their waists under navy blue blazers, are unmistakably police officers. No amount of pretending they weren't there changed that. Everywhere I went people stared. "Who's that woman with those two officers?" No more!

Pierre let me give up Henry on one condition: that I kept security men for the children. It was a small price to pay. The most delightful part of my new-found liberation was how much I rose in esteem in my children's eyes. For the first time I was able to drive them about in my own car, just like everyone else's mother (with a security car behind). We celebrated by buying a cassette player and a number of children's tapes. It was also the beginning of remembering what it felt like to be spontaneous and free again. I started going out for long drives to visit parts of Ottawa, a city I had lived in for five years and knew nothing about.

In some ways, it was the beginning of the end. Having tasted freedom, the sweet beguiling smell of escape, how could I resist it?

Overnight, however, it also improved my relations with the entire security package that surrounded us. I became helpful, even obliging when security was really necessary, and I came to appreciate what it did for us. For instance, the day came when I visited my parents in Vancouver and heard there was a killer on the loose who had read *The Vertical Mosaic*, a thriller about the Canadian establishment. After that he had murdered four teenagers at a camping site and decided to make two million dollars to visit Paris and buy a Rolls Royce. He apparently was looking for a member of one of Vancouver's richest families to kidnap. I was grateful for my security men then all right. Another day a man was seen wandering around 24 Sussex with a shotgun and I got a phone call from the office: where were the children? He turned out to be a harmless fellow, escaped from a mental institution. I figured that I could handle my own safety; but Pierre and the children needed protection. After all, the Canadian record is excellent—in all my years as Pierre's wife I did not have one single frightening incident.

Indeed, the only incidents that befell us were thefts—and those from visitors to the house rather than strangers. One night we gave a reception for about a hundred people at 24 Sussex Drive, a very mixed party to celebrate the opening of a new academy. While handing around the drinks, Ruth, not one of our household maids, but a woman who often helped out on the diplomatic circuit, noticed a man slip a tiny Greek head, given us by the Shah of Iran, from the mantelpiece into his jacket pocket. She made her way to his side, jerked her tray so that a glass of whisky poured over his sleeve, and in a flurry of apologies and excuses whipped the jacket off his back and retreated into the kitchen to clean it. A few minutes later, still apologizing profusely, she was back to return the jacket—minus the Greek head. We weren't always so lucky. Not long after we married Pierre gave me a gold fountain pen with my name engraved on it. After one political reception for the Liberal Association, the pen had vanished from beside the library phone.

The security was one glass wall around me; the screening of my letters became another. As the years went by the numbers of letters from total strangers—of love and friendship, though many, many more of hatred—multiplied many times. I came to see them as a terrible oppressive force on my life, a shattering condemnation of my every move by people who had never set eyes on me. To feel hated and criticized by strangers is a frightening sensation.

In the days following our secret marriage, hundreds of letters poured into 24 Sussex. Dear Mrs. Trudeau, most of them said, congratulations; the prime minister needs a wife; now all will be wonderful. Old ladies sent me recipes for cakes, and patterns for sweaters; wellwishers wrote about their own happy marriages; young women told me of their successful lives with men old enough to be their fathers. I basked in the warmth of their approval.

It didn't last long. Four months after our marriage the Queen came to Canada. Having given considerable thought to my dress, I went out to the airport in a big straw hat, a mid-calf length dress with a pattern of white daisies and brown edging, puffy sleeves and a high neck. That was the time of the gale blowing at the airport, when twice my straw hat danced off into the wind. And did I ever hear about it! "What a shocking dress to wear in which to receive the queen," wrote legions of Canada's matrons. "Who do you think you are? A chorus girl?" The practical sent hints about hat pins and how to tether a straw hat in a gale; the snide cried shame; the busybodies sent advice about what I *should* be wearing: a lime green dress in linen or silk with matching jacket and white accessories. This was the first taste of what was to come: a self-righteous feeling on the part of the great Canadian public that they owned me, that my taste ought to reflect theirs, and that when I fell out of line I should be castigated.

When I was pregnant, letters poured in by the sackful with handy hints about clothes, food, the way to stand and walk, how many hours to rest and what time to go to bed at night. I was Canada's most cosseted lady. One woman wrote to tell me that I must dress my baby in permutations of three: three layers on top—vest, shirt, sweater—three layers at the bottom —diaper, pants and trousers—like some cabalistic formula. Another said I must on no account have the baby at home. The public curiosity and opinion went down to the very smallest detail.

Among the wellwishers there was more than a fair share of nuts. After Justin's birth one woman wrote to say that his

middle name must begin with an E—she suggested Emmanuel—
because that way his initials—J.E.T.—would launch the new
cosmic force into the jet age. A doctor, believing me to be
giving him a bottle, wrote hastily to inquire whether I knew
that milk was poisonous?

From then on, with every event, every birthday, Christmas or
celebration, the mail shot up. The moment I did anything out of
the ordinary—bang! Another two hundred letters. It soon held
me back from the slightest display of ostentation or originality.
Since I insisted on answering all except the real sickies by hand
myself, it meant hours of work. When I was swamped, I got
a little extra help from a girl in Pierre's office. This situation
went on, worsening steadily, until after the 1974 election when
Pierre suddenly realized how badly I needed secretarial help.
It was then that I was given Marie-Hélène Fox as my part-time
assistant, and she took on a team of secretaries to whom we
dictated the replies.

It was a mixed blessing. For one thing it became very easy for
me to leave it all in her capable hands, with the result that
when I did get to see some of the letters that went out in my
name I got furious, and blamed her for tactlessness and formality, and scrunched them all up. They solved that by having
a machine with my signature—two machines to be exact, one
formal, one girlish. So I didn't see anything any more.

This way I missed all the hate letters that started to come in
after some of my exploits on official tours. The few that got
through, delivered by mistake to the front door, or caught up
in my papers, were enough to give me a shock: crazy, cruel
letters written to hurt and destroy.

But I also missed all the encouraging ones, the ones that told
me to keep fighting, that professed admiration for what I was
trying to do. When I went into hospital for depression the mailbag blew up like a balloon—two thousand letters a month. By
the same token I missed the personal letters from old friends,
people coming through Ottawa wanting to see me, and whom I
didn't hear about until they had left: screening took about a
week.

The screening was often arbitrary and absurd, more like
censorship than protection. Prince Andrew wrote me a long
letter, which was opened, probably read, stapled together and

delivered casually, weeks late, even though his name was clearly printed on the back. "Opened in error," said an unrepentant scrawl over his fine hand. When the checks and controls spread to the switchboard, so that friends were curtly told I wasn't at home, and no message taken, I demanded and finally got my own telephone with a private number.

But only when I left Pierre did the full horror of the situation dawn on me. My mailbag had increased 300 percent in my last year at 24 Sussex—at one point I had 950 letters waiting to be answered. The day I walked out of the gates there was no one to protect me any longer. The waves of hatred poured over me, like a rough vengeful sea and I fled in horror from the monster I had unleashed.

"You pot-smoking slut," wrote one man. "Canada is well rid of you." "We'll kill you if we can," wrote another. There were threats and taunts, calumnies and sneers. I had released a genie of vitriol and the poison spread all around me to everything I touched.

"You were damned right to go," wrote a vitriolic woman. "It was about time you left that deviant scoundrel. More is the pity you didn't take the three little boys. You've left them in the hands of a commie. . . ."

A tide of violent hatred was upon me; I ran from it as fast as I could.

THE DREAMS
GO SOUR

W HEN, IN THE LATE SPRING of 1977, I was packing up
my clothes to leave Pierre, I found a sheet of paper
scrawled up and tucked at the back of one of my
drawers. "I am so lonely," it read. "I should be happy.
I am married to a man who loves me and I have a wonderful
baby. But I am terribly unhappy." The date was November
1972. Justin was nine months old.

There is no doubt at all that for much of the time I lived with
Pierre I was deeply unhappy. There was so much that was
good—the babies, the all-too-rare moments that Pierre and I
had totally alone, the trips abroad and the holidays—but there
was also a lot that was rotten. The honeymoon was over much
too soon. As Pierre settled down to married life and no longer
felt he had to court me, so he returned to spend more and more
time at his work, leaving me alone. I waited, and waited, and
waited all day for him to come home, devoting the last hours to
putting on my makeup and my prettiest clothes so as to look
beautiful for him. When he appeared he took *off* his best clothes
and climbed into old, baggy slacks. When I told him how bored
I was, he looked disgusted: "How *can* you be bored when life is
so full, when you have so many options?"

Most of my friends lived far from Ottawa. Those that lived
near kept their distance, intimidated by Pierre's apparently
aloof and unwelcoming manner. All my fond dreams of holding
a salon for artists, intellectuals and the most interesting
politicians, faded. The married women I knew were first embarrassed, then amazed, when I pressed them to let me help
them with their household chores. "At least let me be useful at

something," I begged, suggesting I scrub their floor or do their dishes.

From the beginning of our marriage, Pierre encouraged me to take what laughingly became known between us as my "freedom trips." In the early days these were usually visits back to Vancouver to see my parents, to spend time away from police protection, doing the very things I was now forbidden or impeded from doing in Ottawa: shopping for food, doing the dishes, wandering about the garden without gardeners and security men gawking at me. Sometimes I went further afield, to Boston, New York or even, once, to Rome. Pierre trusted me completely. He saw as well as I did the benefits that came from such sprees. We spoke every night on the phone, I missed him terribly and when I got home we were very close and loving.

There were of course happy patches. The chronicle of our crumbling love affair would be false without them. I made a few intimate friends, with whom I could laugh about the official life, and briefly forget how much a prisoner of it I was. Queen Alia of Jordan was the closest of these.

I met her and King Hussein for the first time when they came to Ottawa for an official visit, immediately after the 1974 election. We took to each other at once. Alia was magnificent to look at: a mass of striking blond hair, green eyes, an irresistible smile. She arrived when I was at my lowest ebb, exhausted and feeling somehow betrayed by the election campaign; despite our victory, or perhaps because of it. Within hours she had taken me in hand, forced me to laugh about our lives, poked fun at my fears.

There was no formality between us: despite her being a Palestinian born on the West Bank, and me a politician's daughter from Vancouver, we were just two girls, sitting and giggling in her bedroom, me in jeans, she in her invariably magnificent clothes, with trunks of silk lingerie and boxes of priceless jewels scattered about the floor. The fact that she understood what I was talking about was enough to comfort me. "You're lucky, don't you understand," she kept repeating. "Pierre will eventually leave politics and you'll be free. Mine is a life sentence." More soberly, she wrote to me on October 17, 1974:

Dearest Margaret,

I finally received your letter, as I was reading it I felt like I was talking to myself. . . . It's not easy to find friends, especially in our positions—if we raged and screamed everybody would think we were absolutely crazy but yet I say only people who have feelings and love in them go through this. . . .

Don't overload him [Pierre], try to control yourself and when he is away, rage, break, scream and cry and get everything out. That is what I have learned to do and it helped me and my husband.

. . . I am scared to death too because I am afraid for his life. I have never felt so insecure in my life as I do now, because as you might know how many assassination attempts he has escaped. I only pray to God everything works out.

They were brave words. Perhaps I should have followed her advice. The fact that I knew she was having a much harder time than I was and yet survived and kept smiling also made my sentence easier to bear. When we went to Amman on holiday in June 1976 I found her just as exuberant, but a little worried. Her extravagance and high spirits were beginning to make her enemies in Jordan and she was now frightened that a plan she had had to put up a monument to her daughter Haiya in the shape of a community center on a prime plot of land in the city was coming unstuck. She had, she admitted to me, been rather haughty and gone ahead without permission, sending in bulldozers. The mayor was furious, and determined to put a stop to it. Alia was decidedly anxious. "I know I have produced a Crown Prince, and that's something," she said to me doubtfully, "but Hussein will be so angry."

Once again we talked, we gossiped, we comforted each other. We even made plans to share a little London house where we could escape to spend holidays together; she had a fantasy that we would join the European jet set and decorate our Chelsea home with all the taste she complained was lacking in her modern Amman palace. She wanted to buy Georgian furniture. She was quick, she was sharp, she was witty. She made me

231

laugh with her stories. I remember she told me that she had just overheard Haiya, then three years old, say graciously to the elder child she and King Hussein had adopted: "*I* am a Princess."

The girl had sat silent for a moment, then replied gravely: "*I* am the Queen Mother."

Our friendship was cemented in the marvelous present of cameras she gave me, which became my third eye, an excuse to leave the house and go walking, the means of being not merely a participant, but a fly on the wall at official functions, as I was in Cuba. I saw her far too seldom, but it was enough to know that she was there. Our relationship became almost telepathic. The days I was most depressed were always those on which my phone rang: "Margaret, are you all right?"

Apart from my close friendship with Alia, I also had some increasingly good times pursuing interests of my own, forwarding causes that I personally believed in. In March 1976, having weaned Micha, I went to California to attend a conference at which Krishnamurti: Yves's guru, a deeply spiritual man, was speaking. I spent five days there, as "Margaret Sinclair," listening to him talk about the evils of structure and authority, and how guilt is a manmade emotion. "All thought leads to sorrow," he constantly reminded us. I came away more convinced than ever that Pierre's solution, to subjugate everything to reason and will, was wrong and that mine, to live from moment to moment, right.

"Why don't you use your mind," argued Pierre bitterly on my return. "You're perfectly intelligent."

Later that year I got involved in the U.N. Conference on Human Settlements in Vancouver and campaigned with Barbara Ward for clean water. "You're like a lovely pot of honey, all those busy bees of the press come rushing to you whenever the lid is off," Barbara Ward said to me somewhat fancifully. "Why don't you find a message and push it?" So I carried buckets of water with the best of them and started talking about pollution and the environment and not whether or not I would be wearing my pink Valentino dress to a dinner with the Queen.

Even so it had begun to be clear to many Canadians that I was not temperamentally suited to the job of First Lady. Not long after Pierre and I were first married the strains of the life had begun to show. I became nervous, jittery, unpredictable. Even my children could not always distract me from feelings of acute tension. My actual "breakdown," when it came, was almost a relief, phony as it was.

After the 1974 election, when Queen Alia had been to Ottawa and gone home again, I took off for one of my more adventurous "freedom trips"; this time without consulting Pierre who had taken Justin off fishing in the St. Lawrence. I was desperate. I phoned him from the airport.

"I'm off to Paris," I told him, "I want to practice my French."

Characteristically, he said at once: "Yes, by all means, off you go."

I had forgotten my passport, but bluffed my way through Orly airport without one, using a special paper given me by the airport authorities, only too happy to be of service. Once I reached Paris I booked for a night into the Hotel George Cinq.

So far so good. Next morning my real freedom trip began. Leaving the press reporters lounging in the front hall I sneaked out of the back door with my suitcase and moved to a small hotel by Notre Dame, overlooking the Seine. I spent several happy days taking photographs, walking around the parks, eating in student cafés.

But I couldn't go on fooling myself for long. I hadn't come to Paris just to recuperate; there was more to my visit than that. I have to have a fantasy in my life; I can't long survive without one. And my fantasy was Yves. I had come to Paris clutching a screwed up corner of paper on which I had written down his last known address: Rue de Blanc Manteau 35. One fine, sunny morning I made my way there and, trembling with anticipation, struck the enormous copper gong that hung alongside the entrance. I heard steps, the key in the lock. The massive door swung back. There stood a middle-aged woman with frizzy, red hair. My heart sank.

"I'm looking for Yves Lewis," I said hesitantly, in my poor French. She looked blank. I tried again. "How long have you lived here?"

"Four years."

"Has someone called Yves Lewis left a forwarding address?"

"No."

Slow tears of frustration started trickling down my face. I had had no idea I cared so much. My frizzy-haired companion was moved almost to compassion.

"*Le monde,*" she said, shrugging her shoulders in a not unfriendly way, "*ça change.*"

I walked the streets of Paris for the rest of the day trying to put my life together again. By nightfall I had decided to move on again. But I still had no proper passport.

I called on our Paris embassy and asked them to provide me with one in the name of Margaret Sinclair. The official was first embarrassed, then dubious. When I went to collect it I found "Wife of the Prime Minister of Canada" stamped all over the first page. I remonstrated. Reluctantly he agreed to provide me with another. Next day I was back. This time the passport, handed somewhat sheepishly across the counter to me, contained: "Wife of a high government official." I left it at that; I hadn't the energy to go on complaining.

Armed with my new credentials I caught a plane to Athens. Greece had a shrine of sorts for me: I went to see the village where Yves had been at school. Then I moved on to Crete. There was nothing sinful or sinister about my trip: I simply needed to be on my own. In Crete I rented a car and drove about the island. I swam, took photographs and had only a knapsack for luggage and a blanket to sleep in. It was precisely what I wanted. I passed the days in a romantic reverie, a soothing daydream of almost adolescent romance. It was like Robert's Creek all over again. After two weeks I was ready to go home.

I caught a plane back to Paris, called Pierre, who had begun to worry about my mysterious disappearance, and told him I was coming home. "Fine," he said, "why don't we go to the Celebrity Pro Tennis Tournament in New York?"

That proved my undoing. I arrived home in that curiously high and edgy state that comes from being too much alone: anxious to make it all up with Pierre, yet resisting every effort on his part. The night before the Tennis Tournament I fell in love. I hadn't looked at another man in four years; it was sudden; it was fantastic. He was a high-powered American; a charming Southerner whose name is of no importance. I became like someone possessed. We danced all evening. I cried all night. When we got back to Ottawa next day I raced up the stairs to our private refridgerator and drank off the half bottle of vodka I found there. Pierre, who caught me at it, was appalled.

"Have you been unfaithful to me in Paris?" he kept on asking. "Have you? Have you?"

We passed a nightmare weekend up at Harrington Lake. Pierre never left me alone. "I know you've been unfaithful. I know it. Otherwise why be like this?" Late Saturday night, exhausted, frantic, I seized a kitchen knife from the table and rushed out into the snow, where I started tearing off my clothes to find a bare spot to plunge the blade in.

"O.K.," I screamed at Pierre. "O.K. I've fallen in love." The confession shocked us both into silence.

"You're sick," was all he said at last.

If I wasn't sick then, I soon became it: frightened, lonely and very mad. When the children ran up to kiss me, I shrank back. When the maids asked for instructions, I panicked. Pierre kept urging me to seek psychiatric help. Finally, my own will worn so thin that I was happy to take anyone's advice, I checked into the Montreal General Hospital under a Dr. Boz. Wendy Porteous drove me—the same woman who that dreadful evening so long ago had put me down about my French. We had an extraordinarily giggly, happy drive down to Montreal: a delicious lunch, lots of wine. I couldn't really believe I was mad. Then she left me.

I had expected the psychiatric wing, and was half curious to meet my fellow inmates. Because of the security, the need for police at that stage to guard me even inside a hospital, I was shown instead into a suite in the urology section, where aging businessmen came to have prostate operations. It reduced me to tears at once. "I want to go with the others," I wailed. They arranged for me to have a round-the-clock shift of private nurses.

Dr. Boz explained the treatment he had in mind for me. "I want to bore you," he said. "I want to make you sleep. Relax."

It was all a bit like *Alice in Wonderland*. "I feel paranoid. I feel everybody is watching me," I said to him.

"Everybody *is* watching you. That's not paranoia. That's reality."

"I feel hostile. I have illusions of grandeur. I think I'm somebody."

"You *are* somebody."

I had come down here to get away from Pierre and think about my marriage in peace. I found myself constantly watched by nurses and fed pills that made my tongue swell and my mind sag. While there Pierre's brother Tip's wife, Andrée, came to see me. She was effusively loving and bore baskets of grapes for me. The tales Andrée took home, fanciful as they were, contained enough to send Tip to the phone to assure Pierre that I undoubtedly had a lover. That night I would have thrown myself from the window had there not been bars across it. It earned me my second shot of morphine in my life to ease the pain.

Though not my lover, my American friend called me every day. I sometimes felt that only he and Alia could understand what I was going through. Gradually I began to take a tentative hold on myself. I weaned myself off the tranquilizers and flushed my daily dose down the lavatory, thus clearing my mind to think. I kept sane by questioning the nurses about their own lives, and brewing myself up little pots of what Dr. Boz, smugly seeing recovery in my domestic chores, took to be tea but were in fact sweet potions of marijuana. I took photographs in the hospital grounds. I wrote to Alia. One Sunday the hospital priest came to talk to me. His words electrified me. "Whatever are you doing here?" he asked contemptuously. "You should be home with your children."

That settled it for me. I called Dr. Boz, and asked him whether I was committed. "No," he replied reluctantly. So I summoned my policeman and prepared to leave. But not before I consented to make an appearance before the journalists who had been thronging the hospital grounds like vultures since my arrival, reporting that I was in hospital for an abortion. I was thin, disheveled, gaunt. "Why don't you leave me alone?" I asked them. "Can't you feel any compassion for me? I don't know how long I shall be here, but I am suffering from severe emotional stress. Please go away." They went, and rather to my surprise my statement brought me sympathy, encouragement and flowers from every corner of the country. The Mental Health Associations praised me for my honesty, and fellow sufferers wrote with understanding. I received three thousand letters. Take up a hobby, said one woman. Bake bread, said another. Start singing, said a third. Good luck, said many more.

They gave me the heart to go home. The most heartening came from the Canadian writer, Gabrielle Roy:

Dear Mrs. Trudeau:

I saw you and listened to you last night on television and I was deeply moved by the note of sincerity that rang through all your comments. Television has not accustomed us to such frank and soul-baring remarks.

I also had the impression that you were not talking for yourself alone but on behalf of all women, that you were speaking for each one of us all more or less enchained. Because the moment we love, do we not fall into a sort of slavery? Doubtless men do, too—who is truly free?—but less perhaps than women for whom love is the center of life and who are thus the most vulnerable of creatures.

As I was listening to you, delighted to hear so many truths said in so few words, I thought that women's plaint through the ages, so long silent, that women's age-old revolt that only love has ever overcome, had found in you a modern expression.

What I appreciated most, during the interview, is the fact that you did not seem to be sorry for yourself but for mankind, poor mankind. It was like a tender prayer, a wish that life could be different, and you said "but one must face reality." A Greek woman would have said "fatality." And I wondered if young women like you, full of the greatest courage there is, that of telling the truth, did not do more than governments to change the world.

Pierre seemed pleased to see me, and I was there in time to accompany him to France and Belgium for the N.A.T.O. summit. It wasn't an easy trip. Pierre continued to eye me with doubt, and I took refuge as frequently as I felt I dared to in quick puffs of marijuana. When I got back to Ottawa the psychiatrist, whom I had agreed should visit me, took Pierre's side: I must get off drugs. Week after week I lay speechless and furious on his couch. Finally I could stand it no longer. I smoked not one but two strong joints before setting out for one of my regular appointments. No sooner was I settled in his office than I began to talk. I told him about my dreams, my childhood, my marriage. A look of profound self-satisfaction spread across his face. "You see," he said at the end of our hour, "you can do it, you know, without drugs." I laughed. I never went to him again.

Meanwhile, on the doctor's advice, Pierre had consented to allow me to fly down to the United States for a brief clarifying meeting with my friend. Both of them agreed that it was merely an unhealthy obsession, best cleared up. The arrangement was that I should have dinner with my friend, agree never to speak or meet again, sleep the night with friends and fly home. It didn't quite work out that way. When I flew home next day I swore to myself that I would never see him again—or that if I did I would leave Pierre. I kept my word.

My new-found popularity with the Canadian public did not last long. No sooner had they stopped praising me for my honesty about my breakdown than they began berating me for accepting Queen Alia and King Hussein's lavish present of cameras. I was hammered yet again when I agreed to christen a supertanker for a Hong Kong shipbuilder called Y.K. Pao, and spent two weeks at his expense with a party of two of my sisters and some friends in Japan.

These were not happy times for us. Pierre, jealous and brooding, took it out on me by leaving me ever more often on my own, and treating me coldly, even with hostility. When we spoke, it was almost always about the children, and even then often words of reproach. Pierre, quite rightly, said I was too harsh, too distant with them. That I wasn't pulling my weight in the home.

I reacted in the unkindest way I could. I went back to smoking marijuana more or less openly in front of him, sometimes, if I was desperate enough, as much as four strong joints a day. (Though never before, then or later did I smoke when pregnant or nursing a baby.)

"Be natural," Pierre used to say, in despair.

"Natural?" I would reply scathingly. "Is this a natural life, sitting four and five hours at a stretch listening to bores and their diplomatic chit chat?"

It became so that Pierre, on arriving home from the office,

would come up not to kiss me, but to sniff me. I brushed my teeth, washed my face and put on scent, but I couldn't stop the distinctive smell of grass lingering in my hair.

From the day I married Pierre we fought about money, pleasantly enough at first, but it proved the material for the most bitter rows of our later years. Early on he gave me 600 dollars allowance a month, to cover everything except major bills. When that never seemed to last the whole month, he doubled it, offering me half his official salary after taxes. My weakness was clothes. On an early freedom trip to Rome with two close friends—Arthur Erickson, the architect, and Francesco Kripacz—I had been swept away by the Italian fashions and returned home with 10,000 dollars' worth of couturier dresses, Valentino models, Lancetti silk dresses, trunks of shoes, bags, hats: I was the best-dressed woman at the 1972 Commonwealth Conference, but Pierre was not amused.

Most of my clothes came from Creeds, the best *prêt-à-porter* shop in Toronto, where, defying Pierre's wrath, I simply let my bills run up. The Creeds were family friends, and Simone knew my taste to perfection. Like all Canadians, she assumed Pierre was immensely rich. Just after my breakdown, on her own initiative, she sent a box of clothes she knew that I would like to 24 Sussex. Pierre let me keep them, but warned it would be the last time.

Two Christmases later, just as I was wrapping the staff presents, an enormous packet was delivered. Thinking it was something I had ordered I opened the box and discovered inside the most splendid white parka jacket, covered in appliqués of birds, and trimmed with ermine. "Dear Pierre," said the accompanying note, "I know you don't have time to shop. I thought you might like to give this to Margaret for Christmas." It was signed, Eddy Creed. When Pierre came home that night I confessed that I had opened a parcel addressed to him by mistake. He read the note, and, without asking me whether or not I liked the parka, ignoring the fact that I had been hinting for one for ages, packed the box up again and sent it straight back.

I never forgave him. Why, I asked myself, should Alia have an open account with Valentino and a hairdresser to accompany her on state visits, while Pierre checked on every dollar I spent, and seemed to begrudge me the smallest luxuries? Alia was never humiliated over small bills. It wasn't as if Pierre didn't appreciate me looking good, and indeed complained when he considered me unsuitably dressed.

Micha's birth was a brief happy interlude in a pattern of increasing unease. It wasn't only that I hated the life—I had become a hateful person myself. A spoiled little bitch. I sulked if I was asked to attend a boring reception, and said I couldn't go because I had a spot on my dress. I soon noticed that at parties people wanted to hear the prime minister's wife talk but that they didn't really listen to what I said. So I talked and talked and talked. I came to like the sound of my own voice.

The colder Pierre became, the more hysterical I got. I took it out on the children, and couldn't stand it when the baby cried, calling out for a nanny to come and deal with him. I refused to take them out any longer on little outings, gradually relinquishing their care almost entirely into the hands of staff. I was quick to lose my temper and take offense. One day a new maid asked to prepare a light lunch, cut an avocado hours before the meal so that by the time I got to the dining room it was brown and lank. I seized it from the dish and hurled it at the wall. On another evening Pierre came home to find me screaming at the boys like a fishwife. Only Mary Alice Conlon, the ex-nun who by now had replaced Tom MacDonald as housekeeper, made 24 Sussex tolerable. She was a gentle, efficient woman and she did all in her power to make it easier for me. When we held her wedding reception at the house I felt as if I was handing over to her my burden of marriage. She was now the bride.

One day I did what in Pierre's eyes was the unforgivable. We were having a frosty argument about clothes, and suddenly I flew into the most frenzied temper. I tore off up the stairs to the landing where a Canadian quilt, designed by Joyce Weyland and lovingly embroidered in a New York loft with Pierre's motto, *"La raison avant la passion,"* was hanging. (Its bilingual pair was in the National Gallery.) Shaking with rage at my inability to counter his logical, reasoned arguments, I grabbed at the quilt, wrenched off the letters and hurled them down the stairs at him one by one, in an insane desire to reverse the process, to put passion before reason just this once. Pierre was icy. Vandalizing a work of art; how low could I sink? (Hildegard sewed them all on again, invisibly and without comment, the next morning.) All of it seemed beyond reason to me.

The end came in a series of inexorable steps. We had a bleak Christmas on the island of St. Lucia, the prettiest of all the Caribbean islands, like Tahiti, volcanic and lush, with crumbling old colonial buildings. It could have been marvelous. Instead Pierre and I lived locked in our own private nightmares, made all the starker by the luxury around us. We swam, lay on the beach, played with the children. I read Carlos Castaneda and wrote pages and pages of letters to Yves, letters I never sent.

Pierre had long pressed me to pursue some interest of my own. "Write," he kept saying. How could I write when I knew that everyone who read my words would try to see in them some deeper meaning? On returning to Ottawa I finally enrolled at the Algonquin Junior College to study photography. It was a highly technical course, and, so long away from the company of students, I felt shy and inhibited. My studies were hardly serious, but they gave me the courage to believe that I could, perhaps, make a professional world for myself again. (Pierre had me followed to make sure I *was* attending school. I was.)

In early spring came our state visit to Washington D.C. I made a brief trip to the United States first to open an exhibition of Canadian artists at the Smithsonian Institution. After the formal opening the wife of our ambassador to the United States, Mrs. Gitana, came up to me and Jane Faulkner, who was with me, and said: "I have arranged for the most eligible bachelor of Washington to escort us tonight." "Ah," I replied, somewhat sadly, "but we are the most ineligible women." Senator Hubert Humphrey had been placed next to me at dinner. "I know I am not the handsomest of men," he said to me, "but will you dance?" His illness was by now well into its final stages, and everyone was surprised to see him jogging away on the dance floor, in a flirtatious, even merry mood. He joked with me about going bald, and talked about dying.

"You aren't bitter?" I asked, moved that someone so ill could seem so cheerful.

"No," he said. "I've got over all that." Within a few months he was dead.

I did see my Southerner one more time. And once more was

enough. I realized that it wasn't he who had destroyed my marriage—simply that I had used him to escape my own unhappiness.

I returned to Ottawa for two days, then turned round and entered the United States as the wife of the Canadian prime minister on a state visit. Our first meeting with the Carters, on the White House lawn, was informal and relaxed. That night, for the official dinner, I put on my white pearl dress, the one I had made for the Micheners' ball after my wedding, and had long considered my favorite dress. It came to three inches above the ankle. (Unknown to me, there was a run in my sheer stockings.)

Next morning there was an uproar in the newspapers. "Mrs. Trudeau and her gaffes!" "Margaret does it again!" My dress, it transpired, had been a disaster. How dare I attend a White House banquet in a dress that didn't reach the ground and in laddered stockings? Mrs. Carter, to whom I apologized, saying I had never meant to show disrespect, was even more horrified than I was at the public reaction. I felt somehow older, more experienced in these matters, when she said to me very seriously that henceforth she would allow no description of the clothes that women guests wore to the White House to be issued to the press. I told her mournfully that it was me, not my dress, that they were after.

We returned to Ottawa once more and at the front of my mind was my earlier pledge that if ever I had anything to do with my Southerner again I would leave Pierre. I might never have kept that pledge to myself and left Pierre if it hadn't been for the news that awaited me.

A few days after our return, moody, undecided and fretful, I went to a cocktail party held by an old friend of mine in honor of Premier Bennett of British Columbia. I was talking to a group of journalists when a man I knew slightly came up to me.

"Hello, Margaret. Have you heard the news? Hussein's wife Alia has just been killed in a helicopter crash."

He could have had no clue what his words meant to me. I started shaking. Tears poured down my face. A friend drove me back to Pierre. Later we discovered that Alia had been killed on the return flight from visiting a man in the south of Jordan who had written to her complaining that he was not receiving proper treatment at the local hospital. She had flown off with Colonel Zasa, King Hussein's closest aide, to pay him a visit. They crashed in a sudden rainstorm.

It was all too much for me. It made a mockery of all our conversations, the way Alia had kept on insisting that everything would turn out well for both of us. Pierre and I discussed our future calmly, with none of the aggravation of the previous months. We both agreed that nothing should happen precipitately. I would leave for a ninety-day trial separation—and we would take it from there.

TAKING OFF

N THE EYES OF THE WORLD my weekend with the Rolling
Stones was the freedom trip to end all freedom trips. No one
but Pierre knew I had already left him for a temporary
separation. To the rest of Canada, to the journalists and
newspapers of the world, my escapade was yet another example
of what a wicked wife I had become, flaunting my infidelities in
Pierre's face.

It was all a ghastly mistake: the truth of that Toronto weekend makes dull reading for anyone who saw the newspapers at
the time. It began innocently and entirely by accident. Pierre
and I reached our decision to part on Friday March 4—our
sixth wedding anniversary. I was packing my cases to leave for
New York when a call came from Penny Royce in Toronto.
"How about dinner with the Rolling Stones?" she suggested,
half joking.

"Why not?" I replied a little bitterly, "I'm free. I've just left
Pierre."

On my previous visits to Toronto I had always stayed at the
Windsor Arms, a small, quiet hotel in the center of the city.
When I reached the airport that Friday, however, I found that
Penny had checked me into the far larger Harbor Castle Hotel,
because, as she explained in the car on our way into town, the
Stones were staying there and we could sneak more discretely
into their suite for the dinner she had arranged. My first
meeting with the Rolling Stones was over drinks. Mick Jagger
was polite and charming. We drank wine. There were no drugs
about.

The Stones had come to Toronto to make some live recordings

244

in the El Mocambo, a small nightclub—a sort of beer cellar that reminded Mick of his first London club appointments. To discourage mobs of hysterical fans, the El Mocambo management had kept their visit a secret and simply announced a booking of the April Wine. When the Stones appeared on stage there was a riot among the tiny audience. It was a spectacular, memorable evening, and it was an honor to be there. Afterwards Penny and I went back to the hotel on our own and had a drink.

At three in the morning there was a loud thumping on my door. I groped my way out of bed, wearing white cotton pyjamas, opened the door and found Paul Wasserman, the Stones' publicity manager, lurching about in the corridor.

"My lady, a gift," he pronounced with rather drunken gallantry, showing me a bottle of cheap Canadian champagne in a plastic container which he held clutched under one arm.

I pointed over my shoulder to my darkened room. "I'm not having a party."

"Take it away."

I laughed. "I don't like sweet champagne at this time of night." He staggered off down the corridor.

Next afternoon, about to leave for New York, I bumped into Ronnie Woods, the Stones' guitarist.

"Hey, where are you off to? Aren't you coming to tonight's session?"

I hesitated. "I'm not a groupie. I can't possibly."

"Why don't you work, then? Take some photographs."

It seemed the perfect solution, like Castro and the radar station all over again. What was I going to do in New York anyway? And wouldn't this be a fine start to my new career? I put on my jeans jumpsuit and snapped away hard with my cameras all evening. Judy Welch, owner of a Toronto modeling agency, who was at the El Mocambo that night, invited me to a party afterwards. I begged off, too exhausted by unaccustomed noise and bright arc lights.

Next afternoon I prepared once again to leave Toronto. This time I heard a timid rattling on my door handle. Outside stood a skinny, pale little boy wearing a jogging suit. He was in tears. It was Marlon, Keith Richards' seven-year-old son. "Where is everybody? Where are they?" he sobbed. "Dad's lying on the floor crying. What shall I do?"

I went with him up to the Stones' suite and found that Anita Pallenberg, Marlon's mother, was out shopping, and that Keith was indeed curled up on the floor in a fetus position, moaning. His case, for possession of heroin for trafficking, was due to come up the next day in court. Marlon and I dragged him off the floor, laid him as best we could on his bed, and I covered him with a blanket. I couldn't just abandon the child, so, clearing a space among the dirty plates, empty bottles and garbage that littered the room, I settled down on the floor to help him glue together a model airplane. He had a lot of very expensive toys he couldn't understand, intended for far older children.

When Mick and the others came back we discussed what could be done for Keith. I was loath to get involved, but since I had good contacts with the various Canadian mental health associations I offered to find a psychiatrist who could at least give evidence for Keith at the trial. They were delighted, and having phoned an acquaintance at the M.H.A., Penny and I went to Ward Island, the hippy community across the water from the hotel, to talk to friends who might be prepared to take in Marlon if both Keith and Anita had to go through a period of rehabilitation.

By this time it was too late to leave for New York that night, so I went off to eat with Ronnie Wood and the Stones' drummer, Charlie Watts. They dropped me back at the hotel before midnight, saying they were off to a recording session. At 5 A.M. I got a call from the lobby: "It's us. We're back. Can we come up? How about a game of dice?" For the Stones, day is night and night is day. Slightly bemused, I climbed into my jeans, and hastily made my bed before the whole group clattered into my room, in high spirits and drunk with the euphoria that comes from an all-night working session.

"O.K. Maggie, put your money where your mouth is," said Mick, teasing me, as one rang down to room service for some champagne and orange juice, and another played the guitar.

"Does it matter what currency?" I asked, since, rather surprisingly, I had a pile of yen with me. We settled down to drink, play dice, smoke a little hash. Mick and Keith disappeared into a corner to work out a new number. It was fun; I was happy to be part of it. At nine o'clock we drew back the curtains on a cold gray morning and ordered coffee. One by one the

246

Stones departed to their own rooms to sleep. Ronnie was the last to leave.

Late Tuesday morning I left for New York. This time, walking down the corridor, I bumped into Paul Wasserman. He looked surprised to see me still around, gave me a wave, and passed on. I never saw the Stones again.

By the time I reached New York the scandal had exploded: "Prime Minister's Wife and Rolling Stones," "Margaret in Hotel Corridor in White Pyjamas," "Sex Orgy in Canadian Prime Minister's Wife's Suite." There was no stopping the rumors, many of them emanating from Paul Wasserman. Too late did Mick ring and warn me: "Don't talk to Wasserman, he's our press agent and is trying to get publicity for us. But he's an arsehole."

Without Yasmin Aga Khan, my great friend in New York, I would certainly have gone mad. She took me in and did her best to protect me from the battalions of reporters who laid siege all night to our front door, and mobbed and jostled us every time we left the house. The Canadian journalists, in town to cover a speech to be given by the Canadian prime minister, were ordered to drop everything and cover me. The second day I took refuge in Richard Avedon's studio on East Seventy-Fifth Street, where I spent about six hours watching a photographic session and eating a delicious lunch. For a moment life seemed sane again. Then Richard switched on a two-way intercom that he had linked to his front door, and we overheard the raucous laughter and crude jokes of the reporters piled up outside. "Hey, Avedon has a bed there, do you think? . . ."

Richard's makeup man, Way Bandy, made up my face to look as good as possible and we braved the street, me in tears.

Later that day Michael O'Flattery, a freelance journalist selling stories to the *Daily Express* in London, trapped me on the phone at Yasmin's. He protested undying friendship, sympathized deeply when in despair I said: "I abdicate," meaning I couldn't stand it any longer. He sold the tape recorded conversation across the world.

It was too late when Paul Wasserman confessed he might have been exaggerating, and that no, he hadn't exactly seen me catch a plane to New York with Mick Jagger and Ronnie Wood. By then I was branded: a promiscuous, irresponsible wife, prepared to go to any lengths to escape her husband. It wasn't made any better when every paper in the world carried the fact that Friday had been my sixth wedding anniversary.

If it was bad for me, it was worse for Pierre. People in Canada yelled "cuckold" when they saw him pass in the streets. Stony faced, he pretended nothing was wrong. When I got back to Ottawa I was in disgrace, total, unredeemable disgrace. It was hardly surprising. The moment I was through the door of 24 Sussex Pierre forced me to listen to a tape he had been sent by his office of the Michael O'Flattery interview. It sounded truly terrible. I protested; I explained what had happened step by step. It was no good. That night we were due to go to a performance of *Romeo and Juliet* at the National Arts Center. I wore my ill-fated Washington dress; I had a black eye.

I couldn't go on. Pierre's position was now intolerable. The break would have to be made official. He spent Easter in California, while I stayed with the children. Not even the sympathetic and tactful letters I received could make me feel any better. One arrived from Rosalynn Carter:

> *Dear Margaret:*
>
> *I understand that our staffs have despaired of trying to mesh our schedules at this time. I want you to know, however, that I took a cue from you and taped some spots for our American Mental Health Association.*
>
> *I look forward to carrying out, at some future date, the plans we discussed for highlighting the needs of our Mental Health Associations.*
>
> > *Sincerely,*
> > *Rosalynn Carter*

Not long after, we drafted a statement together, which was issued to the world from Pierre's office.

> *Pierre and Margaret Trudeau announce that, because of Margaret's wishes, they shall begin living separate and apart. Margaret relinquishes all privileges as the wife of the prime minister and wishes to leave the marriage and pursue an independent career. Pierre will have custody of their three sons, giving Margaret*

generous access to them. Pierre accepts Margaret's decision with regret, and both pray that their separation will lead to a better relationship between themselves.

Overnight Pierre became the most famous single father in the world and his popularity rating rose 17 per cent in the polls. I left for New York, but not before I had received one letter of genuine support—from Prince Charles.

My "independent career" was not quite all that it might have been. Through the kind auspices of Lis and Richard Wasserman, who lived on Park Avenue, I was lent an empty fifteen-room apartment in their block. It was owned by a rich lady from Houston who wanted someone to house-sit while she had the decorators in. My New York life settled down to a kind of routine: sleep till midday, up to the Wassermans', make myself a Bumble Bee Tuna Fish sandwich with sweet pickles and Hellman's mayonnaise on stone ground bread; spend the early afternoon searching for work; the late afternoon at acting classes; and out with friends in the late evening.

Without those friends I would have been truly lost. Rosemary and Gyd Shepherd of the National Art Gallery of Canada saved my reason on more days than I can easily remember. I sometimes felt that they were the only people in the world who weren't busy judging me. Then there were Jane Faulkner and Gro Southam who took me off to the Virgin Islands when Justin, Sacha and Micha all came down with chicken pox in Jamaica and Pierre refused to let me go and nurse them for fear of talk of reconciliation. (There was talk of reconciliation just the same, since we were both in the Caribbean.)

Work wasn't easy to come by. I was inundated by offers—but every enterprise I got involved in turned out to be a con of one kind or another, usually people luring me on and then exploiting me in return for some "exclusive story." *People* magazine offered me work—in exchange for an interview. I took some pictures for them, but the interview was sexy and sensational, a travesty of everything I said. They fooled me again by telling me that Elizabeth Taylor had agreed to have me to tea on her farm at Middleburg, Virginia to take some pictures of her. When I got there, she was furious. There had been no such deal.

I explained what had happened. "What's going on. Don't you know you're being used?" she said to me.

How right she was. Everything I did made news. I couldn't get it right. When the gossip columnists started linking my name with that of the tennis player Vitas Gerulaitis, I began changing my date every night. "Margaret dates a different man every night," read the headlines. My mother called me from Vancouver to ask what was happening.

The greatest con of all was the *Good Morning America* show. It was June 4, 1977. I had been told that my appearance on the breakfast show, presenting a selection of my own photographs, would act as public audition for the job of presenter on the program. When I got to the studio I found that my fellow guest was Anthony Quinn and that we were to be interviewed by a blond, hardbitten woman, a typically plastic Miss Chicago. She was heavily and theatrically made up, her hair a bullet-proof helmet of hairspray.

I began by describing my photography. Miss Chicago beamed. "Now Margaret. You talk with such love about your children. You always say Justin is a prince, Sacha very brave, and Michel an angel. I have to ask you a question that must be on the mind of every one of our twelve million viewers this morning. Have you abandoned your children?"

I had to restrain myself from jumping up, rushing over and messing up her odious straw hair. It almost started what would have been the most popular catfight on American television. I controled myself. "How could you," I asked back. "How could you possibly ask such a question?"

Miss Chicago wasn't the only one who questioned me about my children. The papers were full of stories about wicked, adulterous mothers walking out on their dear little boys. Strangers I was introduced to hinted about motherless children growing up emotional cripples. Even some of the staff at home seemed to have it in for me. On one of my frequent weekends in Ottawa the policewoman who did the night rounds inside the house told me blithely that one night she had heard a pathetic mewing coming from upstairs in the middle of the night. Suspecting a cat had somehow got in, she went upstairs in search of it. She found Sacha curled up in front of my door, whimpering.

Yet my relationship with the children and with Pierre was

growing more healthy by the week. My independence and my attempts to work were giving me a far more balanced attitude to motherhood. I longed for my spells at home, and when I got there, threw myself into loving the children properly, caring for them and actually listening to what they had to say in a way that I never had before. I was a real mother to them at last. When after five days at home, I set off back to New York, leaving them with the two wonderful "care-mothers" I had employed, I left them good tempered and serene. I missed them and was always ready to come home.

A "hard" and "selfish" career girl, capable of "neglecting her children," were not the only insults hurled at me. 1977 was a bewildering year for me; a hard year; the beginning of my new life.

On a trip for *People* magazine to Paris, a promotion tour for Perrier, I found myself sitting next to Bruce Nevins, the company's president, on the plane. I was cross at the unaccustomed discomfort of a long flight, tourist class, and pulled my eye mask sulkily over my face. It wasn't until we landed that I realized who he was. Bruce befriended me in Paris, and on our return to New York I started dating him regularly, though he was diametrically the opposite of any man I had ever dreamed of falling in love with: West Point Military Academy, instructor in guerrilla warfare for the commandos in Vietnam, president of Levis in Hong Kong, strong Nixon supporter. But he was a good friend, a strong, big-shouldered man, with the warmest brown eyes a woman could hope for. We had Sunday brunches at the Tavern On the Green in Central Park, reading the newspapers, and sober, cosy dinners at Elaine's and Nicola's. He worked hard and we shared a warm love. It was some months before I realized with sadness that Bruce, whatever else he may be, is a confirmed lifelong bachelor.

It was while I was with him that I started acting classes. Mornings were given over to private lessons with Bob MacAndrew to prepare me for movie parts. It was a struggle but I grew better and still cherish the day when Bob declared that my best talents as an actress lay in "innovation." Afternoons were more daunting: I had been allowed to audit Wynn Handman's advanced acting class—something of an honor for a total newcomer since Wynn's classes were widely regarded as the finest in contemporary theater. His studio, an old fashioned, run-down series of rooms was above a laundromat on West 56th Street. Classes started at 4:45 every afternoon. For the first months I watched in awe as the professional actors and actresses tackled parts that ranged from Beckett to Shakespeare. I thought my future was made the day he gave me a chance at Erma Bombeck—though I was so overwhelmed by Katherine Hepburn's performance in *Philadelphia Story* that I couldn't stop aping it.

Those were the serious times. Mostly I racketed around New York, getting involved in scenes I couldn't cope with, and people I couldn't understand.

There was my weekend in Las Vegas. I was invited there by a wealthy businessman who groomed his crinkly hair with a blowdryer. He first took me to La Grenouille on St. Valentine's Day and over lunch suggested we go to Las Vegas for the Mohammed Ali fight.

"How can I possibly come to Las Vegas?" I said flirtatiously. "I've got nothing to wear."

And indeed I hadn't. Charmer that he was, he presented me with the best Valentine's present that ever came my way— carte blanche at my favorite store, Ungaro's.

The romance of the present was in sharp and crazy contrast to the actual weekend. The fight was bloody and brutal. The hotel suite where I stayed was quite outstanding in its vulgarity: Cupids spouting water, paintings on velvet, a bar with golden stools, polyester rugs and wall to wall mirrors.

There was my cowboy with whom I played pinball until six in the morning. There were my nights in Studio 54, New York's most exclusive club, and favorite territory of Truman Capote, Andy Warhol, Bianca Jagger and Halston. One night the air reeked of the sweet chemical stench of amyl nitrate and a jerky, stoned blonde was parading about shoving a bottle under people's noses, saying: "Sniff." There was the impresario, Allan Carr's, party for all the beautiful people whose name began with the letters N to Z—John Travolta, Carlo Ponti, Margaret Trudeau—given in a house on Malibu beach encased in a plastic cover with zippers to protect it from the ocean. It took place just after Roman Polanski had been busted for doping a thirteen-year-old girl. When Roman came up to speak to me, I saw a reporter from *People* creeping up behind to get a shot of us together—that's all I need, I thought vanishing behind the potted plants, an imaginary romance with Polanski. There were the many evenings with the "upper decadents" (as opposed to Régine's "top crowd") in our private cliquey basement underneath Studio 54. Bianca Jagger was the Disco Queen, I the Sweetheart. Fast and furious, I searched for freedom at a pace that took me only around in circles. These were no more than desperate attempts at finding how to live, how to survive.

I came to my senses at last after one truly sleazy evening. The party was over; the last of the misfits had wandered off. I was alone, aching. Empty tequila glasses were scattered around the room, and there was a faint smell of stale grass. I tried to sleep, but found myself pacing the room in a growing panic of desolation, willing the cold black world outside to wake and share the misery with me. Looking out of the window as dawn came up all I could see were the garbage cans in the basement area eleven floors below me. I covered sheets of papers with a desperate scrawl: "Help me please."

The lost year was over.

I went to bid it farewell at the anniversary party of Studio 54. The whole of smart New York was there—two miles of solid traffic. On the way through the pouring rain, wearing what Joan Crawford called "fuck me shoes," I saw a dog turd floating past on the rushing water in the gutter like a little boat. I sat in the balcony high above the stage, looking down on all the things I was giving up: the anxious days, the drug-high nights, the phony glamor, the botched friendships, the betrayals. They were none of them worth it.

EPILOGUE

My thirtieth birthday has fallen as I finish this. I'm in Cassis in the South of France making my second movie, *Guardian Angel*. The *Good Morning America* fiasco didn't get me a job as presenter—I was told that I didn't quite seem to represent the middle American housewife—but it did secure me a part in my first film, *Kings and Desperate Men*. I may never make a good film actress or a gifted photographer, but I'm going to try.

I've changed a lot in the past year. Leaving Pierre was like stepping out into Beelzebub's Chaos. I spent a lot of time sinking. I think I'm on the way up again.

Perhaps there comes a moment in life when you understand how really alone you are. My mother warned me early: "Life is a lonely affair. You may share companionship from time to time with those you love, but you are always in the end, alone." Not me, I triumphed indulgently. I have three beautiful sons, who will always be part of me. I had my one romantic fantasy, my ideal: Yves. It doesn't matter that I was never with him. It was enough to know he was there.

One bright September morning in Cassis my leading man, Francis Lemaire, a fine comedian, appeared in the make-up room looking sad and wretched. "Charles Boyer committed suicide yesterday." Micheline, my make-up girl, and I commiserated but privately I couldn't feel too shaken: Boyer was eighty, and his wife had died two weeks before.

"I had even sadder news this morning," Francis went on as I went back to my make-up, only half listening to him. "My best friend's son has also committed suicide." I looked as sympathetic as I could, thinking he would feel better if he talked about it. "You wouldn't know him," he went on. "The father—my friend—was the man who invented the Club Mediteranée."

I froze; waited. And then it came. "His name was Yves Lewis."

Being me, the dramatics were spectacular: I pulled my hair, I raved, I screamed, I cried, I refused to believe him. A great emptiness, like a merciless cold wave broke over me. That morning Francis and I had our most important scene in the film together; it took all the courage I had to go through with it, and only because I knew that my real Guardian Angel was there could I face what was the cruelest reality of my life. In the image of Christ to the last, Yves had hanged himself at the age of thirty-three and a half. My search for him is finally over; but unlike Yves I shall go on surviving.

I see my children for five days every two weeks when I go back home to Ottawa to share with Pierre a life we never had before. I take them to the dentist and buy their shoes. Only now can I love them as they should be loved.

Justin is most like Pierre. He sees no shades of gray, only black and white. Sacha is knowing.

"I have five souls," he said to me at age three. "One is lost and another is searching for it. One is working hard and another is cleaning up. The fifth is just having fun."

Micha is a clown who fights for his life.

Pierre and I like each other very much as parents. We have compromised on schools and pets and he has helped them understand that I need to work, "to explore my freedom," if I'm to be a good mother to them. It's not always easy. The guilt waits to pounce. On one of my most recent visits, Pierre and I took the three boys for a day's canoeing trip; we packed a picnic of their favorite food and the weather was superb. We joked all day long.

"Mommy," said Micha, when I told him I was off to finish my latest film, "don't go."

"She has to go," said Justin. "She's working."

"Why doesn't she work at being a mother then?" asked Sacha petulantly.

Since I left the warm protection of 24 Sussex, Pierre has given me all the moral support he can muster. He has not helped me at all financially, partly because of my stubbornness about being independent, partly because he is loath to aid me to live a life that is apart from him and our sons. Mommy *has* to work.

It is quite possible that Pierre and I could never have made a life together. It wasn't his age or my inexperience, or even the fact that he was Prime Minister. Pierre likes his life programed: the good, Christian philosopher-king who wants to live his life by his will, not by the vagaries of fortune. I spent an awful lot of time trying to please him, yet could never quite escape from my own romantic fantasy or the desire for a life very different from the one I was expected to lead. Quite simply, I preferred being his country mistress; I began to detest being his wife. Now I prefer being alone.

Is it beyond reason for me to hope for a peaceful life, or has my past put me beyond reach of such a dream?

I don't, I realize, come out of this story very well. I have tried at least to be honest.